D0875753

CHICAGO DEATH TRAP

The Iroquois Theatre Fire of 1903

Nat Brandt

With an Introduction by Perry R. Duis and
Cathlyn Schallhorn

Southern Illinois University Press
Carbondale and Edwardsville

Frontispiece: The Iroquois Theatre was Chicago's most modern playhouse when it opened in the fall of 1903. It was situated on Randolph Street off Dearborn, in the heart of the city's busy downtown area. Author's collection.

Library of Congress Cataloging-in-Publication Data
Brandt, Nat.
    Chicago death trap : the Iroquois Theatre fire of 1903 / Nat Brandt ; with an introduction by Perry R. Duis and Cathlyn Schallhorn.
        p. cm.
Includes bibliographical references and index.
1. Iroquois Theater (Chicago, Ill.)—Fire, 1903. 2. Fires—Illinois—Chicago—History—20th century. 3. Chicago (Ill.)—History—1875– I. Title.
F548.5 .B64 2003
977.3'11041—dc21
ISBN 0-8093-2490-3 (cloth : alk. paper)   2002006541

To my grandchildren—
Danielle, Gregory, Kristen, Kaileigh, Sonya, Gabriel, Adlai, and Lucian

Contents

Contents

Illustrations

Illustrations

Acknowledgments

I am indebted to several persons in Chicago and its environs who graciously helped me in the research stage of this book. In particular, I would like to thank three members of the Chicago Public Library for going out of their way to make my work smoother: Lyle Benedict of the Municipal Reference Collection and both Constance Gordon and Andrea Telli of the Special Collections and Preservation Division. Their assistance proved invaluable in my search for material relevant to the Iroquois Theatre fire. Richard Sklenar of the Theatre Historical Society of America in Elmhurst also deserves my thanks. He and his staff of volunteer workers assisted me immeasurably. One of the volunteers, Grant Meyers, who served thirty-one years as a Chicago fireman, helped me to avoid some pitfalls in the contemporary reporting of the Iroquois fire.

Loes Schiller, dean of admissions at Columbia University's Graduate School of Architecture, Planning, and Preservation, was instrumental in my being able to use the school's library.

I owe a special word of gratitude to Bernard A. Weisberger and his wife, Rita Mendelsohn, who opened their home in Evanston to me during my research visit. Bernard, a retired professor of American history, has always been gracious in offering comments and direction about my work. By an amazing coincidence, Rita turned out to be a niece of Max Remer, whose eyewitness account of the fire she provided me for use in the book.

My wife, Yanna, offered her usual astute editing comments and made the manuscript, at least in my eyes, a much better read than it was originally.

Introduction

Perry R. Duis and Cathlyn Schallhorn

The bright lights are on once again along Randolph Street. What had once been Chicago's premier theater district now sports several new and remodeled venues. The old Bismarck Theatre is now the Cadillac Palace. The facades of the Selwyn and Harris front new stages for the Goodman School, which has also opened a new film center named for the late film critic Gene Siskel. Around the corner on State Street, there is the remodeled Chicago Theater. But midway between State and Dearborn is the gem of the street, the Ford Center for the Performing Arts Oriental Theater. Shuttered for decades before extensive renovation sponsored by the automobile company replaced layers of grime with gold leaf, the Ford Oriental is one of the key venues in Chicago's effort to become a major theatrical town.

But few who pass through its doors realize that the building sits on the site of one of the most horrific tragedies in American history: the Iroquois Theatre fire that claimed the lives of 602 people, over two-thirds of them women and children, on the afternoon of December 30, 1903. As Nat Brandt's fascinating narrative reveals, this is a multilayered story that illuminates many aspects of life in the city and on the stage.

The Setting

To place the Iroquois tragedy in proper perspective—and especially to explain the makeup of its doomed audience—it is necessary to understand the social geography of Chicago's region and how its downtown drew people that fatal afternoon. The Loop was really a series of continuously evolving specialized districts. There were wholesale areas on its periphery, newspaper row on the west side, the LaSalle Street financial district, a concentration of office buildings stretching to the south along Dearborn, and two governmental areas, one near the federal courthouse and the other adjacent to City Hall. The construction of the elevated tracks in 1897 and the noise generated by its trains created corridors of low-rent buildings along Wells, Van Buren, Lake, and Wabash that for decades were home to quirky stores, nonprofit organizations, and warehouses.[1]

But by the end of the nineteenth century, two other areas that were of special interest to women were emerging. One was the string of State Street department stores, anchored on the north by Marshall Field and Company and on the south by Siegel-Cooper, the latter claiming to be the largest store building in the world when it was built in 1891. The presence of these stores created a district of unending retail fantasy, a series of enclosed and self-contained shopping experiences fronted at sidewalk level by alluring show windows. Even the elaborate trim on the new Schlesinger and Mayer (later Carson, Pirie, Scott, and Company) store at Madison Street advertised that the place was friendly to women. Dozens of smaller specialty shops scattered up and down the street provided the retail mortar between the big blocks.[2]

The feminization of State Street, moreover, gave the illusion of safety to middle-class city and suburban women and their children. Many arrived in special buses that made the rounds of the depots or crossed bridges from the el platforms directly into stores. Women gazing at the windows could take comfort in the fact that police patrolling the State Street sidewalks were especially on alert for mashers, pickpockets, purse snatchers, or anyone who might spoil an outing. Thanks to the railroads, this same lure of safe consumerism and security extended beyond the city and its suburbs to millions of families living within a radius of a few hundred miles. Dozens of fast passenger trains on some thirty lines fanned out in all directions and brought nearly a hundred thousand passengers a day in and out of six major terminals. Thus, the holiday period gave the opportunity for Midwesterners aspiring to be part of the comfortable middle class to join with thousands of other small-town visitors who came each year to spend money on State Street as well as visit museums.

An outing to Loop department stores often included two other destinations. One was lunch at Berghoff's, Kinsley's, Thompson's, Henrici's, or another one of a tantalizing array of fine restaurants. Most were easily accessible to State Street and promised their own fantasies of consumption. The other treat was to conclude a day of shopping with a play. On some days, it was possible to combine a romantic dinner with an evening of theater, but for many mothers, the best alternative was the afternoon matinee that ended in time for a return home before dinner. The women "have formed little social centers and find that this line of amusement is very enjoyable," noted one trade publication.[3] The northern end of the department store district conveniently intersected with the eastern end of the quickly developing theater area. Although there were a few theatrical houses scattered elsewhere downtown, the Garrick, Powers', Central Music Hall, and others were scattered up and down Randolph. The Iroquois was, in the words of one theater trade journal, "nearest State Street, and the imposing entrance, 60 feet high, leading into a brilliantly decorated lobby, is expected to catch many strangers before they get further up the street." "Randolph Street" was Chicago's Broadway, and it supported hundreds of subsidiary businesses, among them booking agents, publicity photographers, playscript publishers, playbill printers, theatrical lighting and set construction companies, and makeup manufacturers. The presence of some sixty popular music publishers also meant that Randolph was emerging as a Tin Pan Alley second only to New York. Dozens of young songwriters dreamed of selling tunes that might be picked up by some important play or performer. Many of the same trains that took Midwestern shoppers back to their hometowns carried armies of "song pluggers," who were sales-performers hired to make the rounds of music stores to promote new tunes.[4]

While railroads played a critical role in circulating music and bringing out-of-towners to Randolph Street, the trains were absolutely essential to the operation of the entertainment business. After a show closed in New York, its run could be prolonged and made even more profitable by taking it on the road. Productions sought the larger audiences of major cities, especially for such peak theater-going times as holidays, but the long travel between towns was costly. To defray this expense, managers tried to schedule a series of one-nighters or short runs in smaller towns en route. Arranging such tours was a complicated process that involved two sets of booking agents, one for the theater owners and another for the shows. This situation prompted the creation of a trust that was known as the Theatrical Syndicate. It was formed in 1896 when three groups of theatrical booking agents, Klaw and Erlanger, Nixon and Zimmerman, and Charles Frohman, combined their routes. The syndicate simplified things through its ownership of theaters in large cities and exclusive affiliations with those in smaller towns. It could guarantee that a production would enjoy an efficient route and full schedule. Local venue managers could count on a constant stream of productions without the problem of cancellations and overbooking. Actors were signed for a season and guaranteed wages. By applying efficient business practices, the syndicate was able to increase profits for everyone.[5]

But the arrangement carried a price that indirectly contributed to the Iroquois tragedy. Theaters were bound by contracts that forbade them from offering nonsyndicate attractions, thus transforming local managers from entrepreneurs in control of their stages to mere employees of East Coast interests. If they objected in any way, they could be sent the worst shows. Productions were forced to play their assigned route, and those that did not draw well or complained were sent on impossible itineraries that ate up most of the profits in train fares. The syndicate soon began to produce its own shows and favored them in touring by giving them the best routes and by booking them into the larger and better theaters. Shows under this arrangement "double-dipped" by collecting the producer's share of the ticket sales as well as the booking fee. At the same time, syndicate actors could not appear in independent productions. The lack of competition for their services lowered their salaries, but protest meant being banned from syndicate shows. Revolts against the syndicate were generally unsuccessful, but they did result in an atmosphere of greater public criticism and scrutiny of the theatrical industry in 1903. Ultimately, it was syndicate pressure for profit that led to the construction of the Iroquois Theatre and to its opening when it did. The search for larger profits meant that sets and costumes became more elaborate. There was a need for larger venues with larger stages to accommodate more spectacular productions, which, in turn, could pay for the soaring costs of touring. Construction of the Iroquois guaranteed the syndicate a presence in Chicago. By the fall of 1903, its production of *Mr. Bluebeard* was already touring, and high ticket sales during the lucrative holiday season were essential for it to turn a profit. Thus there was enormous pressure on the local managers to get the theater open as quickly as possible, and as a result, it was open in time for the holiday season.

The Painful Effects of the Tragedy

The tragic afternoon of December 30, 1903, set in motion a number of events and reactions. As details of the event and its victims began to filter into the press, what might be called "the shock of misplacement" began to set in. Tragedies often have a way of curiously mismatching people, places, and things that are not normally associated. Nearby businesses were commandeered for emergency purposes—the Sherman House and lounge rooms of Marshall Field's served as makeshift hospitals, for example. What helped make the Iroquois fire so vivid in the minds of the public was the fact that it took place not long after the press had begun to employ half-tone techniques that reproduced actual photographs instead of relying entirely on line drawings and artists' renderings.

The tragedy cast suspicion on every place of public assembly. The city not only shuttered all theaters immediately, but it soon shut down dance halls, dime museums, clubs, the Chicago Coliseum, and other places that accommodated crowds. Inspectors descended on department stores. At least two of the city's leading churches also voluntarily submitted to inspection. Even the Chicago Symphony Orchestra complained that the temporary closing of the Auditorium Theatre, its home, cast a cloud over its financial future.[6]

The tragedy resulted in an immediate and sharp decline in tourism to the city. The number of people entering the Loop each day fell by at least twenty-five thousand in the weeks following the fire. Thousands of families abruptly canceled shopping and theater trips. Downtown department store sales and restaurant receipts plummeted. The usual sale of fancy theater clothes for the winter stage season also evaporated. One trade journal estimated that the number of tourists fell by forty thousand during January 1904 alone. Hundreds of store clerks, waiters, and hotel employees were laid off in a pattern not unlike the sharp decline in tourism that followed the tragedy of September 11, 2001.[7] Instead, many families followed the advice of the *Tribune's* Domestic Science column and stayed home. The writer advised mothers to use the occasion to promote proper moral values, especially among their sons, who would be the leaders of the future.[8]

Actors were also devastated by the event. Chicago theaters remained closed until mid-February. Stranded touring productions went unpaid while they were waiting for the theaters to reopen. Fifty companies reportedly closed their runs. John Drew left what he called "terrible Chicago" early and took his troupe to Milwaukee. James O'Neill's tour, whose continuation had depended on a successful Chicago run, was canceled and returned to New York. Some companies also attempted to make up for the lull by playing one-night stands in small towns near Chicago. But most of the theater industry just suffered. A benefit planned for the Auditorium indicated the extent of the unemployment among those beyond the footlights: 20 percent of the proceeds for musicians, 20 percent for stagehands, 20 percent for bill posters, and 40 percent for actors.[9]

Chicagoans set aside their historic disapproval of theater folk, whose morals were often suspect, and supported the stranded. Mrs. J. Ogden Armour paid the hotel bills of chorus girls so that they could claim their trunks and return to New York. The local Actor's Church Alliance provided bail for women who had been arrested as witnesses. An unnamed department store refunded any money that the chorus girls had spent for costumes and gave them jackets, skirts, and hats. The Immanuel Baptist Church distributed money from an anonymous Arizona donor to unemployed actresses, while many Chicago families offered free housing and board to stage people as well as carfare so that they could search for work.[10]

Then began the commodification of shock and grief. The interior of the Iroquois building had hardly cooled before the first steps were taken to seek economic gain from it. Postcard companies rushed out new printings of cards showing the exterior of the Iroquois, and at least one commemorative spoon hit the market as a keepsake. Music publishing companies also turned out popular tunes based on the tragedy of their Randolph Street neighbor.[11]

The most significant souvenir that any family could buy was a book. Chicago was also a major production center for a genre of popular literature that provided the public with remembrances of tragic events. Almost every major tornado, hurricane, flood, earthquake, assassination, or ship sinking that took place between 1890 and World War I was followed by at least one instant history; over a dozen of them appeared after the *Titanic* tragedy alone. These disaster books, in turn, were a thriving part of what was known as the subscription book business, which was organized to take quick advantage of the public's emotions. The books not only served as keepsakes of the event but also helped to satisfy a news-starved readership's need for the often gory detail. Within hours of the theater fire, printers were already setting type on salesmen's "dummies." These consisted of a detailed title page of sensational subtitles and advertising claims, followed by a makeshift table of contents, a few rewritten news stories, and illustrations lifted from the local press. At the back were a number of ruled pages to record orders. All of this was sandwiched in a cloth cover with elaborate wording and ornament. By January 8, publishers were advertising for salesmen, armies of which hit the city streets and rode the trains that fanned out to countless small towns and farmsteads. While they were taking orders and promising delivery in a few weeks, the publisher was busy rewriting newspaper copy and obtaining illustrations. Within a few weeks, the books were then either mailed or delivered by the salesmen to the buyers.[12]

Time was of the essence in this type of publishing, and this forced a choice between providing a complete account of any subsequent investigation and litigation or making money, and so most accounts are incomplete. The authorship of the major Iroquois book, *Chicago's Awful Theater Horror,* remains unclear, but it quickly came under the ownership of the Reverend Samuel Fallows, a Chicago Episcopalian leader and a popular writer.[13] By the end of April 1904, Fallows's Iroquois book had sold over 30,000 copies, but there would be only 3,799 additional sales during the subsequent ten months. This earned him $4,800, with nothing more due until a total of 60,000 had been sold. "You will probably live in hopes of the sale reaching that figure," advised the Monarch Book Company, "but you know books of such character sell very slowly after the first excitement dies out."[14]

Blame

The public did not have to look far to identify the villains responsible for the slaughter of innocents. The event became the topic of countless sermons on the following Sunday. Dr. William Robson Norman of the prestigious Fourth Presbyterian church said that the fire was the product of "brutal commercialism which is the blight of our fair civilization, in as much as it values dollars much and human life little." "Let no guilty man escape," proclaimed the Reverend Samuel Fallows. Another advised, "Do not ascribe the calamity to the Almighty. He did not do it. . . . Ascribe it to men." Human fault lay mainly with those who enacted inadequate laws, allowed lax inspections, and opened unsafe spaces to the unsuspecting public.[15] Without saying it directly, some divines skirted the issue of morality and commercialized amusements. The tragedy had come at a time when the battle against organized vice in Chicago had just begun, and clergymen, social reformers, and law enforcement officials were expressing their concern about the relationship between the worlds of the brothel and the commercialized amusement. Young people were patronizing dance halls, wasting time and money at baseball games, and hanging around the glitzy world of the theater. For-profit amusements drained pockets and filled young minds with questionable ideas about morality and also placed young women in danger of being recruited into vice. "We are going almost mad in our desire to be amused," warned the Reverend Johnston Myers, who would later help lead Chicago's antiprostitution campaign. "Great playhouses [are] packed to suffocation with a throng who must be excited and entertained. The theater never built character nor strengthened faith in God."[16] That attitude was further revealed in the refusal of a Methodist group to pass a resolution of sympathy with the bereaved families because, in the words of a theater journal, "it would indirectly amount to an indorsement of the theatre as a place of amusement." That denomination was in the midst of a discussion over whether its members could "attend the theatre or any other kind of frivolous amusement, such as the dance hall, the card party and similar entertainments."[17]

The theatrical world was horrified by the fire and even more shocked as details of the conditions in the theater were revealed. Stage publications demanded greater precautions throughout the country and called for punishment for those to blame. In its February editorial, *Theatre Magazine* suggested that the Iroquois managers be held responsible. It cited the numerous convictions of New York managers for safety violations and complained that the punishments were too weak to be effective. The *New York Dramatic Mirror* echoed these sentiments and went on to suggest that greed was the real culprit and blamed the Theatrical Syndicate, calling it an "iniquitous system."[18]

But Chicagoans smelled politics in the tragedy, and the Iroquois Theatre fire proved to be the catalyst for what would become the city's most active period of political reform. During the sixteen months preceding the fire, Chicagoans had seen almost daily headlines about corruption among the building inspectors, including charges of bribes, incompetence, and political pressures to exempt some properties from inspection altogether. During 1903, a city council "graft committee" had found that city employees on every level in every department were willing to sell their power and influence. In 1903, the muckraking journalist Lincoln Steffens had aptly described Chicago "Half Free and Fighting On."[19]

Although scandals continued, the theater disaster contributed to Chicago's brief interlude of political reform. Voters used the next mayoral election to install Judge Edward F. Dunne, an honest Republican who at least temporarily forced a halt to the most blatant corruption. Dunne's first public works commissioner was Joseph Medill Patterson, scion of the *Tribune* ownership and a colorful parlor socialist. (He later authored a radical novel called *Little Brother of the Rich*.) During his brief tenure, Patterson closed numerous public buildings—including the leading department stores—for safety hazards, and even though they quickly reopened, his complaints brought back enough memories of the disaster to force small changes. But honesty in government proved to be as transitory as the outpouring of public grief. Dunne's failure to buy out the privately held traction companies as promised, along with his inability to halt a wave of street crime, ended his regime after a single two-year term. By 1907, the new mayor, Fred Busse, had returned the city to its normally corrupt condition.[20]

Despite the clear influence the Iroquois Theatre fire had on reform in Chicago, the issue of legal responsibility for the tragedy remained unclear. The theater was a semipublic place, that is, privately owned but generally of public access. As such, it joined office buildings, factories, restaurants, saloons, railroad stations, department stores, baseball parks, churches, and other such urban spaces in a legal morass that was only gradually being sorted out a century ago. When the general public entered such spaces, who was liable for their safety? Thus the factory worker who was injured on the job had little recourse against his or her employer for workplace injuries. Typically, customers entering a store had not been specifically invited and paid no admission fee; those injured by a falling elevator in an office building or an escalator of a department store were treated as if they had entered at their own risk. The law was a little less clear in cases where the victim had purchased the right to use a facility or service. Thus, someone hit on the head by an errant baseball or hurt in a train wreck was assumed to have a right to safety and to possess a bit more leverage when things went wrong, but often there was fine print on a ticket that denied liability. It is difficult to generalize about the outcomes of these incidents. Sometimes negligent owners of semipublic places paid hefty penalties. Other times they just walked away.[21]

The final ironies of the Iroquois tragedy involve time and place. The blaze itself was measured in minutes, but its aftermath took years to play itself out. The initial public outrage gradually lapsed into years of continuances that were labeled "AN OUTRAGEOUS INSTANCE OF THE LAW'S DELAYS" by the dean of the Northwestern University Law School. Those remarks, in turn, caused a bitter argument within the legal profession about how prompt justice could really be.[22]

The burned-out shell of the building also escaped becoming what geographer Kenneth Foote has called "shadowed ground," a site permanently stained yet somehow made sanctified by tragedy. Millionaire plumbing-fixture manufacturer Richard Teller Crane, who had lost two nieces in the blaze, tried to use his influence to have the Iroquois shell razed to make way for an downtown emergency hospital that would also serve as a highly visible memorial built by widespread public support. Crane got his Iroquois Memorial Hospital, but widespread public apathy delayed its opening until seven years after the 1903 fire. Even then, Crane had to pay for it himself, and, ironically, its dedication was greatly overshadowed by another fire, this one killing twenty-three firemen and their chief at the Stock Yards. Iroquois Memorial, which was buried in a wholesale district, remained primarily a small outpatient facility operated by the city. During its early years, its central location brought it not only downtown accident victims but also inmates of the vice districts adjacent to the Loop.[23]

The Iroquois Theatre building, meanwhile, was quickly rebuilt inside and functioned for another two decades before it was replaced by a new theater, the Oriental, which eventually became a grimy film house and was then closed down altogether. Saved only because the Cook County court system had filled the upper floors of its office tower with overflow space for state's attorneys, the building has been renovated and is once again the site of a beautiful theater—the Ford Center for the Performing Arts Oriental Theater—approximately one hundred years after the conflagration that closed the original Iroquois so tragically.

Notes

1. Early Shepard Johnson, "The Natural History of the Central Business District with Particular Reference to Chicago," (Ph.D. diss., University of Chicago, 1941); Homer Hoyt, *One Hundred Years of Land Values in Chicago* (Chicago: University of Chicago Press, 1933), 238–90, 200–201.

2. Johnson, 248–54.

3. Quote, *Restaurant Bulletin* 1 (February 1904): 9.

4. Perry R. Duis and Glen E. Holt, "Chicago as It Was: Chicago's Tin Pan Alley," *Chicago* 30 (January 1981): 100–105.

5. *New York Dramatic Mirror,* January 9, 1904, pp. 12–13; Walter Prichard Eaton, "The Rise and Fall of the Theatrical Syndicate," *American Magazine* 70 (October 1910): 832–95; "The Great Theatrical Syndicate," *Leslie's Monthly Magazine* 58 (October 1904): 581–92; 59 (November 1904): 31–42; 59 (December 1902): 202–10; 59 (January 1905): 331–34; Alfred L. Bernheim, *The Business of the Theatre: An Economic History of the American Theatre, 1750–1932* (New York: Benjamin Blom, 1932); Monroe Lippman, "The History of the Theatrical Syndicate: Its Effect upon the Theatre in America," (Ph.D. diss., University of Michigan, 1937).

6. *Chicago Tribune,* January 4, 5, 6, 9, 10, 1904.

7. *Restaurant Bulletin* 1 (February 1904): 9.

8. "Domestic Science," *Chicago Tribune,* January 4, 1904.

9. *New York Dramatic Mirror,* January 16, 1904, p. 14; January 23, 1904, p. 10; February 6, 1904, p. 14.

10. *New York Dramatic Mirror,* January 16, 1904, pp. 12, 14; January 23, 1904, p. 10; January 30, 1904, p. 14.

11. *Chicago Tribune,* January 1, 3, 5, 1904.

12. Duis and Holt, "Chicago as It Was: Fires! Sinkings! Assassinations!" *Chicago* 31 (August 1982):108–10.

13. Some printings of the book bear the name of Marshall Everett, another popular writer. There is nothing in Fallows's correspondence regarding Everett or Fallows's authorship of the book, but there is indication that he owned the rights to it. Fallows was best known to Chicagoans as a somewhat controversial clergyman whose nonalcoholic "home salon" had tried to compete with saloons, but his career writing popular books on religion, travelogues, and biographies had dated back more than a decade. Perry R. Duis, *The Saloon: Public Drinking in Chicago and Boston, 1880–1920* (Urbana: University of Illinois Press, 1983), 199.

14. Samuel Fallows Papers, State Historical Society of Wisconsin, Mrs. L. P. Miller, Monarch Book Company, Chicago, to Rev. Samuel Fallows, Chicago, April 28, 1904, Box 10; and, Quote, W. H. H., Monarch Book Company to Rev. Samuel Fallows, March 4, 1905, Box 11.

15. *Chicago Tribune,* January 4, 1904.

16. *Chicago Tribune,* January 4, 1904; Duis, *The Saloon,* 253–54, 261.

17. Both quotes, *New York Dramatic Mirror,* February 13, 1904; second quote originally from the "Amusement Paragraph," Methodist Episcopal Church, Book of Discipline.

18. Other publications also blamed the East Coast monopoly. The critic for the *Evening Post* denounced Klaw and Erlanger for allowing so much flammable material backstage. The *American,* the Hearst paper in Chicago, criticized the management for attempting to evade the law. One cartoon in *Life* magazine, which began a special vendetta against the syndicate, featured a skeleton, in a costume from the play, standing outside a locked exit door. The caption read, "Messrs. Klaw and Erlanger present 'Mr. Bluebeard,' late of the Iroquois Theatre." Klaw and Erlanger sued *Life* over the use of their name, but when the case came to trial in 1905, it took a jury only five minutes to render a verdict in favor of the magazine. David Belasco, whose company, Independent Booking, tried to create a separate circuit, blasted the syndicate and what it had done to managers. Wilma J. Dryden, "Ironic Prologue and Epilogue to the Iroquois Fire," *Quarterly Journal of Speech* 54 (April 1968): 147–53; *Life* cartoon in John Flautz, *Life the Gentle Satyrist* (Bowling Green, Ohio: Bowling Green University Press, 1972), 177; Patrician Marks, "A Firestorm of Criticism: Metcalfe and the Theatrical Syndicate, 1904–1905," *American Periodicals* 8 (1998): 15–29.

19. The article originally appeared in *McClure's Magazine,* October 1903, and was republished in *Shame of the Cities* (New York: McClure, Phillips, 1904).

20. Richard Becker, "Edward Dunne, Reform Mayor of Chicago, 1905–1907," (Ph.D. diss., University of Chicago, 1971), 24–84, 170–72; Richard Allen Morton, *Justice and Humanity: Edward F. Dunne, Illinois Progressive* (Carbondale: Southern Illinois University Press, 1997), 15; for a defense of the mayor in office at the time of the fire, see Carter H. Harrison, *Stormy Years: The Autobiography of Carter H. Harrison* (Indianapolis: Bobbs-Merrill, 1935), 236–39.

21. The literature on this issue is enormous, but one fine example appeared a few years before the fire: Franklin S. Catlin, "The Liability of a Carrier of Passengers by Elevator," *Northwestern University Law Review* 4 (April 1896): 255–72.

22. F. C. W[igmore], "The Iroquois Theater Fire—An Outrageous Instance of the Law's Delays," *Illinois Law Review* 1 (January 1907): 395–96; Frederic C. Woodward and Frank O. Smith, "The Iroquois Theater Fire—A Flagrant Instance of the Law's Delays," *Illinois Law Review* 1 (February 1907): 429–36; George A. Follansbee, "The Iroquois Theater Cases—Another View," *Illinois Law Review* 1 (February 1907): 437–39; "Editorial Notes," *Illinois Law Review* 1 (April 1907): 606–17; "Correspondence: Judge Kimbrough's Decision in the Iroquois Theatre Case," *Illinois Law Review* 2 (June 1907): 103–6.

23. *History of Medicine and Surgery and Physicians and Surgeons of Chicago* (Chicago: Biographical Publishing Corporation, 1922), 323–24; *Chicago Tribune,* January 9, 1904, October 16, December 24, 31, 1910.

CHICAGO DEATH TRAP

PROLOGUE

One Saturday in the mid-1870s, an extraordinary article appeared on the front page of the *Chicago Times*. It occupied four columns and continued for more than two additional columns inside the newspaper, describing at length and in graphic detail what it called "a Supposititious Holocaust."[1] The headline was ominous: "BURNED ALIVE." And the banks of subheads were harrowing: "The Angel of Death Brings Terrible Mourning to Chicago," "Burning of a Theatre Last night—Hundreds Perish in the Flames," "The Weak Trampled to Death . . ." "Hundreds of Charred and Distorted Corpses . . ."

The fictitious story went on to "report" that the "smoking ruins," located in the heart of the city, were those of "one of the finest theaters in Chicago."[2] It described how once the word *fire* rang through the audience, "many of the people in the gallery"—the topmost balcony that was "overflowing" with theatergoers—"threw themselves to the parquette." Women "shrieked wild, despairing cries and fell to be trampled into eternity by the heels of the wild rushing throng." The loss of life was appalling. There were scores upon scores of "mourning households, and rows of dead bodies at the morgue."

On the surface, there seemed to be no reason why—more than three years after the Great Fire that devastated Chicago—anyone would write, or any newspaper would print, such a terrifying story. There had been a second but less devastating fire in July 1874, when some ninety acres of homes and businesses south of the city's downtown area had been wiped out. But there had not been a recent fire that began in and was confined to a theater. Why single out a playhouse, and why describe the effects of a fire in such a public place in such horrific terms?

1

The article was, of course, a warning. Theaters in general, its anonymous author declared, "are so built and so crammed with inflammable materials that a fire once started in them would in an incredibly short period gain such headway that nothing under heaven could check its mad and devouring career." Chicago theaters in particular, the article pointed out, "are tinder boxes into which humanity are placed by avaricious managers without any regard to their safety. . . . Evidently their only desire is to fill the house, gather in as much money as possible, while they take no heed to the dangers which surround their patrons."

The article—which appeared in the February 13, 1875, issue of the *Chicago Times*—was eerily prophetic. Nearly thirty years later, its gruesome, frightening images would, incredibly, become reality.

1

WARNING SIGNS

Sec. 182. All woodwork, including the under side of floor boards, and also all scenery used on or about the stage, shall be coated with a fire-proof paint. . . .

Eddie Foy was "coming home" to Chicago. Although born in New York City, Foy had grown up in Chicago, and sometime around the time of the Great Fire of 1871, he had begun his career in show business by teaming up with another teenager to sing and dance in beer halls. At heart, though, Foy was a clown with a special talent for silly costumes and broad gestures. He fashioned for himself a purposely squeaky voice. Over the next three decades, Foy's comic antics won him role after role in musical comedies and made him a star on Broadway and with touring companies. He regaled audiences throughout the country, but especially theatergoers in Chicago. He was their Eddie and had entertained them in fantasies such as *Cinderella, Ali Baba,* and *Sinbad the Sailor.*

This time, the forty-seven-year-old comedian was heading a company of 150 actors and actresses, singers, and dancers—the cast of a bit of froth entitled *Mr. Bluebeard.* It was scheduled to open November 23, 1903, as the very first attraction at the spanking new Iroquois Theatre, an opulently appointed playhouse built to house musical extravaganzas.

The company had gone on from a successful run in New York to play Pittsburgh and Indianapolis, and before it reached Chicago, it settled into Cleveland for a two-week stint in mid-October. It was there, at the Opera House, that—looking back now, a hundred years later—a disturbing incident occurred. It seemed a minor matter at the time.

One night in the midst of a performance, a flame spurted from an overloaded electrical circuit and touched fire to a flimsy piece of drapery at the side of the stage. Some of the feathery props in a number called "Triumph of the Magic Fan" caught fire, too. But the flames were quickly doused without the audience even being made aware that there was any trouble. The local fire department was not called, and no report was made to any city authority.

Foy, for one, shrugged off the mishap. It was "well-known to the electricians of the company," he explained, "that in order to obtain the desired lighting effects, they were carrying much too heavy a load of power on the wires." Foy—and apparently everyone else in the cast—was nonplussed by what happened. The fire—"by a piece of luck"—was "quickly squelched," he said.[1]

It is surprising that no one was unsettled by the incident. Theater folk are notoriously superstitious. They fret over the most trivial of circumstances if it is out of the ordinary. They are sensitive to portents. Given their propensity for subscribing to the unusual, it is difficult to imagine that both Foy and his colleagues in the cast of *Mr. Bluebeard* failed to recognize the omen for what it was: a harbinger of tragedy.

That the brief fire prompted no concern whatsoever is perhaps a testament to the real worries a traveling troupe has on its collective mind. The *Mr. Bluebeard* company was going from city to city in a special twelve-car train that was crammed with the show's plethora of costumes and props and the 280 drop curtains that made up its scenery. Just getting the entire company organized before and after each stop was a time-consuming and bothersome chore. Then there were the living arrangements that everyone had to contend with. Unless you were a superstar such as Ellen Terry, a popular leading actor like Eddie Foy could count on earning somewhere between $150 and $300 a week. That certainly was enough to live on comfortably, and Foy planned to bring with him to Chicago his wife, Madeline, and their three young children. They would put up at the Sherman House, a block or so from the Iroquois

Theatre. But other members of the cast did not fare as well. Principals earned from $60 to $150 a week, bit players somewhere between $30 and $50,[2] and, lowest of the low, a chorus girl or boy, $18 to $25.[3] Inasmuch as a hotel room cost, depending on the city and the caliber of the establishment, anywhere from $1.25 to $1.75 a night,[4] that did not leave much for meals or anything other than essentials. Moreover, the company members were expected to pay for the paints and powders they used for their makeup.

The brief blaze in Cleveland was, it can be assumed, bruited about among the cast—how could it not be?—but they gave it less attention than might be expected of veteran performers. Anyway, complacency was endemic. As Foy said, "I had been playing theatres for so long without any trouble with fire that the incident didn't give me much of a scare."[5]

Evidently, a second incident did not frighten Foy or anyone else either. It occurred the following month on the very day that *Mr. Bluebeard* opened at the Iroquois in Chicago. But in hindsight again, it is not astonishing that any danger from fire was then considered remote. After all, the owners of the new theater proudly boasted that it was "absolutely fireproof."[6]

2

"ABSOLUTELY FIREPROOF"

Sec. 185. In every building of Class V a system of
automatic sprinklers [shall be] supplied with water
from a tank located not less than 20 feet above the
highest part of roof of building. Sprinklers shall be
placed above and below the stage; also in paint room,
store room, property room and dressing rooms. . . .

The year 1903 had been a noteworthy one in Chicago. As it drew to a close in the last week of December, one of its leading newspapers, the *Daily News,* summed up the year's achievements. Perhaps the most memorable event was the city's celebration of the first centennial in its history: the founding of historic Fort Dearborn, on the site of Chicago, in 1803. Festivities were held all during the last week in September, attracting descendants of both the Indians who initially made their homes in the region and the pioneers who settled it.[1]

The centennial aside, for some time now Chicagoans had much to be proud of. It was a miracle city, a phoenix risen from the ashes. The Great Fire that occurred in the fall of 1871—a conflagration that lasted two days—had literally leveled the city. The fire had raced across the West Side, destroying homes, shanties, and mills. Winds then swept the flames

over the south branch of the Chicago River, and before long, the city's
gasworks was gone. Office buildings went next, followed by the chamber of commerce building. The courthouse, its bell still pealing, burned
to the ground two hours later. By then, the entire business district was
in flames. Soon, the city's water supply was put out of operation as the
fire headed northward, consuming stores, factories, and mansions in its
wake. The enormous blaze came to a halt when it reached the shore of
Lake Michigan. It burned itself out among squatters' shanties at the far
north end of the city. As the fire died down and spirals of smoke slowly
drifted away in the wind, what was left of Chicago resembled the shelled-
out remains of a war-ravaged city. The fire had covered four square miles,
completely burning seventeen thousand buildings and leaving some 250
residents dead and 100,000 others homeless.[2] Yet, within the short space
of four years, few of the ruins were left to hint at the devastation. Chicago had become a born-again metropolis.

Once known variously as "The Gem of the Prairie," "The Garden
City," or simply "Queen City,"[3] Chicago was now the fastest growing
metropolis in the United States, the nation's "Second City," deferring
only to New York. Its traditional eminence as gateway to the West, as a
major rail hub to points east, west, and south, and for the opportunities
for work that it represented, was still unchallenged. Its soaring population exemplified the city's status. Swelled by immigrants, by 1900, Chicago was the largest Roman Catholic archdiocese in the nation, chiefly
because of the Irish who migrated there.[4] But there were Poles, Swedes,
Czechs, Dutch, Danes, Norwegians, Croatians, Slovaks, Lithuanians, and
Greeks, too—more of them, in fact, than in any other American city,[5]
not to mention the Germans, Italians, English, Welsh, and Scots who
had also flocked to the city. Chicago began the twentieth century with
a population close to 1.7 million persons, and three out of every four of
them were immigrants or the children of foreign-born.[6]

Chicago had increased in size, too, taking under its municipal wing a
surrounding 120 square miles. But its physical expansion and population growth told only a small part of its reputation. For undaunted by
the ruination caused by the Great Fire—on the contrary, inspired by it—
the city had become the birthplace of the skyscraper. Combustible wood
and brick construction was no longer tolerated. Metal beams now carried the great weight that heavy masonry walls once bore. They were cast

iron at first. But cast iron gave way to wrought iron, and wrought iron to steel. The skeletal construction method, together with the development of electrically operated passenger elevators and the so-called floating-raft foundation, which solved the problem of building on the area's soft sand and clay, made the sky literally the limit. Some buildings rose to a height of twenty-two stories. Architects flocked to the city, so many and so innovative that by the end of the 1880s, the era had become known as the golden age of the Chicago School of Architecture.[7] In the almost twenty years between the Great Fire in 1871 and 1890, more than $252 million was spent on new buildings[8]—an impressive sum in an era when a nickel still bought a beer and a free lunch. By then, another structural method was coming into use, one that Chicago was also becoming famous for: reinforced concrete construction.[9]

It was here, in Chicago, that the Columbian Exposition was fittingly held in 1893. Fed through the six railroad depots in the city, millions of sightseers flocked to the ornate exhibition halls and palatial grounds. They crowded the city's downtown streets, too, and were awed and impressed by what they saw, or didn't see. Eighty-two miles of lines made Chicago's the largest cable-car system in the world.[10] An elevated railway begun in 1890 was completed well before the century was out; the girdle of tracks around the very core of the city's business district was called the Loop. But aside from the tracks overhead, there was no forest of dangling electric and telephone wires to mar the urban landscape; the city required utilities to bury their lines as a safety feature and to prevent what was called "a New York type of ugliness."[11] And the streets, so it seemed at least, were safe. Police headquarters in City Hall had a nationally renowned telephone-and-signal system connected to signal boxes surmounted by gas lamps at prominent street corners.[12]

It was the fire department, however, that was the city's real pride. One would have thought that the Great Fire would have stimulated a serious reform of the city's fire department and fire code. Instead, it was the frightening blaze in the extremely dry summer of 1874 three years later—a fire that reminded everyone of the devastation wrought by the Great Fire—that prompted the changes. The so-called "little big fire" of 1874 covered some eighteen blocks, destroyed well over eight hundred buildings—though they were mostly small, cheap wooden stores and dwellings—and killed about twenty persons.[13] Despite the devastation, the pressure for change had come not from Chicagoans but from outside the community. Insurance companies simply lifted their coverage of the city and refused to write new policies until the city's fire protection was improved. The companies, in fact, hired a consultant who drew up the specific bylaws of a new fire code and presented them to the city as a fait accompli.

Not only was the fire code rewritten, but at the city's own bidding, the fire department itself was strengthened. By 1903, the department's alarm system included 2,396 automatic signal boxes as well as an elaborate network of telegraph lines.[14] Its rolls included upwards of twelve hundred men and ninety-two engine companies (including five fire boats), twenty-seven hook-and-ladder companies, and fifteen chemical engines.[15] An alarm in the business district automatically drew at least five horse-drawn engine companies, two truck companies, two chemical companies, and, if the fire was in a structure abutting the Chicago River, a fire boat and hose tender. As many as thirty-five engine companies could be concentrated within twenty minutes at a serious fire in the business district, each of them consisting of a hose wagon and a steam fire engine manned by a captain, a lieutenant, an engineer and his assistant, six pipemen, and two drivers.[16] "I think we have the quickest fire alarm system in the world," Fire Chief William H. Musham declared.[17]

Busy, bustling Chicago. Despite riots connected with strikes and still-lingering walkouts by railway men and livery drivers, business was so good during 1903, reported the *Daily News,* that the majority of manufacturers and merchants had little cause to complain. Even a periodic downturn in the nation's stock market during the year failed to dim the economic outlook.[18]

Ever since the turn of the century, the city's prosperity had been reflected in its flourishing cultural life, for the city was not only a major transportation hub but also the principal center for art and entertainment in Midwest America. It could boast the ever-growing and impressive Art Institute, the Academy of Science, the Municipal Art League, dedicated to beautifying streets and public buildings, a symphony orchestra, and no less than thirteen major public and privately operated libraries. A special attraction for both Chicagoans and day-trippers from the cities and towns within hailing distance were Chicago's thirty-five music halls—vaudeville, burlesque, and legitimate theaters.

The roster of theaters included two playhouses for melodrama and comedy that were already in the process of going up: the Cleveland (named after its owner W. S. Cleveland and not the city) and the LaSalle. Business, in fact, was so good that the veteran theatrical companies that formed a syndicate controlling the Illinois and Powers' theaters believed that there was room for yet another playhouse, especially one with the capacity to mount large-scale musicals. The syndicate was comprised of three partnerships—Powers and Davis of Chicago, Klaw and Erlanger of New York, and Nixon and Zimmerman of Philadelphia.[19] Optimistic about the future, they decided to build the new theater on Randolph Street, between Dearborn and State Streets, in the heart of downtown Chicago. It would be called the Iroquois, and no expense would be spared to make it the city's "most beautiful temple of the drama."

The Chicago partners who completed the syndicate's triumvirate were both well-schooled in the ins and outs of running a playhouse. They had met while working at Hooley's Theatre. Harry J. Powers was perhaps best known for his association with that theater. Hooley's was a landmark playhouse on Randolph Street east of LaSalle Street that over the years headlined such stage luminaries as Eleonora Duse, Maude Adams, William Gillett, John Drew, and Sir Henry Irving.[20] Born in Ireland in 1859, Powers was still a child when his parents emigrated to the United States.[21] Powers began as an usher in Hooley's in 1877 when still a teenager. Competent, eager, self-taught, he was able to slowly progress from one back-office job to another. In 1898, twenty-one years after joining Hooley's, he became its owner. He was two years shy of being forty years old. Powers had the playhouse remodeled and changed its name to his own. The Powers' Theatre was known for its quiet elegance and superior class of bookings.

Though balding and sixteen years Powers's senior, William J. Davis looked younger than his partner. Will Davis—as he was popularly known—had also had a much more adventuresome career. At the age of fourteen, he had joined the Union navy, serving four years until the end of the Civil War in 1865. After the war, he worked for the Internal Revenue Service in Mississippi before moving to Chicago as a railway representative. Once in Chicago, he changed careers again, becoming an advance agent and manager of performing dramatic companies. The career move was propitious. He worked first in 1873 as treasurer of the Adelphia Theater. Three years later, he managed a tour of minstrels to

California and, later, the national tour of an American company known as Her Majesty's Grand Opera Company. Over the years, he was connected with several Chicago theaters. For a short time, he was manager of Hooley's while Powers worked there.[22] He later toured for two years with Gilbert and Sullivan's *H.M.S. Pinafore* before returning to Chicago to manage Haverly's Theater, a reconstructed burlesque house. His wife, Jessie Bartlett,[23] was a noted young contralto whom he met while on tour with *Pinafore.*

Davis was as ambitious and capable as Powers and even more knowledgeable about theatrical matters than his partner. He had, in fact, made such a name for himself in the local theatrical world that he was considered the dean of Chicago playhouse managers. Davis was at Haverly's in 1885 when the popular Ellen Terry rechristened it the Columbia Theatre. He was offered the opportunity to purchase the theater, but instead he allied himself with Al Hayman, a successful San Francisco theatrical producer, and took a ten-year lease on the house. In 1887, he became manager of the newly built Haymarket Theatre, and in 1900, in partnership with Hayman, Davis was primarily responsible for the building of the Illinois Theatre on Jackson Boulevard, a playhouse that he also managed.

According to the syndicate's plans for the Iroquois Theatre, Davis and Powers would both be listed as its resident owners and managers. Davis, however, would actually serve as the president and general manager of the Iroquois Theatre Company. His position fatefully placed him as the individual chiefly responsible for the playhouse's operation.

Determined to give Chicago "its most beautiful temple of the drama,"[24] Davis and Powers chose as the Iroquois's architect a young man with whom they had both worked and in whom they both had confidence: Benjamin H. Marshall, whose design for the Raymond Apartments on North Michigan Avenue in 1900 was the first in a string of apartment houses that would make him one of the city's most popular and successful architects. Marshall had handled the remodeling of the old Hooley's Theatre for Powers, and more recently had designed the Illinois for Davis. He was only twenty-eight years old in 1902, when he first completed the preliminary plans for the Iroquois.

Marshall was enormously gifted. A flamboyant native of Chicago, he had extravagant tastes that he had first developed when, at the age of seventeen, he went to work as a clerk for a wholesale clothing manufacturer. He quickly found he had a knack for designing men's suits and began wearing his own distinguishing wardrobe, one that much later in the twentieth century would be associated with the writer Tom Wolfe: a white suit, white shoes, and a white hat with a black band.[25] After two years, Marshall decided to pursue a newly found interest in architecture, joining as a clerk the architect H. R. Wilson. In a brief two years, without any formal schooling, Marshall was made a full partner in Wilson's firm, which then became Wilson and Marshall.[26] He quickly became known for his penchant for the esthetics of the edifices he designed, supervising not only the design of a building but also insisting on a voice in its decor. Self-taught, highly motivated, and smug, Marshall went out on his own in 1902.

From the beginning, the Iroquois project was plagued with delays. Marshall was the chief culprit. He finished his initial designs for the Iroquois on July 4, 1902, but then dawdled over the completion of the final blueprints. It wasn't until more than five months later, on December 15, that the plans were approved and a permit for the erection of the building was issued.[27]

The plot of land Davis and Powers selected for the theater was an L-shaped lot that turned the corner from Randolph to Dearborn Street, wrapping itself around what was once known as the Real Estate Exchange Building on the corner.[28] An abutting forty-foot-deep vacant lot on the Dearborn Street side of the theater was scheduled in the future to be the site of a twelve-story hotel.[29] The firm selected to build the theater was the George H. Fuller Company, a major construction company with offices in nine cities in the Northeast and Midwest. It subcontracted all fireproofing details to one of the pioneer establishments in the field, the Roebling Construction Company of New York City. However, another delay—this time apparently caused by labor troubles that had inconvenienced builders throughout Chicago for some time[30]—forced postponement of actual construction for seven months until the summer of 1903, when ground was finally broken.

Time was pressing, and one can imagine that Davis and Powers—as the responsible owner-managers in situ—were upset by the delays. They had already missed out on a summer of performances. Now holiday seasons were in the offing, Thanksgiving and then Christmas and New

Year's. These were the most profitable times for a theater, especially one designed to stage costly spectacles. But Marshall was again holding up the work. He was tardy in filing the detailed plans for the theater's immense stage. The main frame of the building went up quickly enough, and the interior was as quickly partitioned off. As of September 25, the interior was ready for plastering, but it wasn't until nearly two weeks later, on October 6, that the plastering was under way. That was aggravating enough, but where was Marshall with the plans for the stage? Before work on it could even begin, the plans had to be approved by the city building department. The reason for Marshall's procrastination is not clear, but it must have been upsetting for Davis and Powers. Would the theater be completed within the next six weeks, in time for the approaching holiday breaks?

Work on the interior was finished on October 12, but still the plans for the stage were not completed. That didn't happen for another week. As a result, it wasn't until October 28 that the stage's elaborate electric lighting system was put in place and work on the stage as well as on interior decorations was progressing at last.[31] Having already lost several months to all the delays, Davis and Powers evidently pressured the Fuller Company to complete the job. They had hoped to open the theater in mid-November,[32] but that proved impossible. The new date they settled on, their fingers crossed, was November 23. The inaugural performance would take place on that Monday evening, three days before Thanksgiving Day and the start of the holiday weekend.

Even before the Iroquois was ready to open, it was attracting enormous attention. "Structurally perhaps," one of the nation's leading engineers wrote, the theater "had no superior in this country or in the world."[33] Its cost was said to run to either $500,000 or $1.1 million, depending on who was quoted,[34] neither figure a trifling sum in 1903. Still, either figure must have included the furnishings and stage equipment, because the building permit issued almost a year earlier gave the cost of construction as $300,000. On the other hand, there apparently were a number of changes made in the original plans. The seating capacity, for example, was listed in the records of the City Collector's Office as 1,692—a trifle less than what turned out to be the theater's actual capacity.[35] The question was, what other changes had been made but not reported?

When the theater was finally ready to open, it did, indeed, live up to the promise of its being the "most beautiful temple of the drama"—a temple that a passerby on Randolph Street could hardly fail to notice. The imposing facade of the Iroquois resembled the entrance to a classical Greek place of worship.[36] Actually, and unwittingly prophetic, the archway was meant to resemble a monument erected in Paris to commemorate the death in 1857 of 150 victims of a flash fire at a charity bazaar.[37] It was of Bedford stone, deeply recessed so that it seemed larger than it really was. Its central feature was a coved arch fifty-two feet high that was flanked by stone columns that, alone, weighed thirty-six tons. The columns and accompanying pilasters rested upon a huge pedestal of St. Cloud granite and were surmounted by a cornice nine feet high. The cornice continued upward to form a pediment in which rested a cartouche surrounded on one side by the semirecumbent figure of a woman representing Tragedy and, on the other side, the figure of a jester typifying Comedy. But a passerby's attention would have undoubtedly been drawn directly above the entranceway to another, lower pediment, this one broken to allow space for the sculptured bust of an Iroquois Indian. Davis, a student of history and collector of Americana—and the one who had chosen the theater's name—had also selected the bust himself. In its background was a screen of ornamental ironwork set with jewel glass that admitted light to the lobby inside.

If the passerby was enticed by the billboards outside announcing the current performance, he, or she, would enter one of the playhouse's five pairs of double mahogany doors and step into the lobby, or vestibule, an elliptical room whose eighteen-foot-high ceiling was beamed and paneled in marble and subtly touched with antique gold. To the left were the ticket windows; to the right, a staircase leading to an administrative office on the second floor as well as to the manager's office on the top, third floor.

Ticket in hand, the theatergoer would then proceed straight ahead through one of three triple-winged doorways into the foyer, or Grand Stair Hall, an imposing room patterned after that of the Operá Comique in Paris and the Congressional Library in Washington, D.C. It was all of sixty feet wide and eighty feet long, its walls of white marble with a colonnade of pavonazzo pillars carrying the ceiling upon groined arches sixty feet above the tessellated floor—"by far the most majestic interior in this city or in this country," its owners declared.[38] Everywhere were tinges of green and rose touched with gold. The skylight above the vast room was of delicately tinted glass revealing cloud forms studded with jewels, lit from behind to create the illusion of stars sparkling in a changing sky. The hidden lights were among the two thousand electric bulbs that illuminated the vast room.

For the convenience of playgoers, ladies' and men's parlors and coat-check rooms were located on either side of the center of the foyer, the ladies' to the left, the men's on the right. Below the latter, reached by stairs, was a men's smoking room.

It must have been difficult not to pause and take in this breathtaking scene. Immediately to the right and left along the outer walls rose grand staircases, each with five landings leading to promenades. Between columns that marched up these staircases were iron filigree candelabra. The wall dado was of white marble. High up along the line of the second story was a succession of arched French windows with little balconies draped in rich oriental colors, their frames set with mirrors that were circled in a velvety red. Hanging from the bosses of groined arches were Etruscan crystal bowl lamps. And in every embrasure, whether along the walls of the hall or on the stairways, were deeply tufted settees upholstered in fine fabrics. They and heavy damask draperies along the walls were of a deep red.

The theatergoer with a ticket for the parquet, or orchestra, floor, continued straight ahead from the Grand Stair Hall through one of the three triple-winged glass-paneled doors leading directly into the auditorium, a space that was almost as imposing as the one just left. It was ninety feet wide, seventy-one feet in depth to the stage.[39] The paneling of the walls was in the French style, while the color scheme was American Beauty red, with neutral tints of green and gold. A wainscot of curly Hungarian ash ran six feet high around the walls.

It was here, in the parquet, that the building took the vertical line in its L shape. Up until now, a theatergoer had been heading northward from the entrance on Randolph Street. But the enormous stage—50 feet deep and 110 feet in width[40]—was to the left, or west. Directly in front, and, of course, facing westward—that is, toward the stage—were nineteen rows of seats, 744 in all, not counting the seats in two boxes on either side of the stage that were almost level with the parquet floor; they could hold an additional twenty-four persons. The rows were slightly curved and divided by three carpeted aisles, two of which ran the entire length of the orchestra, from the first row to the nineteenth. A middle aisle extended only from the ninth row to the nineteenth. The sight lines were impressive. The first row of seats was slightly above the stage line, and behind it the floor was raked. In addition, none of the boxes on either side jutted out into the auditorium to block anyone's view.[41] Moreover, because the balconies above the parquet were built on the cantilever principle, the only columns necessary for their support were behind the last row of seats. As a result, every playgoer had an unobstructed view of the stage.

If, instead of the parquet, the ticket was for either the dress circle (first balcony) or the gallery (second balcony), the theatergoer would have immediately turned on entering the Grand Stair Hall. An usher would steer those going to the dress circle to the staircase on the right, or east, side. Those going to the gallery took the staircase on the left, or west.[42]

The first of the two balconies, the dress circle, was so high above the parquet that the top of the proscenium arch could be seen from every seat. There were nine rows of seats in this section of the auditorium. They held 465 persons, and a single box on either side—above the parquet-level boxes below—held eight persons each. A ticketholder had a choice of three entryways to the dress circle. If the ticket was for the first or second row, entrance was by a stairway that began off the foyer below and was used to reach both the parquet boxes and then, continuing upward, the front of the balcony. If the ticket was for a middle row, the theatergoer had to walk down four steps from either side of the balcony promenade and through a double door. The third entryway, on the east side and leading to the back rows of the dress circle, where the raking was most pronounced, required walking *up* three steps and through a pair of double folding doors. (Those three steps, by the way, were not in Benjamin Marshall's original plans. They were there to correct an error that made it impossible to see the stage from the back row of the dress circle. The balcony had to be tilted more to accommodate the sight line.)[43] Besides aisles running down either side of the rows, there were three aisles dissecting the rows. Each row was about fourteen inches above the next, and steps leading to them were, correspondingly, the same height.[44]

The cheapest seats were in the gallery floor. Like the dress circle below, it had ten rows of seats, with aisles on either side and three aisles dissecting the main body of seats, which numbered 475. This second balcony was, however, even more steeply raked than the dress circle. Each row was twenty-seven inches above the next and required two steps to reach. To enter the gallery, a ticketholder had several choices once the balcony promenade was reached. Each required the playgoer to make one or more turns to the right or to the left in ascending the stairways. The front rows were accessible from a platform stair leading from the top of the west flight of the main stairs. The middle rows were reached by a double run of stairs, the last rows by a triple run of stairs.

Davis and Powers bragged that "a praiseworthy feature of this admirably planned house of amusement" was the number of exits leading off the auditorium. In addition to the "directness" of the entryways through the foyer, there were "far more numerous" emergency doors along "the entire north frontage" and a "large emergency exit" leading across the stage to Dearborn Street from the boxes on the south side of the parquet.[45]

In total, the theater could accommodate 1,724 patrons. In practice, as the owners said, there was "plenty of good standing room on each floor."[46] Following the curve of the parquet, the floor in its rear behind the last row of seats ranged from six to twelve feet in width and could easily handle standees.[47] Similar, though narrower, aisles ran behind the seats in the dress circle and the gallery.

The Iroquois finally opened, as Davis and Powers had hoped, on Monday evening, November 23, 1903. Curiously, however, the building inspector's final report—"Building completed. O.K."[48]—was not dated until two days later. And despite all the pressure Davis and Powers had put on Marshall and the construction company, the theater was far from "O.K."

3

PLAY AND PLAYERS

Sec. 188. In buildings . . . where stationary scenery is used, there shall always be kept for use portable fire extinguishers or hand fire pumps, on and under the stage; in fly gallery and in rigging loft, also at least four (4) fire department axes, two twenty-five (25) feet hooks, two (2) fifteen feet hooks, two (2) ten (10) feet hooks. . . .

*M*r. Bluebeard was a silly musical comedy. The plot was based loosely on the sinister actions of a nefarious character in a popular nineteenth-century pantomime. The stage Bluebeard was nowhere like the ruthless tyrant after whom it was modeled: believed to be either Comorre the Cursed, a sixth-century Breton chieftain who murdered his wives when they became pregnant, or a French nobleman named Gilles de Rais, whose interest in alchemy and witchcraft led, so it was said, to the death of as many as two hundred women and children.[1]

For some reason, the gruesomeness of the subject appealed to English audiences. The story was first presented as a melodrama at Covent Garden in 1791 and subsequently turned into a pantomime at Sadler's Wells. It soon became a staple of acting companies during holiday seasons.[2]

There were any number of versions of the tale. Its basic plot deals with how Bluebeard marries and murders one sister after another; how, against Bluebeard's orders, his latest bride defies him and opens the secret chamber where he keeps the bodies of his former wives; how her sister alerts her brothers to save her; and how Bluebeard himself is killed in the end.

In a ribald version Eddie Foy performed in 1890, Bluebeard's fate was not death but, worse still, being endlessly tormented by his resurrected wives. That version, a local production, was called *Bluebeard Jr.,* with Foy in the lead role. It was nothing at all like *Mr. Bluebeard,* but Foy's name was so indelibly linked with the earlier version that the production at the Iroquois Theatre was often referred to as *Bluebeard Jr.* or a variation on that title.

For one thing, unlike the 1890 version, *Mr. Bluebeard* was an English import, a spectacular production that first played at the Drury Lane in London. It was Americanized for its run in the United States with "Negro melodies indigenous to New York and ditties topical with Chicago cheek and Milwaukee beer."[3] Klaw and Erlanger brought the musical into the Knickerbocker Theatre in New York, paying $65,000 to transport the costumes and scenery to the United States and lavishing a total of $150,000 on it before opening night. The play consisted of three acts with a total of eleven scenes, some of which were elaborate and contained more than one change of backdrops. The costumes and sets for one scene alone, "Triumph of the Magic Fan," were said to have cost $38,000.[4] There were sixteen hundred costumes in all,[5] and a good portion of the money that the producers spent went to pay for shortening the already scanty attire worn by the English female performers because they were "built on a larger mold" than the Americans.[6]

The cast numbered a staggering 280 performers, but that included supernumeraries who, like spear carriers in an opera, appeared on stage for decorative purposes. Except for the members of the Pony Ballet—twelve diminutive English chorines—and the Grigolatis troupe of German aerialists, the rest of the company was cast in New York City.

Although Eddie Foy was not taking the role of Bluebeard and was not on stage all the time, he was headlining the show. This time he was playing Sister Anne, a role that gave the actor the chance for more comic turns, wiggling an unwieldy bustle at awkward moments, often in a direction directly opposite from the way he was moving. The part also called for Foy to do a bit of clowning with two concealed young men cavorting as a Pet Elephant, and for him to sing, in his thin, shrill stage voice, two solos, "I'm a Poor Unhappy Maid" and "Hamlet Was a Melancholy Dane." Dan McAvoy, another veteran comedian, was Bluebeard. Bonnie Maginn, a former Weber and Fields music hall favorite, and Blanche Adams took the female leads. Other roles were played by regulars of the Broadway stage—Adele Rafter, Herbert Cawthorne, Nora Cecil, Robert Evans. Lesser lights appeared as Bluebeard's six pretty wives and his six ugly wives. The latter were performed by men.[7]

Mr. Bluebeard opened at the Knickerbocker on January 21, 1903, to mixed reviews. New York critics agreed that it was "an enormous spectacle." The *Herald* reviewer described the play as "a kaleidoscopic aggregation of beautiful robes, brilliant color effects, wonderful electric tints."[8] The *Times* critic was bowled over by "Girls, girls, girls, nothing but girls—flashing, dashing, entrancing girls!"[9] The play "dazzles the vision with its splendor," the *Clipper* declared.[10] Everyone was taken with the separate ballets in the "Magic Fan" scene, each ballet "representing the six most picturesque countries of the world in respect of fans, with music to match, and scenery that seemed composed of feathers and lace."[11] But the highlight, all the reviewers agreed, was Fraulein Else Haerting of the Grigolatis troupe, who brought the second act to an exciting conclusion. She flew out from the stage, much like Peter Pan, on what was called a trolley wire, strewing pink carnations over the audience, as she swung back and forth between the stage and the top of the gallery. It was, the *Times* man wrote, "a moment of breathless excitement."[12]

Alas, for all the admiring adjectives there were a like number of disdainful ones. The *Dramatic Mirror* was especially negative. Its reviewer said so much money was spent on costumes and scenery that "there was nothing left with which to purchase even a limited amount of brains for the creation of the libretto." As for the costumes, the obviously puritanical critic said, they were "painfully scant": Although "each coryphee must have had seven or eight changes it is doubtful if there was enough material in them all to make for each figure one serviceable article of apparel." The music, the *Dramatic Mirror*'s man added, "was decidedly commonplace. Above all, it was very, very loud, and some of the finales, in fact, closely resembled a subway explosion."[13] The reviewer for the *Sun* described the play as a "monstrous, almost formless piece . . . best described as a series of beautiful ballets, surrounded by a watery waste of silly dialogue." Eddie Foy was "intermittently funny. At any rate he was not so noisy."[14] Dan McAvoy was "simply tragic." The play should have ended "where the fairy from Berlin flies out over the adoring audience and strews her priceless flowers."[15]

Even though the reviews were far from heartening, *Mr. Bluebeard* played twenty-one weeks at the Knickerbocker. It closed in late May and after a brief respite—in which a number of cast changes were made— the production went on tour. Foy was still the star of the show. But Harry Gilfoil, a seasoned performer in many a Klaw and Erlanger production, took over the role of Bluebeard from the lackluster Dan McAvoy. And, as fate would have it, the premiere of the aerialists, replacing the German girl who soared high above the audience, tossing flowers, was now a petit twenty-four-year-old American, Nellie Reed.

The touring company was made up of some 150 performers in all. Supernumeraries, many of whom were children, would be hired locally. The troupe left New York, taking with it the unusually large number of costumes and drop curtains that the play called for. The curtains themselves represented nearly three thousand square yards of material.[16] There were so many of them that when they were suspended from the gridiron above a stage they completely filled the scenic tower, each separated by only a few inches of space.[17] It took eleven miles of manila rope to hang the drops, and about eight thousand square feet of white pine to make up the frames, battens, braces, profiles, and set pieces that held them. Typical of stage sets of the time, much of the scenery was painted on strong linen canvas, but cotton gauze of a texture like mosquito netting was used to create the illusion of skies and to create wispy effects. The drops, whether of canvas or gauze, were all painted with oil paints, which made them slightly less prone to catching fire than unpainted canvas, but hardly fireproof.[18] The manila rope was smeared with oil to make hoisting and lowering smoother. All the scenery—the drops, the rope, the lumber—was highly combustible.[19]

Mr. Bluebeard was booked to play engagements in Pittsburgh, Indianapolis, and Cleveland, biding time, so to speak, waiting until the Iroquois Theatre in Chicago was completed. The brief blaze that occurred during a performance in Cleveland, when an overloaded electrical circuit set fire to a drop curtain, was quickly forgotten.

Eddie Foy was certainly not worried at all about the show going into the new Iroquois. "We were told that the theatre was the very last word in efficiency, convenience, and safety," he said.[20] As a matter of fact, what he and the rest of the cast saw was impressive. "Backstage was far and away the most commodious I have ever seen," Foy remarked.[21] At the south end—stage right—were five stories of dressing rooms for the company reached by both a stairwell and an electric elevator.[22] Dressing rooms for the supernumeraries that would be hired were in the basement. In all, there were forty dressing rooms that could accommodate four hundred persons.[23]

In addition, the Iroquois stage was deep: 50 feet from footlights to rear wall, and 110 feet wide. Looking beyond the footlights into the audience, the auditorium was so wide and shallow that it brought the balconies much closer than they were in other theaters, bonding performer and theatergoer in an unusual manner. The proscenium opening was itself 46 feet wide. Backstage, the steel gridiron that would anchor the drop curtains was 75 feet above the stage floor. At the north end—stage left— were two fly galleries constructed of steel with cinder concrete floorings. "They must have had as much room back there as, or more than they have in the Metropolitan Opera House in New York," said Foy.[24]

There were two exits. One was the stage door in the northwest corner of the stage, leading to the alleyway behind the north wall of the theater, which was called Couch Place. The door was inset in one of the mammoth swinging double doors used to accommodate the loading and unloading of scenery. It led to a wide platform three feet above the ground, which facilitated the moving of sets in and out of freight wagons and was also convenient for performers who arrived by carriage and could step directly into the theater without getting their feet wet in any mud or slush in the street. The other exit was an emergency door on the Dearborn Street side, which looked out on the vacant lot set aside for the planned hotel.[25]

For all its grandiose accoutrements and conveniences, the theater proved to be, Foy later said, "a fool's paradise."[26] Yet, at the time, neither he nor anyone else was shaken when a second incident involving a fire happened. It occurred on the very day that the Iroquois was to open. And later, that night—opening night—an outwardly minor request from some uncomfortably warm theater patrons would, in retrospect, hide a troubling consequence.

4

OPENING NIGHT

Sec. 181. All doors in buildings of Classes IV and V
shall open outward.

Seats for *Mr. Bluebeard* went on sale at the box office on Tuesday, November 17. The play was scheduled to run from November 23 through New Year's, when it was to give way to a production of *Ben Hur.* To make up for time lost during the Iroquois's construction, performances were to be held every night, including Sundays, at eight o'clock, with a holiday matinee at two in the afternoon on Thanksgiving Day in addition to regular Wednesday and Saturday matinees. Ticket prices for *Mr. Bluebeard* were in line with what other theaters in Chicago then charged: $1.50 for a seat in the parquet or in the first four rows of the dress circle; $1 for remaining rows in the dress circle; 75¢ for the first five rows in the gallery, the rest 50¢; and $15 for a box seating six persons.[1] Standing room cost 35¢.[2]

Advertisements touted the Iroquois as "The Theatric sensation of CHICAGO'S CENTURY,"[3] and to take advantage of the much-heralded opening night of the new playhouse scheduled for Monday, November 23, Davis and Powers announced that a special auction for seats would be held a week in advance at the Powers' Theatre. "No resident of Chicago imbued with the proper amount of local pride," the ads read, "can afford to miss the dedicatory performance in the best theater on earth."

Eddie Foy would be in attendance at the auction to "help it along."[4] "CHICAGO ALWAYS LEADS," the ads boasted: "Biggest, Brightest and Best in every other way it now has the theater to correspond." The promotional ploy worked. The house sold out, though Davis and Powers never disclosed what the take was.

The morning of the opening performance found the Grigolatis troupe rehearsing its aerial ballet on stage to the accompaniment of hammers wielded by carpenters, the "swish of scrubbing," and a cacophony of other laborers rushing to finish work on the interior of the Iroquois. The cleaning brigade had to vie with marble fitters for a place to work on the foyer floor, while in the lobby at the front of the theater a "harassed" box-office clerk contended with a long line of ticket buyers hoping to purchase a seat or standing room for the theater's gala debut. "To-night everything will be in perfect order," Will Davis's son assured an observer. "It may look like a big task, but we'll have it done."[5]

Later, in the afternoon, a few hours before the curtain was to rise, workers from the George H. Fuller Company were still busy in the theater. A number of seamstresses and young actresses were in the dressing rooms for supernumeraries under the stage, working together to complete costume alterations. Suddenly, a gas tank in a nearby room exploded. A carpenter, John Bickles, was in a room opposite the one in which the explosion took place. Flames shot over the eight-foot partition between him and the explosion, but he escaped injury. While the actresses and seamstresses fled up a stairway to the stage proper, theater workers struggled to quench the fire, helped in part because there were not many flammable materials in the area. The blaze was put out after only slight damage was done to several dressing rooms, but some of the costumes that were being refitted were destroyed.

The incident had no impact whatsoever on the festivities accompanying the premiere. The workmen and the theater staff involved knew about the fire, of course, and word of the occurrence undoubtedly spread through the acting company. But again, no report was made to local fire officials or to any city authority. Bickles, who was troubled by the fact that the fire was hushed up, voiced his concern. He was subsequently fired by the construction company.[6]

Opening night was a festive affair. The names of the theatergoers—all resplendently dressed in tuxedos and evening gowns—read like a roster of Chicago's social elite. In the boxes and parquet seats were the Booths, Dr. and Mrs. H. H. Brown, the Feltons, the Leichts, the Schuttlers. The Revells had as their guests the Babcocks, while in an upper box, the Plamandons played host to the Ambergs. Edward H. Peters and his wife entertained the O'Garas in their box, while in another box were the Shedds. The Brysons, the Conovers, the Ecksteins, the Kimbarks, the Kennedys, the Trudes—they were all there. Will Davis hosted fellow syndicate member Samuel Nixon and his family, who had come from Philadelphia for the opening. His partner, Harry Powers, was in the parquet with his wife. Benjamin Marshall was seated in a lower box with his father and mother.[7]

Most of the playgoers arrived early, eager to roam through the theater, take in the Grand Stair Hall, and marvel at the decor. "The general aspect of the Iroquois makes for joy," the reporter covering the opening for the *Chicago Evening Post* declared. "The instant you put foot inside you say to yourself it's a cheerful place."[8] "No theater anywhere is handsomer than the Iroquois," wrote Amy Leslie of the *Chicago Daily News.* "Except L'Opera in Paris no theater I ever saw is so resplendently spirited in architecture."[9] W. H. Hubbard, who was covering the opening for the *Chicago Tribune,* was even more rhapsodic. "A playhouse so splendid in its every appointment, so beautiful in its every part, so magnificent and yet so comfortable, Chicago has heretofore not been able to call its own," he declared. "The Iroquois is certainly unrivaled in perfection among the regular amusement places of the west, and it is doubtful," he continued, "if the east can boast more than one or two houses that are its equal." The Iroquois, he said, was "a place of rare and impressive dignity—a theater about as near ideal in nearly every respect as could be desired." "The enterprise which made the erection of the new theater possible," he added, "has given the Chicago playgoers a virtual temple of beauty."[10]

As a reporter for the *Inter Ocean* promised, the production itself provided "a most enthusiastic christening."[11] Leslie of the *Daily News* praised the production, saying "'Mr. Bluebeard' has been rescued from its British stupidity by squandered wealth plain to be seen in the costumes, the tornadoes of brilliant paint and spangles, the armies of dancing, singing and laughing comedians and a ballet which alone is a delight." She made a point of picking out a "pale, fragile little lady" in the chorus—Elise Romaine by name—who made "a hit" of an ensemble number "without reaching beyond the line of the choristers."[12] Hubbard of the *Tribune* was especially taken by the same chorus girl, though he did not know her name. She "captured the audience's fancy by some remarkably clever and expressive eccentric dancing."

Hubbard, for one, however, was just as critical of the plot and music of *Mr. Bluebeard* as New York critics had been. The music, he lamented, "is hopelessly common save bits here and there which are filched from the classics." Still, he praised "the spirited manner in which chorus and principals sing the tunes and the vigorous style in which they dance to them." He thought Harry Gilfoil—who "sings entirely out of one side of his face," and badly at that—made the part of Bluebeard "acceptable with clever imitations." Although the reviewer for the *Chicago Evening Post* found Bonnie Maginn rather "stout" and no longer of "the nimble toe,"[13] Hubbard thought the one-time Weber and Fields star "agile and pretty." However, he reserved his most favorable comments for Eddie Foy, whose personality, Hubbard said, is "so good natured, his humor so infectious, and his cleverness at funmaking so great that he cannot fail to win the tribute of applause and laughter from his auditors." He doted on Foy's "irresistible little tom-cat smile," his "facial expression and absurd 'singing voice.'" Foy was called back time and again for encores, he noted, when the comedian sang "I'm a Poor Unhappy Maid" in "excruciating mock grief" and later when he turned "Hamlet Was a Melancholy Dane" into "a grave-scene that set the large audience in roars."[14]

At intermission following the second act—after Nellie Reed had swung high above the audience, scattering petals on the audience below—there were spontaneous calls from the audience for Will Davis and Harry Powers, and after a few moments Davis appeared before the curtain, but bringing with him Benjamin Marshall. Davis credited "western talent, abilities, and enthusiasm" for the building of the theater. He called on Samuel Nixon to take a bow, pointing out to the audience that Nixon, though from Philadelphia, was also from the west "being a Hoosier." Even the normally self-effacing Powers was at last coaxed up onto the stage. He said it was the patronage of the Chicago public that had made possible the planning and realization of the new theater. There were then loud calls from the gallery for "he whom we call 'Eddie'" to appear, but the orchestra struck up "America" and the audience settled back to enjoy the final act.[15]

A singular circumstance had occurred earlier in the evening as theatergoers took their seats. The later telling of it would cast doubt on the propriety of the Iroquois management. The day had been, for Chicago in late autumn, a mild day, with temperatures in the upper 40s. Decked out in finery, some persons found the theater overly warm, and they complained. George M. Dusenberry, the house manager, had an usher, Willard Sayles, open both the inner set of exit doors on the north side of the building and the heavy outer iron ones they concealed that opened directly to the fire escapes leading down to Couch Place. Dusenberry's order was an exception to the rule, and shortly after Sayles opened the exit doors, Will Davis appeared and ordered Sayles to close the doors "and not to open them unless I got instructions from him." That, said the usher, was the only time he ever received directives from either Dusenberry or Davis. "During my period of employment the fire escape exits at the alley side of the house were always kept locked," Sayles said. Moreover, he added, "We had not got instructions as to what doors we were to attend to in case of fire. The only time we got instructions was the Sunday before the house opened; Mr. Dusenberry called us all down there and told us to get familiar with the house. There was no fire drill or anything of that kind."[16]

5

3:15 P.M., WEDNESDAY, DECEMBER 30, 1903

Sec. 191. The license for each building . . . shall
state the number of persons it has accommodations for,
and no more than that number shall be allowed to
enter such hall at any one time. . . .

For some unaccountable reason that no one could fathom, business at the Iroquois Theatre was not up to expectations after the Thanksgiving week. The box office was enjoying "a fairly prosperous engagement," according to a theatrical publication, but it was not being "accorded the patronage for 'Mr. Bluebeard' which the worth of the offering warrants."[1] Perhaps it was because children were back in school once the weekend was over. By all accounts, *Mr. Bluebeard* was seen as especially fit entertainment for "the little ones."[2]

However, as the Christmas and New Year's holiday season approached, and with it the prospect of school vacations, ticket sales picked up markedly. So it was not surprising that the Wednesday matinee on December 30—despite subfreezing temperatures and slippery sidewalks from a recent snowfall—drew a packed house, the largest the theater had known.[3] Many of the theatergoers were out-of-towners, attracted to the performance as a special treat. And most, whether Chicagoans or out-of-towners, were women and children—mothers escorting sons and daughters, nannies shepherding young wards, a liberal sprinkling of teachers enjoying their mid-winter break, a few shopgirls who had the afternoon off. Sneaking a peek of the house from behind a curtain, Eddie Foy commented that he had never seen so many women and youngsters in an audience. "Even the gallery was full of mothers and children. There were several parties of girls in their teens. Teachers, college and high school students on their vacations were there in great numbers."[4]

With every one of the Iroquois's 1,724 seats taken except for a few expensive box seats that were quickly gobbled up once the house lights dimmed, only standing room was available. There were two hundred standees—a hundred behind the rear row in the parquet, twenty-five more in the dress circle, and seventy-five in the gallery.[5] Those in the narrow space behind the last row in the gallery stood four deep behind the seated theatergoers.[6]

As the performance began, the house manager, George Dusenberry, made a routine check of the theater, making sure that his ushers were in place. There were accordion gates at the top of two uppermost landings that, when pulled across, effectively kept ticketholders in the gallery from being able to sneak down to the more expensive seats in the parquet. Even though the theater was sold out, as was his custom, Dusenberry personally closed the gates and secured them with padlocks.[7] No one would be able to leave the gallery until the intermission, when Dusenberry would unlock the gates so that members of the audience could retire downstairs to the restrooms. He would secure the gates with the padlocks again once the second act had begun.

Backstage, meanwhile, were nearly three hundred performers—principals in the cast, dancers, singers, and supernumeraries, including a number of children playing make-believe animals. With the performers were some two hundred members of the stage crew—wardrobe attendants, scene movers, fly men, lighting operators, property men, electricians, carpenters. Altogether, the theater held close to twenty-three hundred persons.[8]

There had been the usual intermission after the first act. In the dress circle, some women, standees who had tired of being on their feet for so long, took advantage of the break to sit down on the steps in an aisle.[9] Seat holders in the dress circle had to squeeze past them to get in and out of the rows. The women remained seated on the steps, blocking the aisle, as the second act began shortly before three o'clock.

The auditorium lights dimmed and the curtain went up, revealing the chorus, which burst into "Daylight Is Dawning" and then a rendition of "Songbirds of Melody Lane." Harry Gilfoil came on to sing "Beer That Made Milwaukee Famous," backed by Bonnie Maginn and the Pony Ballet. It was Eddie Foy's turn next, and his sketch with the Pet Elephant, which, as usual, went off to great hilarity. As Foy exited to thunderous applause, a double octet—eight chorus girls in fulsome, Victorian-style "Floradora" outfits and eight chorus men dressed in white hussar uniforms—prepared to step onto the stage for a song-and-dance number entitled "In the Pale Moonlight." As was customary during the scene, the lights throughout the theater were turned off. Only the soft light playing on the stage set, an eerie bluish tint, illuminated the theater.

Backstage, about fifteen feet above stage right and adjoining the proscenium wall—what to the audience would be the left side of the proscenium—was an iron bridge and on it a floodlight with a blue gel. It was a calcium arc light powered by electricity but requiring hand regulation to direct its illumination. The light was mounted on a pedestal and had a hood and reflector. It was encased in a closed box to prevent sparks falling on the floor or being blown into scenery. There was an opening in the hood, just above the arc and about two inches in diameter, through which the carbon passed. Such lights required 110 volts of electricity to operate and generated almost 4,000 degrees of heat. Because the light was ordinarily shifted to different positions during a performance, its wire had to be flexible and thus was not enclosed in a metal conduit as were other wires in the theater.[10]

As the double octet of performers waited in the wings for their cues, the operator of the arc light, Patrick McNulty, aimed the flood onto the stage and then, for some unaccountable reason, he stepped away for a moment, leaving the light unattended. No sooner had he left his station than there was a flash of sparks where the electric wires connected to the lamp. Herbert Cawthorne, who played the role of Irish Patshaw, happened to be standing in the wing on the other side of the stage. His attention was suddenly diverted by "a peculiar sputtering" across from where he stood.[11]

Some twenty feet above the arc light, on a fly bridge, where he had gone to see the double octet perform, another lighting operator, W. H. Aldridge, whose calcium light was not needed for the low-lit scene, saw the flash. It seemed about six inches long. As Aldridge watched in horror, a scenic curtain swayed gently against the flare-up. The loose edges of the canvas caught fire, and a flame ran rapidly up the edge of the drop and across its upper end.[12] It was a repetition of what had happened in Cleveland two months earlier.

William McMullen, the theater's assistant electrician, was on the stage below the light bridge, trying to repair a spotlight that wouldn't work. He said he noticed the curtain "swaying" directly above the arc light when "suddenly a spark shot up and it was ablaze in a second." McMullen called to one of the stage electricians, John E. Farrell, to put the flame out. Farrell ascended the ladder to the bridge and tried to do so with his hands, as McMullen coaxed him with urgency.[13]

"Put it out! Put it out!" McMullen shouted.

"I am! I am!" Farrell yelled back as he clapped the flimsy material between his hands.

Some stagehands spotted the flames. "Look at that fire! Can't you see that you're on fire up there! Put it out!"

"Damn it, I am trying," Farrell cried, still clapping at the burning canvas, his hands beginning to get badly burned. A flame shot a foot up. Other curtains in the high loft above him caught fire. Farrell couldn't reach them. He tried throwing the contents of a tube of a chemical extinguisher, a bicarbonate-of-soda mixture called Kilfyre, at the flames, but the powder blew back in his face, nearly blinding him. Crying, "Save yourself," Farrell fell to the stage floor as he descended the ladder, but he pulled himself up and started to run toward the rear of the stage.

Some stagehands grabbed up the long poles used in shifting scenery and tried to beat out the fire. "Hit it with the sticks!" they shouted. "Beat it out! Beat it out!"[14] The house fireman, William C. Sallers, ran up the ladder to the bridge on which the arc light stood, in his hand another tube of Kilfyre. He, too, threw the powder mixture at the burning curtain, but it failed to smother the flames. Sallers yelled to the men below to have the asbestos curtain lowered.[15]

Below him, McMullen repeated the call for the asbestos curtain to be dropped.[16] The assistant stage manager, William Plunkett, pulled the alarm bell. A scene shifter, Gilbert McLean, heard the gong and started yelling also for the asbestos curtain to be dropped, but the man responsible for sending down the curtain "did not seem to understand." The fire was spreading toward the rear of the stage. "Somebody hallooed, 'She is gone. Everybody run for your lives.'" McLean headed for the rear exit. "It was every man for himself."[17]

Nearby, the Iroquois's head electrician, Archie Bernard, was at the theater's massive switchboard, a metal-and-marble box that controlled all the lights in the building. At the time the fire broke out, he had been showing a friend who ran the lighting system at the Powers' Theatre how he changed the illumination patterns on stage. As soon as he realized the difficulty the stage crew was experiencing in bringing the flames under control, Bernard reached down to throw a switch, in an apparent attempt to put up all the lights in the auditorium. But as he did so, pieces of burning curtain fell all around the switchboard and some fuses shorted.[18] The spotlights casting the blue aura over the stage blacked out. The entire theater was now plunged into darkness.[19]

Meanwhile, when the disturbance backstage first started, the performance on stage proceeded without interruption, the music drowning out the noises created by the crew. In the orchestra pit, the conductor, Herbert Dillea, had waved his baton, and the music for the "In the Pale Moonlight" scene began. First, the eight "hussars" of the double octet marched onto the stage, singing. Then the eight girls. One of them, Madeline Dupont, had noticed "just a little bit of flame" as she waited in the wing on the opposite side of the stage with the rest of the "pale moonlight girls." But she paid no attention to it and, on cue, took her place in line and joined the chorus girls as they danced onto the stage. As the chorus line cavorted downstage to the footlights, though, Dupont now saw the flame growing larger. William Plunkett was in the entranceway, ringing the bell to alert the curtain crew to drop the fire curtain. "The curtain will fall in the meantime," the girl next to her, Ethel Wynne, said in an aside to her, "the bells have rung."[20] Plunkett continued to ring the bell as the chorines reached the footlights, still singing.

Up in his dressing room, Eddie Foy—dressed as Sister Anne in tights, a sort of abbreviated Mother Hubbard smock, and a wig with a little pigtail—was tying his shoes when he heard a noise. Thinking it was another ruckus between supernumeraries and stagehands—there had been a quarrel a few days earlier—Foy ignored the rumpus at first. But then some instinct made him decide to look out from his door. Doing so, he heard "the buzz getting stronger and stronger." He was suddenly alarmed. His family was in town, and he had brought his oldest son, six-year-old Bryan, to the theater. With the theater sold out, there was no seat available for the boy, so Foy had arranged for him to sit on a stool on the stage, right next to the switchboard.

Foy ran to the stage, screaming his son's name. As he reached the switchboard area, he saw the house fireman, Sallers, up on the light bridge, trying to put the fire out. By then the two lower borders running up the side of the canvas were burning. Bryan was frightened. Foy seized him by the hand and rushed to one of the exits at the rear of the stage where a number of performers and stage crew were trying to get out. But then Foy suddenly stopped. The image of all the women and children out front in the audience "haunted" him. They had come to see him perform. This was no time to desert them. He "threw" his son to a stagehand, telling him to take Bryan out. Foy paused a moment to watch them running to the rear, then turned and scurried toward the front of the stage where the double octet was performing.[21]

Gertrude Lawrence, the leader of the girls' octet, noticed the flames but thought they would "soon be put out." There was "quite an excitement," but she continued to sing and dance. "I thought if there was an awful fire there would be a panic," she said, "and I thought by working I would quiet people." But when pirouetting, Lawrence saw the fire growing, and when she swung around to face the footlights again the audience was starting to rise in panic.[22]

Large sparks and fragments of burning material were falling, but the double octet continued doing their "turn."[23] In the orchestra pit, Dillea whispered to members of the orchestra to play faster.[24] "Something's happening," Frank J. Holland murmured to his partner, "but don't stop dancing and singing."[25] But then one of chorus girls, Edith Williams, cried out that she was fainting. She managed to dance a few more steps, then collapsed. Her partner, Jack Strause, stooped to pick her up and in doing so saw the asbestos fire curtain starting to be lowered. He took the unconscious young woman in his arms and headed for the stage door.[26]

Two other "hussars," John J. Russell and Samuel Bell, stepped forward to try to calm the audience. Russell told them "to be seated, that everything would be all right, and to quiet down, and quite a number did."[27]

Bell made the same plea, putting up his hands, trying to gain the audience's attention. Seeing the asbestos curtain coming down, he turned to look for his partner, but she was gone. Like almost everyone else, Bell headed for the stage door.[28] Russell, however, raced upstairs to his dressing room, evidently to get his valuables.[29]

Pandemonium had by now broken out backstage. Daisy Beaute, who played one of Bluebeard's six pretty wives, was standing in a wing, waiting to go on in the next scene. Seeing the flames, she said, "I ran for my life without waiting to see anything more."[30] Archie Bernard, the head electrician, had abandoned the shorted-out switchboard and assembled a "chain gang" of stagehands who were trying to help the chorus girls to find their way out. Most were in scanty tights, some were shoeless, and others wore only short skirts and low corsages. They were running wildly and had to be caught and "tossed from one man to another." One of the men helping Bernard was William Wertz, a lighting operator. Several of the chorines were hysterical. "Come on, girls," Wertz urged, "get out of here as soon as possible." He firmly grasped one screaming girl by the arm and led her away.[31]

Lola Quinlan saved the life of her friend, Violet Sidney. They and five others were in a dressing room on the fifth floor above the stage when the alarm was raised. In her haste, Sidney caught her foot and sank to the floor in pain. She had sprained her ankle. Grasping her around the waist, Quinlan dragged Sidney down the stairs to the stage, her right arm and hand becoming painfully burned as she passed flaming scenery.[32]

Ethel Lytle was in another dressing room on the fifth floor, costumed in tights and stockings and waiting for her ballet troupe's entrance later in the show, when the fire broke out. Recovering from a bout of pneumonia, she had slipped on a kimono and was relaxing, reading, when she heard the commotion down below. Lytle jumped up, called to her ballet partners in the scene to follow her, and led the young women to safety.[33]

The youth running the elevator to the top-floor dressing rooms, Robert Smith, could not see and could hardly breathe as he guided the elevator up to the sixth floor. He found one chorus girl there, then stopped at the fifth floor to take on others. The smoke was so thick that he had to search for the girls and then drag them into the elevator. The elevator itself had caught fire and was burning near the control lever. To start the car, Smith had to put his left hand into the flames. But he managed to get the elevator down to the main floor of the stage. Smith was still in the car when the lines holding it parted. He suddenly felt faint, but a passing stagehand saw him in distress and pulled him out of the elevator in time.

High above, four German boys who worked the aerial apparatus in the gridiron, sixty feet above the stage, were marooned. They didn't know what to do. One, some distance from the others, was caught in flames from pieces of a burning curtain that billowed up toward the roof. He jumped. His three companions scampered over the scaffolding and were able to make their way down a stairway.[34]

Nellie Reed, who was waiting in the topmost gallery, ready to swing out above the audience and strew flowers at the end of the second act, suddenly found herself all alone. She managed to get to a stairwell, but fire and smoke roared up the stairs, blocking her path. She was trapped.[35]

Eddie Foy reached the footlights as Strause, carrying Edith Williams, and other members of the double octet began scrambling from the stage. Ethel Wynne "very foolishly" lost her reason and walked back to where she had made her entrance and "unfortunately had to watch the awful sights." Wynne was never able to remember how she got out of the burning building.[36]

Smoke and some sparks were already making their way into the main part of the theater, curling down and around the lower edge of the proscenium arch. "An overture, Herbert, an overture," Foy called out to Dillea, the conductor. Some of the thirty or so musicians who made up the orchestra were leaning out of the pit, trying to persuade members of the audience in the front seats of the parquet to use the passageway on their left that led through the stage proper to the exit in the southwest corner of the stage.

Dillea called out for the musicians to play the overture to *The Sleeping Beauty and the Beast,* a musical that had played Chicago the previous year. They would have to play by memory. His face ashen, his eyes glued to the growing flames above, Dillea beat the tempo with his wand, but one by one the musicians started to drift off. When Sallers, struggling to put out the fire, inadvertently kicked a piece of burning curtain down into the pit, the bassoon player scrambled to get out. Another musician left when an abandoned bass fiddle and a cello began to burn.[37]

Shouting out over the music, but purposely speaking slowly and standing perfectly still although he was excited, Foy at first asked the audience to keep their seats, telling them that the fire was being brought under the control. But when it became clear that the fire was spreading, he called out in short, sharp gasps, "Ladies and gentlemen, there is no danger. Don't get excited. Walk out calmly. Take your time, folks." Between breaths, though, he kept calling out to the wings from the corner of his lips, "Drop the fire curtain! For God's sake, doesn't anybody know how to lower this curtain?" And then, back toward the audience again, "Go slow, people! You'll get out."

Above Foy, the cracking of wooden scenery parts increased, and smoke was growing more dense. The northeast corner of the fly gallery was a furnace. Foy made a last appeal as a fiercely burning piece of scenery dropped at his feet. Another, a smaller one, was caught in a draft and flew out into the auditorium. "Drop the fire curtain," he called out again. He looked toward the switchboard, but Archie Bernard had left it to help chorus girls to escape. Foy shouted for the stage manager, William Carleton, but he was nowhere to be seen. Then for an electrician he knew by the name of "Pete." He, too, was missing. As stagehands, property men, members of the company, and musicians fled, Foy cried out, "Does any one know how this curtain is worked?"[38]

Charles Sweeney, a fly man on the first gallery, kept calling across to Joseph Dougherty to lower the asbestos curtain. Dougherty, in the fly loft at the very top of the stage, was filling in for the man who normally had charge of the curtain. He had finally started it down, but as it descended, one end became snagged and the curtain became lopsided. The other end continued down but got completely stuck when about two-thirds of the way, about eight to ten feet above the stage. The snag was twenty feet below him, too far for Dougherty to reach. Dougherty was surprised that the asbestos curtain had become caught. The drop curtain lowered between acts was only a few inches from the asbestos curtain and had worked without a problem at intermission.[39]

Seeing that Dougherty was unable to unsnarl the asbestos curtain from way up in the fly loft, Sweeney and another fly man in the first gallery reached for tarpaulins and slapped at the burning scenery, but the flames rose steadily along the border and toward the center of the curtain, too far away from them for them to do any good.[40] At the same time, Sallers and some stagehands climbed into rigging below the asbestos curtain to try to pull the curtain down. Frantically, they tugged at it, but the curtain would not budge.

The curtain was snagged on a galvanized iron reflector that held a row of incandescent lights. It was attached with hinges to the north side of the proscenium arch—the right side of the proscenium from the audience's perspective. Ordinarily, between acts, the reflector was swung back into a niche in the wall, enabling both the drop curtain that was lowered between acts and the asbestos curtain, if necessary, to be lowered without any interference. However, it was the duty of Peter O'Day, the lighting operator responsible for the proscenium lights, to swing the reflector out from the wall once an act started, so that it was in place when the lights were needed to illuminate a scene. So, even though the lights were not needed for the dimly lit "In the Pale Moonlight" scene, the reflector jutted out from the wall, effectively blocking both curtains. O'Day could have pulled it back, thus freeing the asbestos curtain, but he was, as he later put it, "at another point of the stage," though he never explained where exactly he was. He could not, he said, "get to the light to push it back again."[41]

With the reflector projecting from the proscenium wall, there was no way the asbestos curtain could be lowered completely. As a result, there was no shield between the fire on the stage and the auditorium.

Foy was still trying to calm the audience. "Don't be frightened, folks! Go slow!" And, in asides to Dillea, "Play." Below him, in the orchestra pit, Dillea and only one musician remained, a "brave, fat little German" who fiddled "furiously." But no one could hear him. The roar of the flames and the screams from the audience drowned out his efforts. Finally, the German fiddler fled the orchestra pit, and Dillea, too. The conductor was in such a rush that he knocked over the podium. Dillea raced through the door behind the pit. It led to a passageway between a prop room and a basement smoking room used by crew members and the musicians. As he ran through the area, Dillea saw several actresses who had fled their dressing rooms. Four of them suddenly fainted. John Russell, the octet member who was still in the building, spotted a pail of water and poured it over the women. Dillea led the way to safety, with Russell and three other men carrying the still-dazed women.[42]

Performers and crew members were in a crush by the exit door in the northwest corner of the rear stage. Many of the young women were at-tired in brief costumes. Two were naked from the waist up.[43] "Seeing that no human power could move the fire curtain, and that the stage was a mass of flames," Sallers, the house fireman, turned his attention to helping the performers. The women were "frantic, and the men not much better."[44]

Maggie Levine was in charge of twelve young girls changing into cos-tumes for a hunting scene in a basement dressing room. "My God, girls, what can be the matter?" she exclaimed on hearing noise from the stage above. A moment later smoke rolled down through trap doors leading to the basement, almost obliterating the room lights. James Gallagher of the men's chorus had the girls hold hands as he led them through the basement to the coal cellar under the sidewalk on Randolph Street. He stopped to help members of the Pony Ballet who were knocked down and stepped on by fleeing chorus girls and men. One, Doxie Marlowe, lay unconscious on the floor and had to be carried away. Reaching the cellar, Gallagher came across a stick and used it to force open the cover of the coal hole. Firemen outside saw what was happening and lowered ladders into the hole. Fifty performers were helped out. As the girls and ballet members struggled out the hole, passersby helped to pull them out and took the shivering performers to shelter in two close-by hotels, the Union and the Sherman House.[45]

Robert E. Murray, the theater engineer, had also been under the stage when he heard the confusion above. Ascending stairs to the stage level, he saw Sallers sprinkle Kilfyre on the burning drop, had witnessed young Robert Smith bravely ferrying chorus girls down the elevator, had been one of the men who tried to jump up and pull down the asbestos cur-tain when it became snagged. As the fire swept through the nearly three hundred drops and threatened the entire building, Murray realized that the furnace that heated the building might explode. He hurried back downstairs to the boiler room and told the foreman to shut off steam in the house and to dampen the fires.

As Murray left the boiler room, musicians and chorus girls came rush-ing toward him, panic-stricken because they could not find a way out. "They tried to take us up the stairs," said ten-year-old Chrystal Haerr, who played a frog, "but the flames made a horrible fence we couldn't pass."[46] Chrystal and a number of other child supernumeraries were among the fleeing performers. One of them, a little girl who played a

Japanese child, was being held in a "death-like grip" by a ballet girl, Elois Lillian. Lillian had seen the girl screaming with fright and suffocating. She grabbed hold of her around the neck and was frantically searching for a way out when Murray appeared.[47] "The basement door was locked," said Chrystal, "but they broke it down and we got out."

It was Murray who got the door to the basement smoking room open. He led the way through it to a coal hole adjoining the boiler room. It was the same chute that Gallagher had opened for the chorus girls. Murray began shoving the girls up the chute and out into the street. When the last girl was through, he quickly ran through the dressing rooms in the basement, where the supernumeraries dressed, shouting for everyone to leave. He found one girl, paralyzed with fear, up against a wall, scratching it and screaming. Murray saw that she got out of the coal chute before he himself crawled out of it.[48]

The last to get out of the coal hole was a member of the girls chorus, Viola McDonald. When the cry of fire rang out, McDonald had told the girl next to her that she would not go out into the streets wearing only tights even if it meant that she would be "burned to death." She ran back to her dressing room to put on a skirt, then heard a crash overhead. Burning timbers blocked her return. McDonald had to crawl on her hands and knees to get to the coal hole. A fireman on the sidewalk on Randolph Street saw her thrust her arm out of the hole and pulled her out.[49]

At almost the same time, James J. Hamilton, a trunk handler, was leading a group of ballet members to another coal hole in the rear of the building. He broke the cover with his bare hands, then lifted men and women in their costumes through the opening. Some of the men were still wearing their helmets. Incredibly, one supernumerary insisted on carrying his spear with him, but Hamilton threatened to brain him if he didn't drop it and move quickly through the escape hole.[50]

Upstairs, everyone was pushing and shoving by the stage-door exit leading to Couch Place. It opened inward, but the crowding made it hopeless to wrest the door open. It was at that moment that Peter Quinn, a railroad agent, happened to be passing by outside and heard their cries. Quinn was able to unscrew the door fixtures with tools he carried with him. Once the exit way was cleared, a stream of excited actors, actresses, and stagehands burst through the opening. Clad only in a flimsy costume as Queen of the Fairies, Annabelle Whitford shivered with cold as she ran out into alleyway. "It was 8 below zero, but we were the lucky ones, even though my hair was burned."[51]

Flames and smoke now filled the entire stage, billowing upwards to the very roof, ninety feet above. But two emergency skylights in the roof that were intended to let out flames and smoke were clamped tight and could not be opened. There was no place for the fire and gaseous fumes to exit. Then, someone managed to open the huge double freight door in the north wall that was used to handle scenery. With both it and the stage exit on the west now open, an immense wave of cold air burst suddenly from the rear of the stage. It was "a cyclonic blast," said Foy, "a flash and a roar as when a heap of loose powder is fired all at once." There was nowhere for the draft to go but into the auditorium, drawn inexorably toward the exhaust vents in the walls behind the parquet and the balconies and carrying with it smoke, heat, and fire. A huge billow of flame leapt over and past Foy. Sweeping under the snagged asbestos curtain, it surged upward to the balconies. Blazing fragments fell over Foy. His wig began to smolder. A fringe on the edge of a curtain was burning just above his head and, as he glanced up, the curtain began to disintegrate.

Feeling he could do nothing more, Foy groped his way through the flames and smoke to find a way out. As he staggered through the blazing curtains, the last of the ropes holding the drops burned through, making sounds like explosions, and the entire loft collapsed, crashing down and bringing with it tons of burning material. Foy saw "another great balloon of flame" leap out into the auditorium, "licking even the ceiling." He was the last person to leave the stage.[52]

Considering how many persons were backstage and the disorganized, panicky behavior exhibited by them, the number who died in the fire on stage was relatively small: five persons in all, out of the nearly 300 involved in the production of *Mr. Bluebeard*. They were aerialist Nellie Reed, a minor bit-part actor named Burr Scott, a twenty-two-year-old usher, and two female attendants, one fifteen years old, the other twenty-two. Except for them, and although some suffered burns and other injuries, all the members of the troupe, the supernumeraries, the stage crew, the orchestra, and the theater staff were able to escape.

It was a totally different story in the auditorium.

6

IN THE PARQUET AND BOXES

Sec. 194. The stand-pipes, electric wires, hose, foot-lights and all apparatus for the extinguishing of fire, or guarding against the same . . . shall be at all times made and kept in condition satisfactory to and under the control of the Fire Department, the Commissioner of Buildings and the Fire Marshal of the City of Chicago.

Joseph Dimery, who worked for the company that provided the lighting fixtures for the Iroquois Theatre,[1] was a good friend of Will Davis and Harry Powers. He had lunched that Wednesday with both men and told them that he was planning that afternoon to attend *Mr. Bluebeard* with the young daughter of friends who were staying with his family. Davis offered him seats in one of the lower boxes that he and Powers reserved for guests. But Dimery arrived late at the theater. The matinee performance had already begun. Although nobody was seated in the box, tickets for all the seats had been sold to a theater party. So Dimery and the girl had to be content with standing room at the side of the parquet, near the box. Looking over the auditorium, Dimery was pleasantly surprised. "I never saw a prettier audience," he remarked to the girl, "so many ladies and children and all so beautifully gowned."

Dimery saw the flash of fire when the floodlight shorted during the second act, but being "well acquainted with the construction of the building," he believed there was no danger. He knew the theater had an asbestos curtain. He even took it upon himself to shout for everyone to keep their seats. The building was fireproof, he called out.[2]

Both the box that had been offered to Dimery and the one next to it on the left side of the parquet were taken by Mrs. Rollin A. Keyes of Evanston, who was entertaining a group of young ladies in honor of her daughter Catherine, home for the holidays from a school in Washington, D.C. The Keyes theater party had dallied over lunch and missed the entire first act, arriving at intermission. They had been seated only a short while when the second act began. Some fifteen minutes into it, as the double octet was performing, one young woman leaned across to Mrs. Keyes and asked if she smelled something burning. They then noticed some of the musicians in the orchestra pit pointing upward to a flame that was creeping along a curtain. "The people were wonderfully calm, it seemed to me," said Emily Plamondon. She and her sister Charlotte—the daughters of a wealthy Chicago heavy-machinery manufacturer who had, incidentally, attended the opening-night performance—were seated in the box closest to the stage.

Everybody appeared to be obeying Eddie Foy's remonstrations. Instead of rushing for the doors, the audience "gazed for a moment at the stage," as if contemplating "how they would escape." Some people in the balcony crowded forward to get a better view of what was happening. Just then the shrill cry of a woman caused women and children in the audience to jump to their feet, terror stricken. As smoke began to fill the auditorium, people screamed frantically for help. Flames now lit up the stage. Emily suddenly heard a "confused rumbling noise" that filled the theater "from the pit to the dome." It was, she realized, "the sound of a thousand people preparing to leave their seats." The rumble of footsteps from the balcony was soon drowned out by the cries for help from theatergoers trapped within the rows of seats, struggling to get into the aisles and to safety.

Before any of the young women in the Keyes theater party could leave their seats, the flames had spread to the first row of the parquet and, as stagehands were struggling to pull down the asbestos curtain, Emily Plamondon saw "a great gush of fire then spread to the draperies over the boxes." Mrs. Keyes and the young women left hastily, leaping ungracefully over the railing of the boxes. Looking up, Emily's sister Charlotte saw many patrons in the first rows of the dress circle who could not manage to get up the aisles jump for safety into the parquet below. She was shocked when several men in the audience pushed and pulled women and children aside "as they fought like maniacs to reach the exits." Several little children were trampled underfoot. Although Charlotte was unaware of it at the time, two children struggling up the aisle were the daughters of executives who worked for her father's company. The two young girls were hand-in-hand, trying to reach the back of the parquet when a heavy-set man dashed between them, breaking their hold. The girls were separated. One fell and was trampled by fleeing theatergoers.[3]

"We plodded through the aisles," Emily said. Charlotte was knocked down by a man. "I was so terror stricken," she said, "that I gave way and sank into one of the orchestra seats." After that, Charlotte could remember little. "I think I lost all reason." Charlotte thought she "must have been walking on prostrate bodies" as she struggled to reach the lobby. She only came to her senses when she became caught between the crowd and a marble pillar in the Grand Stair Hall. "The pain revived me," she explained. "I know I was almost crushed to death, but it did not hurt. Nothing could hurt with the screaming, the agonized cries of the women and children ringing in your ears."

The crush of people was "terrible," Emily said. Once the doors were broken open, however, all the young women in the Keyes party were able to escape, though most of them had their clothes ripped to shreds. Charlotte, her knees trembling, found herself on the street outside the theater, "the dead and dying" all around her.[4]

In an upper box on the other side of the theater from the Keyes party were two former professional baseball players: Frank Houseman, who had pitched briefly for Baltimore of the American Association,[5] and Charles Dexter, who was with the Boston team. They had also arrived late at the theater and found that, other than standing room, the only tickets available were for two remaining seats in an upper box on the farther, north side. The first act was in progress as they carefully made their way up a lightless circular stairway to their seats. Houseman stumbled several times. "This is a dark stairway," he remarked. "This is funny they don't have a light or something here."

It was Houseman who first spotted a spark on the opposite side of the stage. He saw a man—it was John Farrell, though he did not know his name—trying to beat out the flames with his hands. Houseman pointed out the burning curtain to Dexter. But his friend was not concerned. The stagehands would put it out, Dexter said.

Houseman, however, felt uneasy. He remembered the dark stairway they had ascended. He suggested that they return to the floor below, where he surmised there would be an emergency exit. With that, Houseman left the box, urging the couple who shared it with them to leave also. The two men became separated. Dexter lost sight of his friend when he stopped to strike a match because it was so dark on the stairs. Reaching the parquet floor, he walked on his own to one of the lower boxes. Eddie Foy was on stage, urging people to stay calm. Dexter decided to leave the theater when he saw burning scenery begin to fall around the comedian. By then, however, everyone else in the audience had risen and was bolting for ways out, people running over one another in their frenetic search for an exit. Dexter took in tow a group of little children who were wandering aimlessly without any adult nearby. He looked around for an exit, but saw no sign for one. Then he spotted some heavy damask drapery on the north wall and intuitively shoved it open. Behind the drapery was an iron door held shut with what he took to be a crossbar. Dexter grappled with it, but whether he pulled it up or down, it would not budge. Finally he beat on the door with all his strength. It gave way. Leading the children out into the alleyway called Couch Place, Dexter looked back. "A wave of fire" was "sweeping over the whole inside of the theater."

Ahead of Dexter, Houseman reached a different parquet-level exit leading to the same alleyway. People around him were "screaming and halloing." Like the door that Dexter found, this one also did not have a sign indicating it was an exit, but Houseman figured out that it was. He recognized the lever holding the door shut. It was a bascule lock—a device popular in European theaters but virtually never used in American playhouses and totally unknown in Chicago theaters. Fleeing playgoers who could not figure out how to open the exit doors fitted with such a lock were certain that the doors were purposely bolted shut.

Houseman, however, had one like it at home. So he had no trouble with the lever.

Once outside in the alleyway, Houseman for a few moments tried to help people from the dress circle jump from a fire escape that was ten to fifteen above the ground. Its final rung of steps, evidently frozen, could not be lowered. Houseman persuaded a few of the fleeing theatergoers to leap, breaking their fall as they fell into his arms. But then others higher up on the fire escape began jumping, too. Houseman pulled bodies out of the way as people plunged from above. One man fell on three bodies, started to get up and then was struck down by a woman who fell on him.

Feeling it was too dangerous to stay in Couch Place, Houseman ran to Dearborn Street, then around the corner at Randolph to the front of the theater. He managed to wedge himself past fleeing theatergoers and into the parquet section as Eddie Foy was still pleading for the asbestos curtain to be lowered. Off to the side, Houseman saw some drapery and a young fellow that he took to be an usher standing by it, doing nothing. "Where does this lead?" he asked. The youth replied, "Outside." Houseman had no trouble with the lever. When he got the door open he found that it led to an iron door with another bascule lock. Before he could get it open, a "big blast came out from the stage." Houseman fled.[6]

As panic now spread throughout the audience, an unusually calm Chicago housewife found herself thankful that she had not been able to purchase a ticket for a seat. Mrs. James Pinedo had taken standing room instead and had been able to wiggle herself between other standees on the extreme right of the parquet floor. From her vantage point, she saw the arc light short out and then someone—it was Farrell—using his hands to try to put out the flames. Mrs. Pinedo made a conscious effort not to move. "I was afraid of precipitating a panic," she said. "I simply turned my head and I saw what I supposed was an exit. I couldn't tell."

What Mrs. Pinedo saw was the drapery hanging in front of one of the emergency exits on the north wall. It was unmarked, but Mrs. Pinedo, a theater-going regular, "naturally supposed," she said, that the folds of the damask masked a way out. Calmly, Mrs. Pinedo put on her rubbers, preparing to go out into the cold, slippery streets outside. Eddie Foy had then appeared on stage, and, to her astonishment, she said, she never saw an audience "who were saner." For at least two minutes, while the sparks turned into flames and Foy tried to assure the audience that there was no danger, everyone "sat perfectly still." However, when a "big ball of flame" came out from the stage and fell on the heads of those seated in the front rows, panic spread throughout the audience.

Mrs. Pinedo realized it was "time to get out." She walked "quietly" to what she took to be the emergency exit that she had located only minutes earlier. A man was already there. He had torn aside the drapery but could not open the door. The man asked an usher to unlock it, but the usher had no idea how to do so. Mrs. Pinedo joined the man in trying to force the door open, without success. Finally the man induced the usher to try. They were both fiddling with the unfamiliar bascule lock when an explosive rush of wind shot through the theater as the freight door in the back of the stage was opened. Mrs. Pinedo was astonished. The blast of air not only blew the iron escape door open, but it also was so strong that she, the man, and the usher were propelled to safety into the alley outside.[7]

By happenstance, before the fire on stage broke out, standing near Mrs. Pinedo behind the rear row of the parquet was teenage Sarah Knisely Dreher, her younger sister, and her mother. It was the wedding anniversary of the youngsters' parents. Mrs. Dreher had taken her daughters shopping and after lunch planned to send them home while she stayed in the city to have dinner with her husband. But after lunch, Sarah and her sister begged their mother to be taken to see *Mr. Bluebeard*. Mrs. Dreher gave in to their pleas and they went to the box office. The only seats available were in the gallery, several flights of stairs up. Mrs. Dreher was reluctant to sit so high in the theater, but her daughters nagged her. They climbed to the top of the steep gallery, but once they got there Mrs. Dreher was too nervous to remain. "Girls, I just can't stay here," she said. So back down the stairs they went. When they reached the lobby, Mrs. Dreher gave an usher a dollar to allow them to stand behind the seats in the parquet. He showed them to places behind the last row, right next to a door. It was an emergency exit, unmarked. Sarah's sister hung her beaver hat on the door.

As soon as scenery began dropping into the orchestra pit, Mrs. Dreher announced to her daughters, "We're going." The three of them, mother and two young girls, started, but Sarah's sister went back to retrieve her hat and when doing so tried to open the exit door. She couldn't. The three then walked quickly toward the entranceway, the mother tripping several times over a row of spittoons that lined the back of the parquet wall. Each time she fell to her knees, the girls reached down and pulled her up. They finally made it to the doors to the lobby, but the ones they tried were also locked.[8]

Seated six rows from the back of the parquet, Harold C. Pynchon and a schoolboy friend also tried to escape by what they took to be an emergency exit on the north side of the theater, but they, too, could not get the door open. The two youths turned and fought their way into the Grand Stair Hall, only to find that one of the doors to the lobby was locked, as well. Pynchon kicked through the glass panel of the door and squeezed through it. His friend never made it.[9]

Joe Graham and Dorothy Bour were also able to kick one of the doors open. The two youngsters—both were twelve years old—had decided to flee "despite" all Eddie Foy's assurances that there was no danger. Near them, in the tenth row, four women fainted. "All the others seemed dazed and just sat still."[10]

Bessie Letts and two visiting friends she had grown up with in Iowa had seats two in from a side aisle in the fifth row of the parquet. She wondered what had prompted her father to pay the extra $1.50 for the tickets, because he knew she would have preferred to sit in the first row of the gallery. That was her favorite place when going to the theater. Her father's choice was, as it turned out, a fortuitous stroke of luck.

When the fire started, Bessie heard someone clapping their hands offstage. Again, that would have been John Farrell, trying to stamp out the flaming drop curtain with his hands. Within minutes, there was a blaze of light, and "in just an instant," the entire stage was on fire. One of Bessie's friends moaned, "Oh! Fire!" and everybody around them began screaming. The three young women rose up, but two men sitting next to them urged them to keep calm and sit down. They did. Bessie's hair was done up in a then fashionable pompadour hair style. As burning material flew out from the stage, the heat from it was so strong on her face and back, she thought her hair would "surely" catch fire. So she stood up again and, looking around, she discovered to her amazement that, without saying anything to her, her friends had gone "and so had everyone else." Instead of leaving by the side aisle, Bessie scrambled along her row to the center aisle. A "rush of people" knocked her hat, scarf, and purse from her arms. Reaching the rear of the parquet, Bessie tripped over the train of a woman's skirt. Stumbling, she reached out and grabbed hold of the back of the coat of some man who was fighting his way up the aisle. Desperately grasping the coat, Bessie was pulled by the man into the theater foyer.[11]

The woman whose skirt Bessie tripped over might very well have been Mrs. Eva Katherine Clapp Gibson. She and Mrs. Emma Schweitzler had seats together, also in the fifth row. The two women were seated about halfway in from the aisle. They managed to get out of the row, but Mrs. Gibson fell when someone, perhaps Bessie Letts, stepped on the back of her long dress. Mrs. Schweitzler begged for someone to help Mrs. Gibson, but no one stopped to do so. Crawling on her hands and knees, the stricken woman edged her way up the aisle.[12]

Although all the aisles were now choked with people who had fallen down, Georgia Swift was able to grope her way from her seat near the stage all the way to the rear of auditorium. As she struggled through the panicking mass, she passed a little boy, about seven years old she thought, who was lying in the aisle. "Won't you please, please, help me," he cried out. Miss Swift stooped to pick the youngster up, but the crowd around her was too thick and the crush too strong. She seized the boy by the arms but was knocked over him and fell on her knees in the aisle. Miss Swift struggled to her feet, but she couldn't turn back to the boy. The onrushing people pushed and shoved her toward the entranceway. "The memory of his eyes will haunt me while I live," she said.[13]

Eleven-year-old Winnie Gallagher fared better. She and her aunt were in the third row of the parquet. The youngster managed to climb over seats and the heads of terror-stricken persons to get out, but she was thrown about and trampled, her clothes torn to shreds.[14]

George E. Smith and his wife were trying to make their way around the crush of people when Smith spotted, to his left, a young girl raise her arm, then sink down as some people fell on her. Caught by the fallen bodies, the girl nevertheless was able to give Smith one arm, then the other. He pulled her free. But in the struggle, her clothes were ripped off. Smith and his wife led the girl, naked and bruised, to safety.[15]

The first intimation of danger that Winifred Carona had was when she saw one of the girls in the double octet "look upward and turn pale." Winifred looked up, too, seeing "the telltale sparks shooting about through the flies." Winifred, who was with three friends in the seventh row of the parquet, took Eddie Foy's cautions to heart when he stepped forward and urged everyone to keep calm. All four young women stayed seated. But when they realized that a "seething mass" behind them was struggling for the exits, they rushed from their seats. Winifred stumbled over the body of a woman who was trampled almost beyond recognition. For an instant, Winifred thought "it was all over." But someone— she never knew who—lifted her up and carried her to safety.[16]

Walter Flentye had no idea how serious the situation was. In fact, as incredible as it seems, despite all the tumult around him, he seemed impervious to any thought of danger. Flentye and a friend were in a back row of the parquet "handy to the entrance." Heeding Eddie Foy's appeals, Flentye kept his seat. But when his friend left, he got up, too, and nonchalantly went to retrieve his umbrella and a valise from the checkroom. In the Grand Stair Hall, Flentye noticed there were a number of "almost frenzied" women around the entranceway and a man was carrying a woman. It still did not dawn on him that anything was the matter. Blasé, Flentye got his belongings and stepped back into the Grand Stair Hall. He placed his valise and umbrella on a settee and was leisurely putting on his overcoat and hat when he saw, through an open door leading into the auditorium, "a mass of fire" strike the front seats of the parquet and belch out into the theater. Still seemingly unconcerned, and despite the throng of fleeing theatergoers who were now racing headlong into the hall, Flentye found without difficulty the only doors that were unlocked in the hall and lobby beyond. He left the theater, waited to get across heavily trafficked Randolph Street, then walked across the street to a police officer who stood in front of a store. It had suddenly occurred to him that he ought to tell the officer what he had witnessed. By that time, however, a group of patrolmen was running down Randolph Street toward the Iroquois and fire engines rumbled into the street, their bells clanging. It was only then, Flentye said, that he finally realized "what a terrible thing I had escaped."[17]

Flentye may have passed Mrs. William Mueller in the Grand Stair Hall, but if he did so, the encounter did not register with him. She had been seated with her two daughters in the second row from the back of the parquet. The youngsters, five and seven years old, had gotten restless, so Mrs. Mueller had taken them to the ladies' lounge in the Grand Stair Hall. But then the children wanted to return and see the show. Mrs.

Mueller took them in hand and started back when she saw, in one of the tall mirrors in the hall, the reflection of flames from inside the theater. She hurried back to the lounge and asked the maid there for the children's wraps, saying that something was the matter. The maid assured her that everything was all right. "I won't give you the things now," she said. "I'll go and see what is the matter." Mrs. Mueller demanded the wraps but the maid refused. Just then Mrs. Mueller heard a cry of alarm and, grabbing the children, she ran toward the entranceway. The first of the triple-wing doors she reached was locked. She tried the next one. It, too, was locked. Mrs. Mueller fainted. So did her oldest daughter.[18]

Meanwhile, in the lobby, several men were on line in front of the ticket window, planning on purchasing seats for one of the remaining performances of *Mr. Bluebeard* before the show's run ended over the coming weekend. Already, people were at the doors to the lobby, trying to find one that could be opened. Two men who had just purchased tickets were leaving the lobby. Without being aware of what was happening inside the theater proper, one man said to the other, "That's a mean trick, to lock the doors so people can't get out." The man wondered "if there is a policeman around here." The other man said he wasn't going to bother about the matter, and the two walked away.[19]

Ebson Ryburn was on the ticket line, hoping to obtain seats for the evening performance. There were several men ahead of him. Suddenly he heard a commotion. Several persons rushed out from the theater. Ryburn thought it was a scare at first. He went and held the door open. It was the only door leading into the lobby from the Grand Stair Hall that wasn't locked. The ticket buyers on line ahead of him were trying to open the other lobby doors but couldn't. They were locked on the inside.[20]

One of the other men waiting on line for tickets, John C. Galvin, tried to get the westernmost door open. A crush of people were banging at it. Gesturing, Galvin tried to pacify them, but it was useless. He saw a woman being trampled. Galvin was finally able to kick out the panel of the lobby door. Men, women, and children fled through it, through the lobby, and into the street.[21]

Ernest Stern kicked out the other door. He had been standing in the dress circle with his sister when the fire broke out. They both managed to get down the stairs but were pushed aside by the mob fighting their way through the only open door. Stern could see Galvin in the lobby on the other side trying to open the locked door. Stern went up to one of the other doors and kicked out the glass.[22]

Just arriving, firemen had to fight their way to get inside the theater as the mob of terrified theatergoers streamed through the now opened doors. Fortunately, because their fallen bodies were near the doors, the firemen quickly spotted Mrs. Mueller and her oldest daughter. The woman had been kicked in the eyes and bruised while lying helpless on the floor. The firemen picked them up and carried them out of the theater. Some man picked up her youngest daughter and literally threw her over the heads of the crowd of people. She fell upon the pavement outside but was not badly injured.[23]

Sarah Dreher, her sister, and her mother were saved, also. As were Bessie Letts, Mrs. Gibson, and Winifred Carona. So, too, were most of the audience in the parquet. With some exceptions, they were able to take the familiar way out of the theater. They simply retraced the steps they had taken to enter the theater, turning to the right at the rear of the parquet and exiting into the Grand Stair Hall, and from there into the lobby. Or, in a number of cases, they were able to use one of the emergency exits on the north wall that had been forced open. Nevertheless, without any exit signs to guide them or ushers to direct them, and because so many of the doors beyond the Grand Stair Hall as well as emergency exits on the north wall were locked, the exodus had erupted easily into panic. That so many did escape was a miracle.

Theatergoers in the balconies above them were not that fortunate.

$$7$$

IN THE DRESS CIRCLE AND GALLERY

Sec. 179. All aisles and passageways [in buildings of Classes IV and V] shall be kept free from camp stools, chairs, sofas and other obstruction, and no person shall be allowed to stand in or occupy any of said aisles or passageways during any performance. . . .

The "cyclonic blast" that swept over Eddie Foy's head like an explosion when the scenery doors at the rear of the Iroquois stage were swung open curved under the snagged asbestos curtain. It carried flames and gaseous fumes in an arc over the parquet and into both the dress circle and the gallery. The sudden draft was so unexpected that many people were caught in their seats and asphyxiated. Those who had abandoned their seats before then, searching for a way out, were gasping, their throats on fire, their hair and clothing singed or burning. Panicking, many could not find a way to escape. Those who managed to make it to a stairway found themselves caught in a human traffic snarl. Hundreds died.

James Strong, a board of trade clerk, was standing with his mother, wife, and niece in the rear of the gallery. They tried to get to the stairway that led down to the dress-circle level, but it was too crowded. So they ran down the aisle by the side of the gallery rows and down a short flight of steps to the middle entranceway. But the door there was locked. Strong threw himself against it without success. He then stretched on his toes as far as he could and smashed the glass transom above the door with his fist. Strong hoisted himself up and through the transom. But once on the other side, in a hallway, he found the door secured with a hasp and padlock. Just then a theater carpenter happened to run by. Together, the two men tried to break open the door, without success. "We worked at the padlock like crazy men, but could make no impression upon it," Strong said. "Nor could we break the door." The carpenter boosted Strong up to the transom in the hope that he could pull his family on the other side through it. Strong got the upper portion of his body through and saw his family below, "but just at that second the flames swept through the balcony and smoke poured over the transom." Strong felt himself suffocating, lost his grip, and fell back into the hallway outside. On the other side of the door, his mother, his wife, and his niece lay dead.[1]

Other survivors also told of horrifying experiences. Mrs. W. F. Hanson made it out of the theater only because someone seized her. A man presumably, but she never knew who it was. Dazed, she was tossed and dragged along an aisle and lost consciousness. But everyone else in her theater party—eight relations—were killed.[2] Two young schoolgirls slid down the banisters from the upper balcony, making it to safety. A young boy hoisted a younger girl onto his shoulders. Holding her feet fast, he said, "Now use your fists and fight for all your worth." The boy bent his head and forced his way through the mob.[3] In the clamor to get out, however, a girl thought she had her younger brother by the hand, but when she reached safety, she found it was another boy. Her brother was nowhere to be found.[4] Dr. Charles S. Owen was the only one in a family theater party of twelve persons to get out of the theater alive, but even so his injuries proved fatal.[5]

Anna Woodward escaped only because she was a large woman and frightened. She feared she would have trouble getting out of the gallery because of her size—she weighed 180 pounds—and because there were so many standees crowded behind the last row and the steps from her seat were so steep. So Woodward decided to leave when she saw the arc light sputtering. She stepped down to the dress circle but had to break a glass partition with her umbrella to get any farther. Halfway down to the Grand Stair Hall, she heard "the roar of the crowd" coming after her.

Woodward hurried, but the crowd overtook her, knocking her down. She managed to struggle up and, walking over bodies that had fallen, made it to a lobby door.[6]

Rose G. Payson and her sister-in-law joined a group of people headed for a door in the gallery that they took to be an exit. But they could not open the door. Everyone turned to try to retrace their steps down the three flights of stairs to the Grand Stair Hall. As they exited the top entranceway of the gallery, people stumbled and fell on top of one another. Soon, bodies began piling up as fleeing theatergoers tried to climb over those who had already fallen and were themselves crushed or smothered. Some of them did make it down to the level of the dress circle, but once there, they found themselves in a jam of people exiting from the middle entry to that balcony. "By that time, " Mrs. Payson said, "people were rushing out screaming and falling on top of each other. Some [were] fainting and unable to gain their feet. We kept pushing and squeezing our way to the lobby floor. There we found a more desperate crowd screaming and pulling off their burning clothes." The two women made it out. "Victims were piled in a pyramid and others falling on them."[7]

The convergence of those fleeing the gallery and those exiting the dress circle created an impenetrable tangle. With the theater in darkness except for the glow cast by the flames in the auditorium, the panic remained unchecked. Covering his mouth with a handkerchief, seventy-year-old D. W. Dimmick made it down from the gallery to the dress-circle level. He was shocked. "People were packed like cordwood." Dimmick squeezed past many who were "writhing on the floor." He caught hold of the arms of one woman who was alive but lying near the bottom of a heap of bodies, trapped by her feet. He pulled her out. Dimmick then tried to rescue a man who was also caught by the feet. He braced himself against the stairs to get a purchase and began tugging, but he was unable to pull the man free.[8] Those still upright started down the stairwells to the Grand Stair Hall the same way that they had come up on entering the theater. They found their way blocked by the locked accordion gates. Soon, as fumes from the burning scenery spread through the theater, the people fell, choking, and died, their bodies creating another pile of corpses at each of the gates.

Instead of turning and heading back down the way they had reached the gallery, another group of fleeing persons headed straight out of the top gallery entranceway. They stumbled down stairs outside the upper entrance, tripping and falling on one another on the very steps that had been added in the construction of the theater so that the tilt of the gallery provided an unimpeded sight line of the stage. Ahead was a corridor at the end of which was a door. The door led to the offices of the manager at the front of the theater looking out on Randolph Street and also to the stairwell connected, two levels down, to the right side of the lobby. It was an escape route. But the door was bolted shut. These people, too, were asphyxiated.

Outside, in the alley behind the north side of the theater, a clerk scrambled up the drop staircase of one of the fire escapes and quickly climbed to the top of the stairs. The iron door of an emergency exit leading off the gallery was stuck. The clerk, J. W. McMeen, tugged frantically at the door, finally forcing it open. So many people then tried to push their way out of the exit that many were thrown to the ground.[9] Only about a dozen persons made it down the fire escape to safety. One was George E. Berry. He had lost consciousness when the sheet of flame shot out along the ceiling toward the gallery. When he came to, his wife and his sister were lying beside him on the floor. Berry lifted his wife but was knocked down by someone rushing past him. He then tried to lift his sister, but her body was brushed out of his arms by the crowd. Berry returned to where his wife lay fallen, but a mob of fleeing persons swarmed around him and caught him up, carrying him along. He found himself at an upper exit leading to the fire escape. Bodies were heaped in a great tangle, "hands and feet sticking out of the pile, but they were all motionless and limp." Berry crawled to the top of the heap and fell over onto the fire escape on the other side. He made his way down the stairs to the ground.[10]

A number of persons were able to escape from the dress circle using the fire escape stairwell. Dr. Lester Sackett, his wife, sister-in-law, and eleven-year-old daughter reached it after scrambling over the seats behind them. But as they started down the fire escape, their way was blocked by two confused women headed in the wrong direction. They were coming *up* the stairway. Sackett turned them around and they all descended the emergency stairs.[11]

For Harriet Bray, what was supposed to be her Christmas present turned into a dreadful nightmare. Clothing and hair singed, the eleven-year-old girl had to jump the remaining twelve feet to the ground from the fire escape. Her father caught her in his arms. "I'll always remember," she said, "crawling beneath the legs of the horses who pulled the fire equipment, how they stood motionless in the face of all that chaos."[12]

The fire stairs, however, soon proved a futile escape route for those fleeing the gallery because once people bolting from the dress circle opened the iron exit door to get onto the stairs outside the building, they left the heavy door jutting out from the wall. Ordinarily, the door should have been opened before a performance, swung back flush against the wall, and pinioned there. But it had been shut tight, and as theatergoers fled from the dress circle they left the door standing at a right angle to the wall, sticking out across the fire escape and effectively cutting off the escape route for everyone above it.

Seeing their way blocked by the open iron door off the dress circle, several people on the uppermost landing climbed over the railing and dropped to the alley below. One of them was schoolgirl Ruth Michel. Ruth had slipped on the narrow grating of the iron ladder and fell to the next landing. Scared that she would not make it down, she squirreled under the railing. The men down in Couch Place yelled at her not to leap. But, she said, "I knew I had to jump or else burn up, because the flames were coming up so right behind me."[13]

Below, in the alley, W. G. Smith saw a man, his wife, and two daughters step out onto the fire escape from the dress circle. Flames swept up from a window below them that had been blown open. The clothing of the woman and the children caught fire. The man tried to beat out the flames only to get burned himself. Realizing that delay meant death, he dropped the children ten feet to the ground, then helped his wife to jump before leaping himself. Smith took up one of the children and carried her to his store on Dearborn Street. Employees carried the others to the store. When Smith returned to the alley, a group of screaming women, all hatless, their faces scorched by the intense heat, were huddled on the fire escape. Smith shouted to them to wait, that firemen were coming, but one leapt as he spoke.[14]

Frank J. Sanchez noticed another woman about to hurl herself from the fire escape. He got directly underneath her in a crouching position and allowed her to fall on his back, timing the drop so that he could bend downwards and break her fall. Picking the woman up, and wrapping her in his overcoat, Sanchez carried the woman into a nearby store. Her face was badly burned.[15]

Two other men ran up with a blanket. They were engineers from the old, historic Tremont House across the alleyway, which had been taken over early in the year by Northwestern University to house three of its professional schools.[16] "Jump one by one and we'll catch you," one of the engineers shouted to the women high above. Holding the blanket at the ends, the engineers formed a cushion for the women as they dropped from the fire escape, one after the other. The two men rescued twenty women before the flames "got so terrific" that no one could climb out onto the fire escape. One of the engineers, Morris Eckstrom, said he saw "a dozen women and children and some men, through the open door to the fire escape, fall back into the flames."[17]

The commotion in the alleyway attracted the attention of some law students who, although it was vacation time, were studying in a library in the rear of the third floor of the Northwestern University Building. At the same time, a group of painters working in another room on the third floor also heard the noise from the alleyway. Together, students and painters carried planks and ladders to the back window of a lecture room that faced an emergency exit of the gallery of the theater high above the alley. They ran out a ladder across the narrow gap and a man fleeing the inferno inside the theater managed to crawl across it. Another man behind him tried, but the ladder slipped on the ice-covered sill of the lecture room and he fell to the ground lifeless.

The painters quickly positioned the planks across the gap between the building and the theater and dropped to their knees to anchor them. "Come on," they called out. Sixteen-year-old Hortense Lang was the first to cross, dragging her eleven-year-old sister Irene. "I was going to jump," she sobbed to the painters, "but I thought of my mother." Behind them came thirteen-year-old Carrie Anderson, who was guiding two smaller children across the makeshift gangway.[18] In all, a dozen persons edged their way over the planks. The last to cross was Alice Kilroy, a Chicago school teacher. She had been a standee in the gallery and was certain that she would have burned to death had not the planks been laid across the gap. As it was, she was badly burned.[19]

Kilroy was no sooner drawn inside the Northwestern lecture room than a "pillar of fire" bursting from the theater struck the wall of the school building. Across the narrow alley, women and children still on the exit landing of the theater died there, the bodies of some dropping to the ground. Firemen rushed into the school and up to the third floor to cross the planks with a hose in order to spray water into the gallery, but the flames made them retreat. With them was Fire Marshal John Campion. "Is there any living person here?" he called out. No one answered. "If any one here is alive," he shouted again, "groan and make some sound. We'll take you out." Again, no one responded. Campion ordered his men to fall back. As they edged backward over the planks, the fire in the theater billowed once more.

Other firemen had brought nets into the alley below to catch the bodies hurling from above. But the nets were black and difficult to make out in the gloom of Couch Place, so many people missed seeing them and leapt haphazardly into the dim space. Oddly, the bodies of those who had first jumped and died provided what one observer called "a thick cushion" for those who leaped after them. Watching from his office in the medical school quarters of the Northwestern building, William A. Dyche saw firemen using their hose carts to carry away victims. He estimated there were hundreds of bodies lying in Couch Place.

Dyche called the alleyway "the valley of death."[20]

The Iroquois Theatre was Chicago's most modern playhouse when it opened in the fall of 1903. It was situated on Randolph Street off Dearborn, in the heart of the city's busy downtown area. Author's collection.

Harry J. Powers was co-owner of the Iroquois Theatre. Special Collections and Preservation Division, Chicago Public Library.

The architect of the Iroquois Theatre was twenty-eight-year-old Benjamin H. Marshall. Billy Rose Theatre Collection, The New York Public Library for the Performing Arts, Astor, Lenox and Tilden Foundations.

William (Will) J. Davis was a co-owner and the man responsible for managing the Iroquois. Special Collections and Preservation Division, Chicago Public Library.

The special pride of the Iroquois Theatre was its richly appointed Grand Stair Hall. The stairways led to the dress circle and gallery. The latter was closed off with pad-locked accordion gates during performances. Special Collections and Preservation Division, Chicago Public Library.

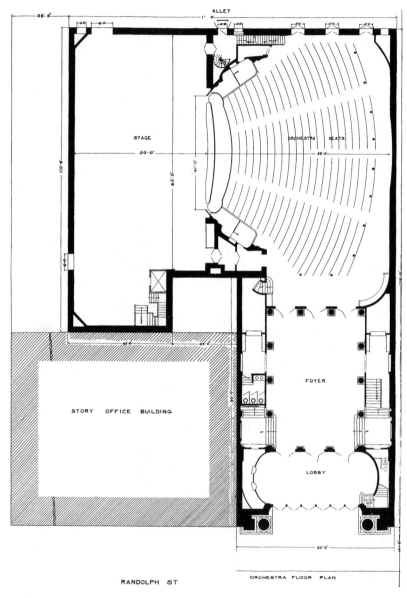

The lobby and foyer (Grand Stair Hall) of the Iroquois led directly into the orchestra section, which was also called the parquet. *Inland Architect and News Record*, February 1904. Author's collection.

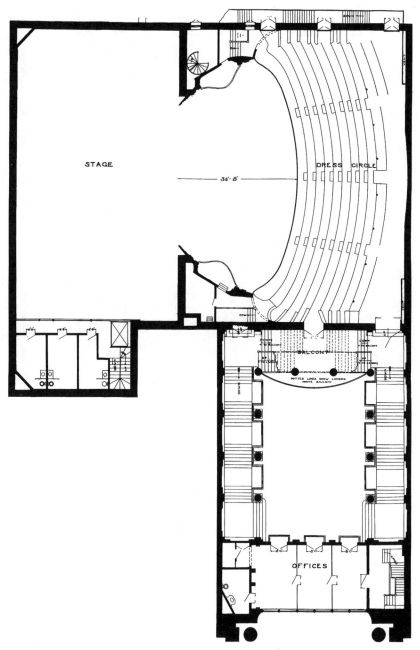

The dress circle floor was reached by stairways on the east and west sides of the Grand Stair Hall. Note the exhaust vents on the east, or right, wall. *Inland Architect and News Record,* February 1904. Author's collection.

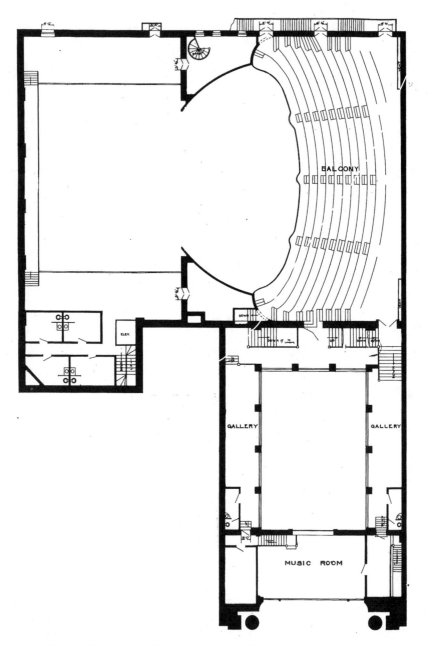

Once the top floor was reached, theatergoers still had to navigate turns on staircases to reach entrances to the gallery (second balcony). Note the vents behind the seats on the east, or right, wall. *Inland Architect and News Record,* February 1904. Author's collection.

Eddie Foy as Sister Anne, shown with the costume of the Pet Elephant, performed the comic antic in the second act of *Mr. Bluebeard*. When the fire broke out, Foy, dressed as he is here, ignored his own safety to go out onto the stage to try to calm the audience. Billy Rose Theatre Collection, The New York Public Library for the Performing Arts, Astor, Lenox and Tilden Foundations.

The double octet of the "In the Pale Moonlight" number was performing when sparks from a shorted spotlight ignited a drop curtain (indicated here by the cross) on stage right—the audience's left. All lights in the auditorium were purposely turned off during the dimly lit scene on the stage. Billy Rose Theatre Collection, The New York Public Library for the Performing Arts, Astor, Lenox and Tilden Foundations.

Nellie Reed, the flying aerialist who showered the audience with flowers, was trapped high above the stage, awaiting her cue, when the fire started. She never made it to safety. Billy Rose Theatre Collection, The New York Public Library for the Performing Arts, Astor, Lenox and Tilden Foundations.

A crowd of relatives and friends jams the sidewalk outside the Iroquois Theatre. The time is about 4 P.M., approximately forty-five minutes after the fire broke out. To the right of the theater is Thompson's Restaurant, which became a makeshift hospital during the rescue operation. Chicago Historical Society.

A fire pump in action in Couch Place, behind the north wall of the theater. Fire escapes from the balconies and emergency exits from the parquet fed into the narrow alleyway. Note the open double freight doors immediately to the right of the fire pump. Chicago Historical Society.

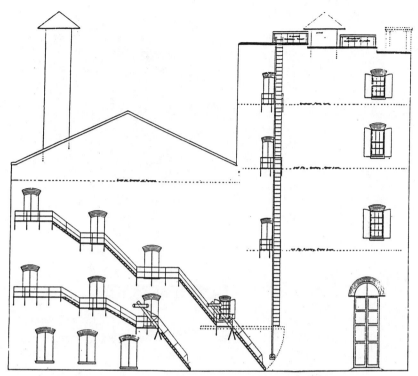

The diagram of the north wall of the theater shows the fire escapes from the gallery and dress circle as well as the exit doors off the ground-floor parquet. The last rungs of the emergency stairs were initially frozen and could not be lowered. The fateful immense double freight door is to the right. Not shown is the stage door that was inset in one wing of the freight door. It opened inward. Panicking members of the cast and theater crew jammed the stage door, making it impossible for anyone to get out. From "Report of the Fire at Iroquois Theater," Chicago Underwriters' Association, Chicago Historical Society.

Theatergoers fleeing the gallery from the topmost entryway collided with those exiting by the middle entrance, causing a gridlock effect. Bodies here were piled ten feet high. Author's collection.

Bodies of victims also piled up at two accordion gates that were shut and padlocked to keep playgoers in the gallery from sneaking down to seats in the dress circle or the parquet once a performance began. Chicago Historical Society.

The identification of bodies proved a grim task for members of the families of victims. A total of 602 persons died in the Iroquois Theatre fire. Author's collection.

Seventy-five standees were crammed into the narrow space at the back of the gallery. The door at the farther end was locked at the time of the fire. Chicago Historical Society.

A portion of the parquet and boxes along the north wall were visible from the stage. Most theatergoers in the orchestra section of the auditorium were able to flee to safety. Copyright © Bettmann/ CORBIS

Piles of rubbish and twisted metal were all that remained backstage. The charred remains of the theater's massive switchboard are behind the patrolman. Above him is the iron bridge on which the short-circuited floodlight stood. Author's collection.

Firemen use a blanket to carry a body up a balcony aisle. Many persons in the gallery died in their seats of asphyxiation when a blast of gaseous fumes and flames shot through the auditorium. Author's collection.

Had the skylights been open, the gaseous fumes and flames would have vented above the stage, as indicated in this diagram, which was made after the fire. The fire curtain is incorrectly shown as being level halfway down. Actually, the right edge caught on a reflector light. The left side of the curtain continued to descend until it was eight to ten feet above the stage. It could not be moved farther because of the snagged right edge. *Fireproof,* February 1904. Author's collection.

8

THE RESCUERS

Sec. 192. Every portion of any building . . . devoted to the uses or accommodation of the public, also all outlets leading to the streets, and including the open courts and corridors, stairways and exits shall be well and properly lighted during every performance, and the same shall remain lighted until the entire audience has left the premises.

It was, Arthur C. McWilliams thought, a "gray afternoon."[1] The temperature stood at eight degrees above zero.[2] "An icy gale" howled through the streets.[3] Huddled in coats, scarves, and hats, pedestrians leaned into the wind. Many still donned rubbers or galoshes, fearful of slipping on the frozen remains of the recent snowfall.

McWilliams was walking down Randolph Street when he saw some sort of excitement ahead, where the striped canopy of the new Iroquois Theatre spanned the sidewalk. People were running out of the building. Astonished, McWilliams saw "puffs of smoke." He quickly strode toward the theater.

A block away, Max Remer saw the smoke, too.[4] A fifteen-year-old errand boy, Max had just finished delivering a batch of messages and was through for the day. Although his family expected him home, Max ran toward the source of the billowing black clouds.

By coincidence, three clergymen were walking in the vicinity. One, the Reverend Albertus Perry of Simpson Methodist Episcopal Church, was passing by the Iroquois when a crowd of "madmen and hysterical women" fled from the theater.[5] Perry ran into the theater lobby. Through the glass-paneled doors he could see inside the theater proper that men "were beating" against locked exit doors, while women crowded by the doors "with the desperation of death stamped upon their faces." Perry did not think he could do anything to relieve the situation, "for there was nothing within the power of mortal man to do to stop the horror." "Overcome by the terrible sight that had met" his eyes, and so numbed that he could not figure out how to help the panicky theatergoers, the minister reluctantly turned away.

Bishop Samuel Fallows of the Reformed Episcopal Church had been shopping in the Marshall Field store at the corner of Randolph and State and happened to be passing by the theater, also, when the surge of fleeing theatergoers broke into the street.[6] Like Rev. Perry, he raced into the lobby. But instead of feeling hopeless, as Perry did, Fallows, a former chaplain with a Wisconsin infantry regiment during the Civil War, pushed and shoved his way into the Iroquois's elegant foyer, intent on trying to help. He, too, though, was horrified: "God forbid that I ever again see such a heartrending sight."

At almost the same time, Bishop Peter J. Muldoon of St. Charles Borromeo's Roman Catholic Church was strolling along Randolph Street with one of his parishioners, Thomas J. Quigley, when they heard a commotion up ahead.[7] Together, Muldoon and Quigley, an amateur songwriter, hurried down the street toward the source of the unusual noise.

As a man ran down Randolph, shouting news of the fire, no one was more surprised than William A. Brady.[8] A well-known New York theatrical producer, Brady had that day arrived in Chicago to see how his play, *The Pit,* was doing at the Garrick Theater, not far from the Iroquois. Satisfied with the attendance there, Brady had "sauntered" down Randolph and was passing the Iroquois when Harry Powers, the theater's co-owner, spied him. "Running over with exultation," Powers had invited Brady inside. "Come on in, Bill, I want to show you what a real house looks like," he said. The second act of *Mr. Bluebeard* was in progress as the two men reached the back of a box close to and virtually on a level with the stage. Eddie Foy was finishing a comic monologue, and as applause rang out, Foy started to make his exit. Recognizing Brady, he stopped and leaned over. "Happy New Year, Bill," he said. "Same to you, Eddie," Brady responded. Brady then turned and looked up into the auditorium. It was "jammed to the ceiling with children and young boys and girls and their parents celebrating the holidays." Brady boasted to Powers that he had just as good a house at the Garrick, "but it won't come to so much money." The two men then shook hands, and Brady left the theater.

Brady headed back to the Garrick Theater and wasn't more than a hundred feet down the sidewalk when "a man came tearing past" him, "gasping in the cold, and shouting: 'The Iroquois Theater's on fire!'" Brady turned and ran back. He was able to get into the Iroquois's lobby in time to see "a queer thing" happening in the box office: "the treasurer and his assistant frantically packing up money and tickets, paying no attention to what might be going on inside." Suddenly, plate glass that separated the lobby from the foyer inside burst into shards, and "a roaring loop of flames" shot out, striking the far wall and curling back in again, "slowly heating the place like an oven." Brady found himself "in the midst of a frightful stampede. It was as if I had been plunged into a nightmare without any warning. There were the most terrible yells and shrieks and cries of agony and fear coming from the theater." He had a sudden frightening thought: suppose the audience watching *The Pit* at the Garrick Theater learned what was happening when the play broke at the next intermission. Some of them might have relatives or friends attending the Iroquois. Brady hurried back down the street to the Garrick, hoping to avoid a panic there.

Peter Quinn was curious.[9] Quinn, who was chief special agent of the Atchison, Topeka, and Santa Fe railroad system, was returning to his office after attending a trial in the nearby criminal court building when he saw a man run up Dearborn Street, colliding with several pedestrians and stopping only when he reached a policeman at a crossing. The man spoke hurriedly to the officer, who then rushed excitedly away. Wondering what was going on, Quinn followed the man back down Dearborn Street and into the alleyway called Couch Place on the north side of the Iroquois Theatre. As he reached the stage door, Quinn no-

ticed that the door was slightly ajar. He could hear some sort of disturbance behind it. Still unaware of what the trouble was, Quinn peered
in. A crush of screaming performers and stagehands, so many and so
wedged together, had made it impossible to budge the door, which
opened inward. Fortunately, Quinn always carried in his pocket a number of small tools. He immediately started to unscrew the metal attachments that held the door in place and, with the aid of other men who
had reached the alley to help out, managed to force the shrieking crowd
inside the building back far enough so that the door fell away. Waiting
until the last of the scantily clad performers had made their way out and
clearly still unaware of the extent of the fire inside, Quinn stepped
through the door and found himself on the back of the Iroquois stage.
It was "a seething furnace."

The fire inside the theater had begun about 3:15. Almost fifteen minutes passed before an "unexcited" stagehand walked in the door of Engine Company 13 at Dearborn and Lake Streets and told Michael J.
Corrigan, an apprentice fireman, that there was a problem at the nearby
Iroquois. By law, the theater was supposed to have its own alarm callbox,
but it didn't. The young fireman went outside and saw smoke billowing
from the theater. He quickly ran over to Fire Box No. 26 to sound the
alarm. The time was 3:32 P.M.[10] Within seconds, Corrigan's own company
was on its way.

Two blocks away, at the fire department's headquarters in City Hall,
Fire Chief William H. Musham and his assistant, John Campion, were
sitting in Musham's office, talking over old times and congratulating each
other on their luck.[11] There had been more than six thousand fires in
Chicago in 1903,[12] but not one was serious. Suddenly, an alarm came over
"the joker." Told by the telegraph operator that it was from the Iroquois
Theatre, Musham, who had battled the Great Fire as a young fireman
more than thirty years earlier, experienced a sudden pang. He felt certain there was going to be "a catastrophe." Musham's remark was not a
matter of clairvoyance. As it turned out later, he had every reason to
believe a tragedy was in the making. Both he and Campion sprinted from
the office, Musham grabbing his overcoat but not stopping to put it on
until he got into his buggy. By the time the two men reached the theater, First Battalion Chief John Hannan and the men of Engine Company 13 as well as Truck 6 were already there. They had positioned a

pumper in Couch Place, where two fire escapes led down from the balconies inside. Musham quickly realized the seriousness of the situation. He ran to a fire box at the corner of Randolph and Dearborn, perhaps thirty yards or so from the theater, and, using his code as fire chief, punched in another alarm call. The time was 3:41, exactly nine minutes after the first alarm had been received.

At almost the same time that Musham and Campion arrived at the alleyway behind the Iroquois, Police Chief Francis O'Neill and his assistant, Herman F. Schuettler, reached the theater's entranceway on Randolph Street.[13] O'Neill had been in the city council chambers, attending a hearing into charges against one of his lieutenants, when an officer approached him and whispered to him the news of the fire. O'Neill immediately ordered all captains from a dozen police stations to bring their men. He himself raced to the theater, arriving there as a group of firemen headed into the building. O'Neill followed them, rushing blindly up a staircase through dense smoke. They all stopped abruptly when they came to the head of the stairs. Ahead of them, blocking the way, was a wall of bodies ten feet high. "Look out for the living," O'Neill shouted. "Try to find those who are alive."

Amazingly, Louis Guenzel saw what he benignly described as "some commotion" outside the Iroquois and shrugged off the notion that anything was the matter.[14] Guenzel, a Prussian-born architect, was on the opposite side of Randolph Street, walking with a friend, Dr. Walter Wever, the German consul in Chicago, whom he had treated to lunch. True enough, Guenzel couldn't make out what was happening across the street. A traffic jam blocked his view. Several streetcars had stalled in front of the theater, and a row of delivery wagons were backed up against the curb. So he and Wever continued on their way, totally unaware of what was transpiring a mere twenty yards away. As the two men leisurely strolled away, there was no reason for Guenzel to think anything was amiss. An architect who designed public buildings, he was well aware of the Iroquois's reputation. The theater was touted as representing the latest advances in theater construction and safety. Guenzel, of course, had no idea he would actually be feeling his way through the theater the very next day. He imagined that the noise coming from outside the theater was simply the audience leaving after a matinee performance. "We paid no further attention to the matter," he said.

Like Guenzel, many of the first passersby outside the main entrance of the theater had no idea what was occurring inside the Iroquois. They paused, attracted by the commotion and the sound of fire engines approaching, but stood quietly, watching and wondering, until the onrush of victims turned the street into a bedlam.[15]

However, S. I. Shane, the president of a local lumber company, realized how serious the situation was. Aware that it was important to relieve the "awful crush" of people trying to get out of the theater, Shane joined some other men in breaking the fastenings of the easternmost outer doors. "The people coming out of the pitch-dark theatre seemed frantic," said Shane. "Many had become separated from their friends in the wild rush, and after they reached the vestibule made desperate attempts to get back into the theatre." Shane and the others tried to prevent the distressed theater patrons from returning, but it wasn't until firemen and the police arrived on the scene that some semblance of order was restored.

Chicago's mayor, Carter H. Harrison Jr., was away on a hunting trip south, but the finance committee of the city council was meeting that afternoon. Immediately upon learning about the fire, its chairman, William Mavor, ordered the fire, police, and public works departments to do "anything needful, spend anything" to care for the victims. "The Finance Committee will be your authority," he declared. One of the committee's members, Alderman Walter J. Raymer, had already bolted the meeting on hearing the news of the fire. His wife and three children were at the Iroquois, part of a theater party that his oldest daughter, Abbie, had arranged for her seven girlfriends who made up the Felmiva Pleasure Club. They had seats in the dress circle, but as Raymer discovered on reaching the theater, they had all escaped when a man managed "by sheer strength of his hands" to break through the glass pane of a locked door. Only one of Abbie's friends suffered any burns, though they were severe.[16]

Within ten minutes of Mavor's decision, 150 men and 70 wagons from the public works bureau were put at the disposal of the fire and police departments.[17] At the same time, Dr. Herman Spalding, the senior official in the city's health department, personally telephoned physicians in the downtown district, asking them to get to the Iroquois Theatre to help with the injured. His staff called hospitals, nurse associations, and schools and told operators at switchboards in downtown office buildings to notify every doctor in their building. Heeding the calls, more than 100 doctors and as many as 150 nurses dropped what they were doing and hastened to Randolph Street. Meanwhile, a telegram was sent to Mayor Harrison, informing him of the fire.[18]

The police drew a cordon around the front of the theater, trying to make room for the removal of the living and the dead and to prevent relatives from getting into the theater and blocking the rescue efforts. It was a thankless task. "My God, my daughter is in there, my daughter is in there," cried one frantic father, trying to beat his way past the line of policemen. Behind him were scores of other men. "My wife is there!" shouted another. "My boys are there!" still another. "My family is in there!" a fourth. One man did squeeze through the struggling line and got into the lobby, where he wandered about, cracking the glass of the smashed skylight under his feet. "My wife and three daughters were here," he pathetically told an officer as he was led out.[19]

As a fire engine pulled up in front of the Iroquois, Arthur McWilliams, who had stayed outside the theater, went over to see what he could do to help. Two firemen asked him to hold the reins of their horses while they rushed inside. People were erupting from the theater, some with their clothes on fire. The frightened people ran down Randolph Street like "wild animals." More fire wagons pulled up in front of the theater. The firemen jumping down from them saw McWilliams holding the reins of the other engine's horses and took him to be a fellow firefighter. They gestured that he join them. McWilliams found himself in the middle of the first rescue team to enter the theater. "We held a rope and each others [sic] hands as we groped into the dense smoke." The lead fireman suddenly dropped the line, shouting back, "There must be a dozen dead in here!" He came back carrying the scorched bodies of two children, one on each shoulder.[20] The bodies of two women in their midtwenties, their arms tightly locked around each other, were found in one end of the orchestra pit. They had apparently fallen from the balcony above.[21]

A "professional pedestrian"—a threadbare, red-nosed "Weary Willie" street bum[22] named Dan O'Leary—was with a group of firemen who made it up to the balconies. On the first landing as they went up, they passed the bodies of three women and a little girl. In the second balcony,

O'Leary discerned through the smoke the bodies of fifty to a hundred people. "I shouted to see if anybody would answer my voice," he said, "to see if there were any persons still alive there, but there was no response." O'Leary began to help, carrying down bodies to the ground floor. He was in the midst of doing so when the first policemen arrived. On entering the theater, they had encountered some thieves who, attracted to the tumult inside the building, were picking the pockets of the dead lying on the sidewalk and tearing rings from fingers. Seeing the bedraggled O'Leary carrying a body, they mistook him for one of the "ghouls" and threw him out of the theater, threatening to arrest him if he came back.[23]

William Corbett was on his way up to the balconies when a "fear-frenzied little woman" begged him to save her two children, who had seats in the gallery. Corbett started up, though some firemen warned him that he might be in danger. Undaunted, Corbett groped his way upward, stumbling in the dark over bodies on the staircase, until he reached the upper balcony. It was, he said, "positively the most sickening spectacle I ever saw. They were piled up in bunches, in all manner of disarray. I grabbed for the topmost body, a girl about 6 years old. Catching her by the wrist I felt the flesh curl up under my grasp. I hurried down with the little one, then back again, each time with the body of a child." Exhausted, and feeling that what he was doing was in vain—"everybody was stark dead"—Corbett "turned and fled," saying he "never again want to go near the place."[24]

Back from putting in another alarm call from a nearby fire box, Fire Chief William Musham was in the Grand Stair Hall, directing his men in putting out the fire inside the auditorium, when one of his men and a newspaper reporter approached him. With handkerchiefs over their mouths to avoid choking to death, the two men had crawled up the stairs leading to the dress circle, scrambling over bodies, the fireman at one point grabbing the reporter by the arm and exclaiming, "Good God, man, don't walk on their faces." They tried to get into the balcony, but the doorway was jammed with dead persons. They immediately returned downstairs to tell Musham that if anyone was to be saved, prompt action was necessary. Musham immediately ordered all his men in the vicinity to abandon fighting the fire and to go at once upstairs. As Musham himself started up the stairway to the dress circle, he ran into "a mob of people rushing down from the first balcony. They were falling on the stairs and being trampled upon."[25]

Coming up behind him, Police Chief O'Neill and his assistant, Schuettler, took over the direction of rescue efforts in the balconies, O'Neill assuming command in the dress circle while Schuettler directed police officers and firemen in the gallery.[26] The body of a dark-haired girl who looked to be about twelve years old lay impaled on the iron railing of the dress circle. She had evidently jumped or fallen from the gallery above. In a far corner of the gallery lay a child, about one year old, all but his baby shoes ripped from his body. He was trampled beyond recognition. Once in a while, a moaning cry was heard and the shout would come, "Some one alive there boys. Lively now!"

The victims of the fire still alive—suffering from burns and bruises and still gagging, trying to breathe—were relatively few, and they were close to death. Bishop Muldoon moved among the dying in the gallery, giving absolution to Catholics among the injured and, "at the top of his voice," begging people "to put their trust in God and to calm themselves."[27]

Frustrated because there were so few survivors whom they could help, all that O'Neill and Schuettler could do was watch as firemen and police officers "crawled back and forth in the tiers of seats, hunting the dead." The smoke was heavy, and the rescuers worked with difficulty. Every so often, they would pause and sit down, their faces almost touching the floor, trying to get a little air. Bodies were found all through the gallery, some in a sitting position, others fallen forward with their heads resting on the seat in front "as though in prayer." All were terribly burned. The bodies were laid in a hallway until blankets could be gotten and the corpses carried down.[28]

Outside, meanwhile, some firemen ran into Marshall Field's store a block away and came out carrying blankets to put over the fleeing victims, most of whom left the theater half-naked or with charred clothing. Merchants at dry goods stores sent over not only blankets but also rolls of linen and packages of cotton to be used in binding up the wounded. A nearby hardware store supplied scores of lanterns so that rescuers could see inside the dark, smoke-filled theater.

Hearing word of the fire, Alexander H. Revell drove by carriage to the Iroquois. Shepherded by a maid, his daughter Margaret and a young friend had gone to see *Mr. Bluebeard.* On reaching the theater, Revell immediately ran into the maid, who was hysterical. But between her rantings, she managed to tell him that the two children were safe. So Revell hastened into the theater to help. He got up to the balconies, searching for victims still alive, only to find so many dead—"poor women and their little children, with clenched fists raised as though trying to beat their way to safety, and stricken down in the very act."[29]

Nearby, also assisting in looking for anyone who was alive, Bishop Samuel Fallows was appalled. He encountered a young actor, still costumed and with a gaudily painted face, wandering aimlessly about the balcony. How he got up there, he could not tell, "for he was nearly crazed with fear." "I have been in wars and upon the bloody battle field," Fallows said, "but in all my experience I have never seen anything half so grewsome as the sight that assailed my eyes when, with the aid of a lantern, I was finally able to penetrate the inky darkness of that balcony. There was a pile of twisted and bleeding bodies, ten feet high, with blackened faces and remnants of charred clothing clinging to them. Some were alive and moaning in their agony. But others—and, oh, by far the greater number, were dead!"[30]

Max Remer, the teenage messenger boy who was one of the first to spy the smoke coming from the theater, saw people being carried out as fire engines, ambulances, and hearses crowded the street in front of the Iroquois. Max helped to bring men, women, and children to the sidewalk. "Some of them were dead, some were dying, and others were gasping for air." Some of the donated blankets were used to muffle the flames in the victims' clothes, others to cover the dead and dying. Max remained at the theater for hours, until finally Fire Chief Musham called all the rescue workers together to tell them no more could be done. Max took a trolley home, where his anxious parents, unaware of the fire, were worried about where he was. He arrived dirty and tear-stained. "I bawled all the way home," he said. "I couldn't help it."[31]

Arthur McWilliams said it was difficult to tell who was dead and who was alive. The bodies piled along Randolph Street "didn't look dead," he said. "They looked just as tho they had gone to sleep."[32] There were so many bodies lying in heaps upon the sidewalk that firemen and policemen ran over to the Water Street market—now the site of Wacker Drive—and commandeered horses, wagons, and drivers to take the dead and living to hospitals. One problem they ran into was that striking livery drivers, unaware of the extent of the disaster, refused to man any of the appropriated vehicles. One livery proprietor said he went into a saloon next door to his stable, where many of his drivers regularly congregated, and asked them to volunteer to man his twelve carriages. "What you doin', kidding us," one of the pickets said. "It's none of our funeral," said another.[33]

Sheriff Thomas E. Barrett, who arrived on the scene with twenty deputies, had "never witnessed such a scene" in all his life. "On all sides were heaps of mangled and charred humanity. We carried out so many injured and dead that at last they grew so numerous that we were unable to keep count of them. Such a dreadful sight I trust I will never be called to witness again. Crazed men fought to get within the corridors, thinking to find their loved ones among the piles of corpses that filled every available foot of space. Strong men with tear blinded eyes stood on the sidewalk and called loudly the names of their loved ones as though there were a chance of the dead hearing. We did all we could to lessen their grief, but such scenes can never be forgotten in a lifetime."[34]

Doctors waited at the entrance to the theater with stethoscopes in hand. As soon as a body that looked as though it might possess life was carried out, it was examined at once. If alive, everything possible was done to revive the victim. As soon as ambulances, police wagons, or any sort of conveyance were available, the injured were whisked away to hospitals or to offices of physicians in the neighborhood. Soon, all the hospitals, dispensaries, and clinics—Samaritan, Central Homeopathic, Illinois Charitable Ear and Eye, Michael Reese, Presbyterian—were crowded with victims. A quick, temporary count at the hospitals listed 160 injured men, women, and children.[35]

Dead persons were placed in piles on the sidewalk. The corpses were unceremoniously tossed into whatever cart or wagon was handy, and once the vehicle was filled with stacked bodies, it left for a mortuary. One large truck ordinarily used for conveying freight to rail depots was so heavily loaded with the dead that its two horses were unable to start. Police hailed a huge electric delivery wagon from Montgomery, Ward, and Company, but the press of people was so great that, even though the driver clanged his gong incessantly, he could not turn off State Street to get near the Iroquois. Occasionally, a body would be identified and efforts would be made to remove it directly to the dead person's home. One such victim was the wife of a brewing company president. Her body was taken to her home on Woodlawn Avenue.[36]

There were so many injured and so few ambulances to take them to hospitals that before long, many hotels and stores in the vicinity of the theater opened their doors and became temporary shelters. Thirteen victims were cared for at the Sherman House, a block and a half from the Iroquois Theatre. Nearby on Dearborn Street, Kohlsaat's Restaurant and Bullard and Gormully's store also became havens for the wounded. At the latter, twelve persons, almost all from the balcony, died within ten minutes of being carried into the store from the poisonous gases they had inhaled.[37] Many of the injured women were taken to the Marshall Field store, where an improvised hospital was set up on the eighth floor. Maids in charge of the toilet rooms acted as nurses. Supported by friends, women weak with faint staggered through crowds of shoppers to the elevators. One whose children were unaccounted for went into convulsions.[38]

Bishop Muldoon came from ministering to the dying at the Iroquois Theatre to help a priest from Holy Name Cathedral attend to victims who had been brought into the Northwestern University Building. Overwhelmed by the great number of sufferers, Muldoon announced that he would give general absolution to all Catholics among the victims. As the two priests with uplifted hands besought God to pardon all, noted a reporter, "the poor mangled men and women who lay in dozens on the floor seemed to realize" that they were dying. "Many, though crazed with pain, ceased to moan and fastened their fast-dimming eyes upon the two priests. After absolution was given many of them barely able to move feebly stretched out their hands imploringly to the priests for a hand clasp and a word of sympathy before they passed away."[39]

It soon became evident that by the time firemen arrived at the Iroquois, the disaster had already run its course. It had taken only about two minutes from the moment of the first spark from the arc light until all the upper scenery was in flames. Three or four minutes later, the loft above the stage was completely filled with fire and smoke. Trapped inside the theater, members of the audience began suffocating within five minutes from the first spark.[40] The initial fire alarm had not even been turned in by then. When it was, the response was prompt for those horse-drawn days. Firefighters were on the scene within minutes—Chief Musham claimed within probably two minutes after that first alarm,[41] others said within a little more than five minutes. However, whether two minutes or five was moot. By then, most of the victims had already suffocated. And except for a few scattered and dying flames, the fire in the theater was extinguished within thirty minutes of its start.[42] The only thing that could be done was to search for survivors and treat the injured.

9

THE NEWS SPREADS RAPIDLY

Sec. 184. There shall be over the stage of every building . . . a flue pipe of sheet metal construction . . .
opened by a close[d] circuit battery; a switch to be
placed in the ticket office and one placed near the
electrician's station on the stage, each to have a sign
with these words printed on it: "Move switch to left in
case of fire to get smoke out of building."

An unusual performance was taking place at the Garrick Theater a
little farther down on Randolph Street. New York theatrical producer William Brady had rushed back to the Garrick after he witnessed the fire at the Iroquois, afraid that his audience there would panic
if it learned of the disaster. Brady found the manager, Jake Shubert, in
the lobby, informed him of what had happened, and told Shubert not
to let anyone into or out of the theater. Brady then hurried backstage
and cornered Wilton Lackeye, the star of *The Pit,* who was waiting for
an entrance cue. He urged Lackeye, an actor well known as a raconteur,
to use his wits to keep the audience from leaving the theater during intermission. *The Pit* was performed in four acts, and one intermission had
already been held. That still left two intermissions before the play's con-

clusion. So at the end of the second and third acts, the versatile Lackeye went out in front of the curtain and told funny stories, successfully keeping "every soul in the theater in his seat." All the while, Brady and Shubert "held the fort" at the front doors, not permitting anyone to enter or leave the theater "though many made desperate attempts to do so." Despite the crisis at his Iroquois Theatre, Harry Powers came over. His wife and children were in a box and he wanted to get his family out. But Brady refused him. "Not a soul goes into this theater," he said.

"By 3:30 all of Chicago knew what was happening," said Brady. "And fathers, mothers, brothers, sisters and friends of people who had gone to the matinee that afternoon were crowding around the Garrick, half mad with anxiety, not knowing whether their loved ones were in the Iroquois or the Garrick." When, at 5:30, the show let out, the audience was amazed to find the Garrick lobby "crowded with hundreds of persons, desperate men and women waiting to see if their loved one had been in our house or in the Iroquois. Fathers would rush up and grab their girls in their arms; mothers would look and look until every soul had left the house, then turn away sobbing."[1]

The news of the fire spread rapidly through Chicago by word of mouth, by telephone, and by the city's newspapers. Once they learned of the fire, businessmen with families at the matinee performance tried to get through to the police and fire departments as well as to area hospitals, anxious to learn what had happened to their loved ones. Relatives phoned each other, frantic for news about their sons, daughters, and grandchildren. Telephone lines were so swamped that the day shift of operators was held over and by evening twenty-two hundred operators were on duty at all the central stations to handle the flood of calls. The manager of the Chicago Telephone Company said callers were so distraught that they shouted "unintelligible stuff" rather than numbers to the operators. "All of our downtown lines and connections were busy every minute." Wednesday represented perhaps the first time that telephone communication played a role in a tragedy of major proportions. As it was, that day turned out to be the biggest single business day in the Chicago company's history, a bigger business, the manager supposed, "than any exchange ever did before."[2]

Newspapers had dozens of reporters drop what they were doing and reassigned them to covering the story of the fire. Other newspapermen took it upon themselves to rush over to the theater. Charles Collins, a cub reporter for the *Record-Herald,* happened to have interviewed Harry Powers at the Iroquois only hours before, asking him a few questions about "the eternal problem of ticket speculators." Collins heard of the fire when he stopped at the office of the rival *Inter Ocean* to see a press agent. A clerk casually mentioned to him that a fire alarm had come from the Iroquois. Collins immediately phoned the *Record-Herald's* day city editor to ask for instructions.[3] Arthur Sears Henning of the *Tribune* had just finished covering a financial story at a bank and, following routine, phoned in to the paper's city desk. He was told to report at once to the assistant city editor, who was at Dyche's drugstore at the corner of Randolph and State Streets. Henning hurried there to find the editor, surrounded by twelve reporters, assigning each to cover a different aspect of the story. One of them, Richard Henry Little, went off, his "heart in his mouth," because he believed his sister planned to attend a matinee at one of the downtown theaters with a friend. Another *Tribune* man, Clifford S. Raymond, had been married the night before at the residence of the newspaper's managing editor and was on a honeymoon vacation with his bride at a Loop hotel. He heard about the fire when he went on an errand to City Hall. He rushed over to the Iroquois Theatre.[4]

The *Daily News* had its first afternoon edition out by 4:30 P.M., an hour and a quarter after the fire broke out. "EXTRA" a three-column box on its front page screamed: "FIRE PANIC AT IROQUOIS. Big Crowd at Theater Matinee Thrown Into Awful Confusion by Flames." As details of the story developed, coverage by the *News* grew from a two-column lead article on its front page to, eventually, taking over almost the entire newspaper. The *News* published editions at 5:30, 6:30, 7:30, 9, 10, and 11 P.M. A final edition, a wrap-up complete with a list of the known dead, interviews with survivors, feature stories dealing with the rescue operation, the construction of the Iroquois Theatre, and the reaction of its owners and city officials, came out at 5:30 the next morning.

With the demand so pressing for any kind of conveyance to carry injured victims or the dead to hospitals or mortuaries, and with so many bodies clogging the sidewalk, many of the seriously injured and dying were taken to Thompson's Restaurant, adjacent to the Iroquois Theatre. A few late luncheon patrons quickly abandoned the place as rescuers carried body after body into the restaurant. The marble-topped tables were cleared.

Dead and dying alike were lifted onto the tables, chairs, and counters if there was space available. Others lay on the floor. One woman was even placed on top of a display case for cigars because of the lack of space. At one point, bodies were being brought in so rapidly that for more than an hour there were two streams passing in and out of the doorway, one of men carrying bodies, the other of men returning to bring more inside.

Before long, there were eighteen doctors working in the restaurant, which became, in effect, a battlefield hospital. Surgeons, many with tears running down their cheeks, bent over the bodies, searching for some sign of life. "She's dead," a doctor would call out. "Next!" The cold and stiffened form of a victim was tossed quickly under a table while another body took its place.

The victims were horrible to see: a man whose entire face except for the back of his head was burned away; women with arms or legs gone; a little boy whose hands were burned off, his tiny wrists red stumps; a young girl clothed only in the shreds of a turquoise-blue silk petticoat, dead of suffocation; another girl, still wearing a holiday dress of velvet with a silk petticoat, also suffocated.

The scene inside the restaurant became frenetic as, amidst the carnage, howling, screaming parents and friends struggled against a police cordon to get into it. Some actually managed to squeeze their way into the restaurant to hunt for a child or spouse. But it got so crowded that the physicians had difficulty trying to treat the victims.

The scene in the restaurant was so charged with confusion that, seeing the need for order, state senator Albert C. Clark, who happened to be in the neighborhood when the fire broke out, jumped on a table, shouting for everyone to make room for the doctors. Policemen quickly cleared the area. "We want a captain," a doctor cried out. "I nominate Dr. G. Frank Lydston." All the other physicians agreed and Lydston, a noted and respected local physician, took over immediately. The doctors formed a line and, marching past Lydston, were assigned to different tables, three to a table. There were only enough nurses to assign one to each table. Lydston also assembled a small force of medical students to bring supplies of brandy, hot water, and hypodermic stimulants from Dyche's drugstore down the block.

Amidst the groans and writhing bodies, the doctors at one table labored to induce artificial respiration in a girl, about sixteen years old.

Every moment or two, one of them would listen with his stethoscope for heartbeats. There was no sign of burns on the girl. When they forced her eyelids open, her eyes were still bright. Stimulants were tried and finally nitroglycerine was injected, but to no avail. After an hour, the doctors had to give up.

Not far away, a nurse and two physicians tended to a boy who suddenly, after ten minutes, opened his eyes. "What cher doin' to me?" he asked. He was alive and would make it. The doctors' attention was suddenly diverted to another table, where a spark of life was also detected in a young girl. "Strychnia quick," a doctor said to the nurse. The nurse stumbled over a dead body as she hastened back with the medication. Meanwhile, the girl's hands went "cold as snow." The doctor ordered the nurse to chafe them. The nurse rubbed the girl's hands, but they were already stiffening. It was too late. Her body was laid with a pile of the dead.

William McLaughlin was still alive, though barely. The nineteen-year-old nephew of Dr. Frank W. Gunsaulus, pastor of the Central Independent Church, McLaughlin was in Chicago to attend the wedding of the clergyman's daughter, Martha, scheduled for Saturday. A sophomore at Ohio Wesleyan University, he was severely burned while helping others to escape from the theater. McLaughlin, in pain and choking, was carried into Thompson's, where a medical student from Ohio Wesleyan noticed the fraternity pin he was wearing, Delta Tau Delta. A doctor asked whether McLaughlin wanted the pin removed from his vest before someone stole it. The youth said no: "It's been a pal of mine for a while, and I would not like to have it taken off now; just let it . . ." His voice trailed off. McLaughlin was removed to Presbyterian Hospital, where he soon died.[5]

Among the physicians working on fire victims was Dr. H. L. Montgomery, who had served with the Army of the Potomac during the Civil War and had also attended victims of the Great Fire of 1871. "I have seen the wreckage of explosions," he said. "But I never saw anything so grimly horrible as this."

Charles Collins, the ambitious cub reporter from the *Record-Herald,* was able to get inside Thompson's, hoping to find survivors to interview. Some tables, he saw, had been moved against the walls to serve as ledges for a temporary morgue. Bodies were like "heaps of tattered clothing with faces uncovered, some in fixed grimaces of terror, some in repose." One woman in particular attracted his attention. She had been stripped to the waist in her attempt to escape—"a nude torso like a plaster cast in the ancient Greek rooms of an art museum, silent, white, and beautiful."

Collins maneuvered his way around the chaos and through a service door into the kitchen. In a corner, a scullery maid was glumly peeling potatoes. On a chair, attended by a nurse, was a man whose head, face, and hands were swathed in bandages.

Collins looked around for the owner of the restaurant, J. R. Thompson, but he was nowhere to be found. Thompson, he later learned, was one of those desperate men trying to get into the Iroquois Theatre. His seven-year-old niece Ruth was missing. Her grandfather, a younger brother, and two aunts had gotten out safely, but Ruth was nowhere to be found. Thompson had even tried to jump across an air shaft between his restaurant and the theater, but a bakery chef talked him out of it. Ruth, it turned out, had become separated in the parquet while, "as if on signal, everyone stood up and crowded into the aisles." Carried along by the mass of people, her feet only occasionally touching the floor, Ruth was hurtled toward a door that led onto the stage. As adults surrounded her, pushing her out of the stage-door exit that led to Couch Place, she saw little, hearing only screams and shouts. Suddenly, Ruth fell down without warning and, as "waves of black cloth streamed" over her, she thought she was dead. Actually she had fallen to the ground from the raised platform outside. The "waves of black cloth" that streamed over her were a "torrent of people." They swept over her without touching her and she was able to get away and enter a brightly lit store, where she was eventually found. Her brother John, who had wiggled his way to the rear of the parquet and into the Grand Stair Hall, was passed over the heads of the crowd to safety in the theater lobby. He then knew enough to walk into his uncle's restaurant next door.[6]

Collins was surprised that, aside from the scullery maid in the kitchen, the working areas of Thompson's Restaurant were bereft of waiters and cooks. It turned out that they were busy outside rescuing victims. They had raised a ladder from the roof of a shed in Couch Place to a window in the rear of the theater building. Standing on its topmost rung, the head cook, C. Little, had women and children jump into his arms. Catching them, Little then passed them down to other men on the ladder below. They saved fifteen people in all. One woman, though, jumped before

Little was braced to catch her. She fell into the alley, fracturing her skull and dying instantly.[7]

When, finally, friends and relatives were permitted to enter the restaurant, Stanley Waterloo, a reporter for the *Inter Ocean,* stood in the doorway, watching as they passed along the long rows of the dead who lay on the tables "all covered decently and silent." But around them there was "no silence." As an "impromptu" shroud was lifted, a relative or friend would shriek until, Waterloo said, "the cries of agony seemed blended."[8] A group of priests and nuns appeared, searching for two young girls who had gone to see *Mr. Bluebeard* with a convent sister. They found one of the girls in the restaurant, among the dead. Later, the other girl was found dead, too.[9]

The first thing a *Sun* reporter, Katherine Kennay Brookes, saw on entering Thompson's Restaurant was "a pile of children and men and women four feet deep and fifteen or twenty feet square, a mass of crisped humanity: arms and legs and headless trunks." The entire dining room was permeated, she said, by "the sickening smell of burned human flesh." Near the kitchen was a woman who had been resuscitated, her face so badly burned that she was unrecognizable. Brookes was surprised by a "sudden stir" at one of the tables. A doctor thought he had discovered signs of life in the body of another woman. A crowd of doctors surrounded the table on which the woman lay. "They administered oxygen, gave hypodermic injections of whiskey and brandy and finally of boiling hot coffee." After nearly an hour's labor the doctors gave up. The body was "unceremoniously thrown into a blanket."[10]

Charles Collins, in the meantime, had gone looking for members of the cast to interview. Entering the lobby of the Sherman House, he came across a "haggard and nerve-shattered" Eddie Foy.[11] The comedian had emerged from the Iroquois, looking for his son Bryan. An icy gale was howling through the streets, making Foy's teeth chatter. He could not speak. A stranger offered him his overcoat. Other "kindly people" offered their coats to chorus girls who were dressed in skimpy costumes. Suddenly, Foy spotted Bryan across Dearborn Street, still in the keeping of the stagehand who had shepherded him out of the theater. He took the boy up in his arms and started toward the Sherman House. As they walked away, he heard shouts of "Oh, thank God! Oh, thank God!" It was his wife, Madeline, hastening down the street with their two younger children in tow. She had had a premonition of disaster when she heard a fire engine clanging past the window of their hotel room. Now, she threw herself into Foy's arms, then seized Bryan and kissed him.

Foy did not sleep that night. "My nerves did not subside to normal pitch for weeks afterward," he said. Although he was one of the few individuals who, without regard for their own safety, had selflessly attempted to help others, Foy was hard on himself. So many persons who had come to see him perform in *Mr. Bluebeard* had died or suffered serious burns and other injuries. All he could think about was that he had failed them. "I was enraged almost to the point of madness because of my inability to do more."[12]

10

MORGUE SCENES

Sec. 180. Emergency exits and stairways shall be
provided outside of the walls. . . . These emergency
exits are to be kept free of obstructions of all kinds,
including snow.

As the day drew to a close, a quick count of bodies at the various mortuaries reflected the shocking extent of the disaster. There were 160 bodies inside Jordan's, 75 more in wagons outside that undertaking parlor on East Madison Street, waiting to be attended to. Rolston's counted 75 inside the mortuary, 100 more in wagons outside in Adams Street. Buffon's on Wabash Avenue held 50 bodies. Scores of other bodies were at Carroll's on Wells Street and at Perrigo's on State. With space at midtown funeral parlors at a premium, three wagons, each with eight to twelve bodies, carried victims outside the district to the undertaking rooms at Gavin's on North Clark Street and Sheldon's on West Madison. Other bodies were taken to the county morgue on Polk Street or were in the morgues of the hospitals where the injured and dying had been taken.[1]

Everywhere, the scenes were heart rending. Fathers and mothers went despairingly from one morgue to another, searching for their children. Grief-stricken husbands looked for wives. Anguished grandparents hunted for families. Hundreds gathered outside each mortuary, pressing to enter. Weeping women beat upon the doors, but entry was refused. Police, assigned to handle the throngs, had to turn away the grieving relatives for the time being. Bodies at Jordan's were packed so closely together—stretched out upon the carpets of the little chapel and on the bare floors of the preparation room below—that it would have been impossible anyway for anyone searching for a relative or friend to pass through the rooms.[2]

As it was, identification of the bodies was difficult because of the severe burns that so many of the victims suffered. At one point, Police Chief O'Neill had a list of fifty-seven girls and young women, ranging in age from nine to about twenty, who were "burned beyond recognition" and unidentified.[3] Cook County Coroner John E. Traeger issued an order that no one be permitted to inspect bodies for two hours in order to give undertakers the chance to arrange the bodies. Two patrolmen were specifically charged with searching each corpse for letters, cards, papers, or other possible marks of identification. Even bits of shoelaces were saved. They were all placed in sealed envelopes with whatever valuables that were found and then numbered. A handkerchief, for example, led to the identification of a boy whose features were unrecognizable. It was found in the pocket of the boy's suit at Rolston's and was enough to identify him as thirteen-year-old Hoyt Fox. He and his mother, sister, and brother all died in the fire.

By midnight, as the result both of tracking down the owners of personal items and of relatives being able to recognize bodies, more than four hundred of the dead were identified.[4] There were, however, instances of wrenching mistakes, which were almost inevitable considering the condition of many of the corpses. After hours of fruitless searching, Herbert Lang thought he had found the body of one of his two missing daughters at one of the morgues. Two detectives helped him carry the child to his carriage. But upon reaching home, Lang discovered that both daughters were safe. They had become dazed and had been wandering the city aimlessly. Lang immediately returned to the morgue. "There were some strong points of resemblance," he explained, "and I concluded it must be she."[5]

In a similar case, Mrs. Lulu Bennett was so distraught by what might have happened to her sixteen-year-old daughter, Gertrude, that she asked a friend to tour the morgues and look for her. The friend identified what appeared to be the girl's body at Rolston's, and the corpse was conveyed to Mrs. Bennett's residence. She looked at it and turned away with a moan. "That is not my Gertrude," she said, "take it away, take it away. There has been some terrible mistake made."[6]

Before Traeger's order was given and a crowd grew outside Jordan's, G. E. McCaughan, a counsel for the Rock Island Railroad, managed to get into the mortuary. A friend had told him that the body of his seventeen-year-old daughter, Helen, was there. But when McCaughan arrived, there was no corpse there that resembled her. He spent hours searching for her.

McCaughan was not the only person trying to find a child. To help to at least speed the process, a dozen policemen at police headquarters in City Hall were busy all night taking down the names and descriptions of missing persons. A young man supplied the names of seven girls, all from the Englewood neighborhood, who had not been heard from. Mrs. L. A. Rose was searching for her three children. As the names of victims became available from morgues, the temporary shelters, and hospitals, lists were posted in police stations, where many anxious families went to find out what had happened. But sometimes the crush of people at a station house was so overwhelming that, instead of allowing the people to enter inside the building to read the posted lists, a patrolman would step outside with the latest list and, in a loud voice amidst the silence of the crowd, slowly read off the names. As he did so, every so often there was a spasm of sobbing when a name was recognized.

The searching, finding, and identifying were anguishing, and clashes between overwrought parents and the police were bound to occur. By midnight, more than a thousand persons were in front of Jordan's, demanding entry. The waiting line ran for several blocks. It took twenty policemen to keep order. At one point, a little woman dressed in black broke from the line and rushed to the door of the funeral parlor. As she was pushed back by a policeman, she exclaimed: "My boy is in there. You have no right to keep me from him." She rushed toward the door again, but before she could reach it, she fell fainting into the arms of the policeman.

At Rolston's, police had to fight to keep back the hundreds of people who struggled to enter the undertaking establishment when it finally opened its door at two in the morning. Once inside, scores of women fainted before they had gone a dozen steps, and men staggered as they walked down the aisles, all overwhelmed by the sight of corpse after corpse after corpse. The bodies lay, thirty deep, in furrows, "their ghastliness brought out by the glare of the electric lights." The dead included a child in a Fauntleroy costume, his golden curls in vivid contrast to the scarlet color of his face, for his facial skin had been torn off. The marks of boot heels were plainly visible on his cheeks. His chest was crushed.

Some of those who viewed the bodies were struck by the look of "resignation" on many of the faces. A friend who identified the bodies of Mrs. F. Morton Fox and her three children was particularly impressed by the appearance of their visages—"almost with a smile of faith," he said, "so serene were their countenances." Her thirteen-year-old son's "smile of courage" was "one of the most noble sights that I ever saw," the friend said. "It seemed to me that I could see the brave little fellow trying to reassure his mother and facing death with a heroism not expected of his years."[7]

"In one respect," a reporter wrote, the bodies were all alike. "The left arm of nearly every victim was held stiff and close to the side, while the right hand was outstretched as if warding off peril."[8] It was such an outstretched hand that attracted the attention of Patrick O'Donnell. Walking through the aisles at one morgue, O'Donnell, a wealthy brewer, suddenly stopped to examine a woman's hand that extended from beneath a sheet. On it was the ring he had given his wife for Christmas. O'Donnell knelt and kissed the hand.[9]

Another O'Donnell, but no relation, Simon O'Donnell, superintendent of the Union Stock Yards, lost two grandchildren in the fire, together with their nurse. He had given them money to attend the theater as a holiday treat. He went from funeral parlor to funeral parlor, barely able to handle his grief.[10]

In some cases, almost entire families perished in the fire. Only one member of the Moore family of Hart, Michigan, survived. Eight others, representing four generations of Moores, died.[11] Morris Eger and his wife lost their three daughters and two young grandchildren.[12]

Residents of Kenosha, Wisconsin, were stunned by the losses of two of the city's leading families. The Cooper brothers, Willis and Charles, both perished in the fire. A millionaire, Willis was a leading fund-raiser for missions sponsored by the Methodist Episcopal Church as well as a one-time prohibition candidate for governor of Wisconsin. He was general manager of the Chicago Kenosha Hosiery Works, the largest stock-ing-masking plant in the world. Charles, who was the factory manager and headed the sales force, was associated with a number of organizations, including the Kenosha Hospital Association. A popular figure among his workers, Charles had innovated profit-sharing at the plant, which had become known as the place "where the life of the worker is flooded with sunshine."[13]

The other Kenosha family was the Van Ingens. The father, H. S. Van Ingen, was the former manager of the Chicago office of the Pennsylvania Coal Company. The mother was a sister of the commandant of the Newport Naval Reserves in Rhode Island. Following a family holiday custom, all seven members had gone to Chicago for a matinee theater party, with dinner at a hotel planned for afterwards. Only the mother and the father survived, both severely burned. Their children—Grace, twenty-three; Jack, twenty; Ned, nineteen; Margaret, fourteen; and Elizabeth, nine—all died in the Iroquois.[14]

Chicago authorities were overwhelmed not only by the urgency to identify the bodies of victims but also by the problem of keeping track of the number of dead. Too late, they discovered that at first many families had been permitted to take away the bodies of their members from a morgue. James Blackburn wrapped the body of his horribly burned thirteen-year-old daughter, Ethel, in his overcoat, procured a cab, and went to the Northwestern rail depot to catch a train home to Glen View.[15] We know her name and age and who her father was and where they were from only because the incident was witnessed and reported. Other people simply laid claim to a body and left with it. In the confusion that day— as well as with the concern and sympathy of police officers for bereaved relations—they carted the corpse away without anyone recording the name, gender, or any other pertinent information. In one such case, an unidentified man got into a cable car carrying in his arms the body of a little golden-haired girl wrapped in canvas cloth. As he took his seat, the conductor approached and tapped him on his shoulder, saying, "I'm sorry, but the rules of the company do not permit the carrying of bodies in this manner. I must ask you to leave the car." The man rose and with his free hand thrust a revolver into the conductor's face. "This is my daughter," he said. "I have tried in vain to obtain a cab or a carriage. I am taking my baby home to her mother, and I intend to take her on this car." The conductor retreated and the cable car continued on its way.[16]

11

IN MOURNING

Sec. 209. All buildings of Class V, with accommodations for 1,000 or more persons, shall have at least one three-inch iron stand-pipe and metallic ladder combined in the street or alley, on the outside of the building, from ground to roof, with hose attachments close to a window or door at each floor or gallery.

On May 1, 1865, the special funeral train festooned with black crepe that was carrying Abraham Lincoln's body from the nation's capital to Springfield, Illinois, reached Chicago. At every stop along its slow journey, thousands of Americans gathered, heads bowed, grieving for the assassinated president. The public mourning was unprecedented. The death of no other leader in the nation's history had evoked such a mass reaction. Sudden, unexpected, the shooting of Lincoln, even after four years of cruel, bloody civil war, shattered people in the North. Everyone, it seemed, shared in the loss. It was as though a family member had died. The phenomenon would not be repeated again on a national scale until almost the middle of the twentieth century, and then too frequently after that—for the death of Franklin D. Roosevelt in 1945, following the assassination of John F. Kennedy in 1963, in the aftermath of the terrorist attacks on the World Trade Center and Pentagon on September 11, 2001. In Chicago, fifty thousand persons escorted the hearse bearing Lincoln's coffin to the Cook County courthouse, and twice that many witnessed the somber cortege as it made its way through the streets. That night and the next day, 125,000 people, it was estimated, filed by the bier inside the building to pay their respects to Lincoln.[1]

For many Chicagoans, that memory lingered. Now, almost forty years later, all Chicagoans bore another grief, stunned by the enormity of the Iroquois disaster. The city, the *Chicago Record-Herald* said, had become "a house of woe."[2] It seemed as if almost everyone was related to or knew one of the victims. Or, if they weren't related, or weren't even an acquaintance, they were shocked by the number of victims, particularly by how many women and children were involved. To citizens who had weathered the Great Fire of 1871, or the lesser one in 1874, it was unbelievable that a disaster on the scale of the Iroquois Theatre fire could occur within a city that had, supposedly, learned a lesson about catastrophes.

Never before, and never since, have so many persons been killed in a fire in America. In terms of the toll of human lives, the Iroquois Theatre fire was—and still is—the worst fire in the nation's history. In all, 602 men, women, and children died as a result of the conflagration. The toll was so extraordinary that the Cook County coroner's office, too overwhelmed to perform a postmortem on every individual, took the expedient of declaring that, no matter how badly burned or mauled the victims were, they all had died of asphyxiation.[3]

An initial list of victims, prepared by the office of Coroner John Traeger in the latter part of January 1904, before more than thirty more victims died of their injuries in hospitals, bears the names of 570 individuals. Most—300—were Chicago residents, but the rest came from as many as twelve states other than Illinois and as many as eighty-five other cities and towns, mostly in the Midwest.[4] As might be expected, they represented a cross-section of the holiday matinee audience. Of them, 420 were female, 150 male.

By far, the largest number of the total number of dead, 201, were boys and girls, most of them nine years old or older, though there were more than a handful of victims in each age group between three years and eight years. As many as twenty-five of the children were only fourteen years old, twenty-four were seventeen, and twenty-three were twelve.

The next largest segment of the dead were housewives, 147 of them in all, most of whom were between thirty and forty years old. The female victims also included thirty-nine teachers, two principals, and one retired teacher. Among the other dead females were twenty-nine domestics, four nurses, four milliners, three seamstresses, four dressmakers, a phone operator, and a waitress.

Male victims included nine blue-collar workers, six salesmen, four administrators, four farmers, three government workers, two teachers, two dentists, two clergymen, and two railroad men.

According to the coroner's list, the youngest person to die was a girl of two years, the oldest a man of seventy-six.[5]

Back from his aborted hunting trip, Mayor Carter Harrison issued a proclamation asking Chicagoans to forego any New Year's Eve celebrations on the day after the disaster. The city usually greeted a new year with a raucousness of sound—screeches of steam whistles, trumpet blares, volleys of cannon fire, the ringing of bells, the tooting of revelers' horns.[6] All that, Harrison said, would be "particularly objectionable." "I would particularly ask all railway officials and all persons in control of factories, boats, and mills," he said, "to direct their employes not to blow whistles between the hours of 12 and 1 o'clock."[7]

The mayor's request was unnecessary. Chicago was plunged into mourning. Every train arriving in the city that Thursday morning, December 31, bore relatives of the victims. The lobbies of hotels were filled with grieving families. From dawn until far into the evening, crowds continued to press into the morgues, some mourners arranging to have their dead kinfolk conveyed home, others planning funeral services within one of the city's cemeteries, and still others grimly searching for missing mothers, fathers, or children.

The coroner's office was besieged with requests to view bodies. Less than twenty-four hours after the fire, a total of 336 persons were still listed as missing and almost two hundred bodies had yet to be identified.[8] To facilitate the identification of victims, the office issued permits allowing anxious mothers and fathers to gain admittance to any morgue or hospital. E. C. Fready, president of the Strohber Piano Company, identified five bodies of the six persons who were in a theater party hosted by his wife. Each body was in a different morgue. He was still searching for his sister. Dr. W. D. Alexander finally found his son Boyer. He identified him by the watch he had given him as a birthday present. The boy's body was headless. Harry Wunderlich discovered the body of his seven-year-old daughter, Helen, at the county morgue. Still missing were his thirty-five-year-old wife, Pearl, and her father. Fourteen-year-old Marjorie Edwards was identified by her father when he matched a swatch of cloth he was carrying with the skirt her mother had made for her. The teenager's face was unrecognizable. Postmaster F. A. Freer of Galesburg, Illinois, spent the day searching for his wife and daughter without being able to find them. Mrs. B. L. Stoddard of Minonk, Illinois, had the same experience. She was supposed to have attended the performance of *Mr. Bluebeard* herself but had become ill and stayed home. She spent fruitless hours trying to locate the bodies of her daughter, Zedell, thirty, and her son, Donald, eleven.[9]

Telephone and telegraph offices were still swamped with inquiries. At the telephone exchange, every available operator was again pressed into service, and for hours it was impossible to make connections to some outlying exchanges. Carrier boys from Western Union and the postal service lugged great bundles of messages. The private wires of the stock exchange and board of trade were loaded with inquiries and answers.

In no mood to celebrate, every traditional dinner, dance, and New Year's party was either canceled or postponed. With young William McLaughlin dead, the marriage of his cousin, Pastor Gunsaulus's daughter, was canceled. The charity dance given by the Young People's Club was postponed, so, too, the children's party of the Catholic Women's League. The Standard Club decided not to hold its traditional New Year's ball. The Arche, Lakeside, Social, and Hamilton Clubs dropped their plans for festivities. The annual dinners of the Concordia and Lincoln Clubs were called off. The Waupanseh Club postponed its leap-year dance. Alpha chapter of Beta Tau Delta sorority of Hyde Park called off its dance at the Chicago Beach Hotel. Theta chapter of Zeta Beta Tau postponed its dance until a later date. The Menoken Club postponed indefinitely its stag party because a prominent member of the club had lost his daughter and three grandchildren. The annual ice carnival presented under the auspices of the Sleipner Athletic Club, which ordinarily attracted entrants from throughout the West and an audience of forty thousand fans, was canceled.[10]

All during the day, firemen working by calcium light checked every nook and cranny in the Iroquois Theatre, sometimes finding a body that had not been uncovered before. In one section of a balcony, a little girl was found. Her hair had been burned and her face badly scorched by flames. In her lap was a fur muff; oddly, it was untouched by fire.[11]

Policemen, meanwhile, gathered an unusual assortment of personal effects from the theater. They scraped up debris from the Iroquois floors and sifted it through a sluice box, similar to those used in mining camps. More than a thousand dollars in diamonds and other precious stones were recovered as well as $276 in coin and currency, and 195 wallets containing $884.33. The goods the police found, 4,530 articles in all, also included 33 sealskin coats and a miscellaneous lot of astrakhan, otter, mink, Persian lamb, bearskin, and other fur garments. There were 259 ladies' and misses' cloth hats, 93 men's and boys' overcoats, 263 other ladies' hats, 100 girls' hats, 240 pairs of rubbers, 30 pairs of shoes, and 50 opera glasses. Fifty diamond rings were found, also earrings, stickpins, and other articles of jewelry.[12]

The year 1904 slipped in at midnight Thursday with scarcely a sound to be heard. What few pedestrians were out looked with scorn at a messenger boy blowing a tin horn on LaSalle Street and a man doing the same on Wabash Avenue. Streets everywhere were hung with crepe, and everywhere—in residential neighborhoods as well as downtown—sidewalks were virtually deserted. A few restaurants were open, but there was no music to herald in the new year. At Rector's, floral decorations were taken down and sent to hospitals. Surprisingly, the members of the Pony Ballet showed up at the Hotel Wellington, where the cast of *Mr. Bluebeard* and friends from other theatrical productions had planned a New Year's Eve celebration. William Brady was the only other person to appear. It was, the New York producer said, "the saddest holiday I ever spent." Brady and the young ballerinas sat talking "glumly against the silence. It was the same everywhere else that night."[13]

In past years, streets downtown were festooned with lights that illuminated the entire business district. But not now. Electric signs and other illuminations were turned off, an eerie phenomenon for an otherwise "gay, wicked, noisy Chicago" that was "clothed with gloom such as it had never before known." Hardly anyone wished anyone else a happy new year. "The greeting for the day," Charles Collins of the *Record-Herald* noted, "was seldom spoken."[14]

Friday, New Year's Day, was grim, and the next day, Saturday, January 2, even gloomier. At the mayor's suggestion, the day was set aside for the burial of the dead. Flags flew at half staff. City Hall was shuttered, and all businesses were asked to shut down, too. Chicago on a normally busy Saturday came to a virtual standstill. The stock exchange never opened. The board of trade closed at eleven in the morning.

Embarrassed by their initial reaction to news of the fire, livery drivers did an about-face and declared a ten-day truce in their strike, offering to drive hearses without compensation. "The disaster is too great to be ignored and we have done what our sense of humanity and good judgment dictated," their union leader declared. However, mortuaries had to hire nonunion men anyway to handle the huge volume of funerals.[15]

A silent, wind-driven snowstorm clothed the city in white. The empty streets that had marked New Year's Day the day before were now filled with procession after procession filing slowly to Chicago's several cemeteries, the horses pulling the hearses and carriages stepping gingerly through the slush, sometimes slipping. They headed to Graceland on North Clark Street, or Oakwoods on Greenwood Avenue, as far out of the city as Forest Home in Oak Park or Waldheim, more than three miles west of the city limits, or Rosehill, seven miles away. From dawn until into the evening, funeral corteges moved through the streets in the blinding storm. White hearses bore the bodies of children, black ones the bodies of adults. Long lines of carriages followed the hearses and the plain black wagons that had been preempted for the occasion as they wended their way. At noon, church bells throughout the city tolled a solemn dirge, "The Dead March in Saul." Those hearing it stood hatless in the snowstorm, their heads bowed.

Sometimes the homes of several of the dead were within a few blocks of one another. Six funeral corteges formed in one street alone. At some churches, three or four hearses stood idly outside in the snow, waiting their turn as one funeral service followed another inside the chapel. More than a thousand members of the Chicago Turnbezirk joined in services at Social Turner Hall for seven members of the gymnasium club.

Grief was widespread, every sect and denomination affected. A crowd of a thousand mourners jammed the home of Ludwig Wolff on Washington Boulevard. In his living room, the minister of St. Andrew's Church officiated over the coffins of Wolff's daughter and three young grandchildren. The largest funeral procession for children ever witnessed on the South Side—there were seventy-five carriages—followed the white hearse bearing the children of William Dee after services at the Dee home on Wabash Avenue conducted by a Roman Catholic priest. A priest from the Church of Our Lady of Lourdes celebrated mass at the home of Mrs. Louise Ruby for her two married daughters, both members of his parish, then a minister from the Bethlehem Evangelical Church read the service for Mrs. Ruby, who had also died in the fire. A Congregational minister read the Twenty-third Psalm at Forest Home over the graves of the two daughters and two grandchildren of Jacob and Elizabeth Beder. Services for Eva Pond, her sister, and her two children were held in their home on Lyman Avenue, with a minister from All Saints' Episcopal Church leading the prayers. The four bodies were then taken to Beloit, Wisconsin, for burial. A little frame church on Congress Street that was still adorned with Christmas decorations was the scene for services for Mrs. Mary W. Holst, daughter of a former Chicago police chief, and her three children, aged eight, ten, and thirteen. The largest funeral at Oakwoods was that of Dr. M. B. Rimes, his wife, and their three children, aged five, seven, and ten. They were buried together in one large grave. The two Lange children—Herbert, seventeen years old, and Agnes, fourteen—were mourned at services at the Johannes Evangelical Lutheran Church. Emma D. Mann, supervisor of music in the Chicago public school system, and her fourteen-year-old niece, Olive Squires, were buried at Rosehill after ceremonies at the Centenary Methodist Episcopal Church.[16] Rabbi Emil G. Hirsch conducted the service for teenage sisters Hazel and Helen Regensburg at their parents' home on the South Side, then excused himself to go to the home of Dr. Joseph Zeisler, whose seventeen-year-old son, Walter, a student at the University of Chicago, had also died in the fire.[17]

Scores of dead were taken to the various rail stations in the city for transport back to their homes. It seemed as if there was hardly a village or town within a radius of a hundred miles of Chicago that had not been affected in some way by the fate of the dead or the injured. Every train leaving the city that day, no matter what its destination, carried at least one casket. Two double funerals, both headed for the same rail depot, passed slowly through downtown streets at the same time. One bore the bodies of two sisters, the other the bodies of a brother and a sister.

In Chicago itself, two hundred victims were buried before darkness set in, so many that undertakers had to make up schedules to allot time during the day to convey the bodies in the available hearses.[18] The main thoroughfares leading south and west toward the graveyards were crowded all day with corteges going to and coming from the burial sites. Sometimes a few hundred feet from one freshly dug grave there was another, and a short distance away still another.[19]

And all during the day, while the silent snow fell and the corteges carried their sad burdens and tears flooded the eyes of the mourners, there were still heartbroken families going solemnly from one morgue to another morgue to another morgue, trying to locate a wife, a husband, a son, a daughter, a grandchild.

VICTIMS OF THE FIRE

Photos and captions from *The Great Chicago Theater Disaster* by Marshall Everett, 1904.

Lucile Bond, 4123 Indiana Avenue, Chicago. Daughter of Mr. and Mrs. George R. Bond and granddaughter of Benjamin Moore, ten years of age. Her mother did not attend the matinee and her father was absent in Nome, Alaska, where he holds a government position.

James Paul Brennan, Chicago. Jimmy Brennan, as he was generally known, was the son of Mr. and Mrs. P. G. Brennan, and, with his mother, was burned in the fire. He was eleven years of age, sturdy and bright.

Louise Dee, Chicago. The child of William Dee, who was killed with her brother at the Iroquois fire. She was not burned, but is supposed to have been suffocated or died of shock and exposure.

Natalie Eisendrath, 10 Crilly Court, Chicago. Mrs. S. M. Eisendrath and her daughter, Natalie, ten years of age, were both lost in the fire. They were in the first balcony and were smothered and crushed. Natalie was a bright child and an especial favorite in church entertainments.

Sibyl Moore, Hart, Michigan.
Daughter of Mrs. Perry Moore, 13
years old, who also perished in the fire,
and granddaughter of Benjamin
Moore. At the time of the calamity her
father was on his way home from
Nome, Alaska.

Amy Holst, 2088 Van Buren Street,
Chicago. The daughter of Mr. and
Mrs. Wm. H. Holst. Amy was seven
years of age and a pupil of the Sumner
School. She, with her mother, brother,
and sister, was a victim of the fire.

Gertrude Holst, 2088 Van Buren Street, Chicago. Gertrude was ten years of age and with her younger sister, Amy, and her older brother, Allan, was a pupil of the Sumner school. All were burned in the fire. The picture was taken some time ago when she was a flower girl at a wedding.

Donald D. and Dwight M. Hull, 244 Oakwood Boulevard, Chicago. Two nephews and adopted children of Arthur E. Hull, 8 and 6 years of age, who with his daughter, Helen, and wife, were burned to death. Mr. Hull headed the movement for safe theaters.

Helen Muriel Hull, 12 Years old, Chicago. The daughter of Arthur E. Hull made one of a little theater party organized by his wife for the amusement of the three children. All the party perished.

Dora L. Reynolds, 421 E. 45th St., Chicago. Dora attended the fateful matinee in company with her mother and her cousin, Ruth Stratman, of Dodgeville, Wis. Both the girls were burned to death.

Josephine E. Reynolds [no relation to Dora L. Reynolds], E. Ravenswood Park, Chicago. The daughter of Mrs. [Barbara L.] Reynolds who perished with her mother in the theater disaster was only seven years of age. Both were burned beyond recognition.

Myrtle Shabad, 14 Years old, 4041 Indiana Avenue, Chicago. Myrtle and her brother Theodore, attending the grammar grades, were at the matinee with a girl friend, Rose Elkan. They all met death in the fire.

Theodore Shabad, Chicago. Theodore was a bright boy, eleven years of age, and, as stated, formed one of the merry party of three which met their fate on that terrible afternoon.

Mrs. Maria E. Brennan, 608 Fulton Street, Chicago. Mrs. Brennan was the wife of P. G. Brennan, connected with the stereotyping department of the "Chicago American." Before marriage she was Miss Maria Hogan. Mrs. Brennan and her boy were lost.

Miss Melissa J. Crocker, 3730 Lake Avenue, Chicago. Miss Crocker was for seventeen years a teacher of the higher grades in the Oakland school, coming to Chicago from Princeton, Illinois. She attended the theater with a friend, Mrs. L. H. Pierce, and a little girl of Plainville, Mich. All were lost.

Mrs. Teresa M. Danson. Mrs.Danson was the daughter of Mrs. Sands. She was married in 1902 and perished with her mother and sister in the theater fire.

Miss Mayme A. Decker, Chicago. Daughter of Mr. and Mrs. Myron A. Decker, who, with her parents, met her death in the fire. She was thirty-three years of age.

Myron A. Decker, 3237 Groveland Avenue, Chicago. Mr. Decker, who, with his wife and daughter, perished in the fire, was a prosperous real estate dealer, 65 years of age. He had a particular horror of fire and seldom attended a theater. Only one member of the family survives, a daughter and bride of a few months, Mrs. Blanche D. Kinsey, wife of Carl D. Kinsey, of the Chicago Beach Hotel.

Mrs. Anna H. Dixon, 100 Flournoy St., Chicago. Mrs. Dixon attended the matinee with her two daughters, 15 and 9 years of age respectively, all being lost in the fire. She was the wife of A. Z. Dixon, a well known West Side grocer.

Herman Fellman, 3113 Vernon Avenue, Chicago. Mr. and Mrs. Fellman attended the matinee with their little girl, twelve years of age, and their mothers. All except Mrs. Fellman and her daughter perished.

Mary Herish, 710 S. Halsted Street, Chicago. A Russian girl, only eighteen years of age. She was one of only three or four of that nationality to lose her life in the disaster.

Mrs. Mary W. Holst, 2088 Van Buren Street, Chicago. Wife of Wm. H. Holst, and daughter of ex-Chief of Police Badenoch, who, with her three children, Allan, Gertrude and Amy, perished in the fire. She was identified by her husband by means of her wedding ring and a diamond ring.

Mrs. William C. Levenson, 268 Ogden Avenue, Chicago. This victim of the Iroquois fire, 28 years of age, was a Russian by birth, and left a husband and two children. The latter were girls, four and two years of age, respectively.

Mrs. Barbara L. Reynolds, 1286 E. Ravenswood Park, Chicago. Mrs. Reynolds, her daughter, sister and sister's two boys attended the theater together. When entering the auditorium she remarked: "What a death-trap!" Soon afterward she and her little daughter were burned. Her sister and boys escaped.

Mrs. Amelia T. Sands. Mrs. Sands went to the theater with her daughter, Mrs. Danson, of Pullman, with whom she was visiting, and her younger daughter, Miss Jessie Sands. They all perished.

Mrs. Emma Steinmetz, 2541 Halsted Street, Chicago. Mrs. Steinmetz was fifty-one years of age and the wife of O. T. P. Steinmetz. She was born in Galena, Ill., her maiden name being Emma Garner.

12

A STATE OF SHOCK

Sec. 186. It shall be the duty of the owner, lessee or manager of every building of Class IV and V, during the performances of which programs are issued, to cause a diagram showing the exits of such building to be printed on such programs.

Situated as it was for so many years on the edge of the western frontier, Chicago had won a reputation as a no-holds-barred kind of city, where corruption was endemic, brothels and gambling dens flourished, labor strife was perpetual, and greed its motto. That image, often still realistic, persisted. Those who lived outside the city tended to look down their noses at immoral, ribald Chicago. So it was surprising that the Iroquois Theatre fire stimulated the wave of sympathy that it did. Telegrams poured into City Hall from cities and individuals all across the United States, and from Europe as well, expressing sorrow at the great loss of life. The response was remarkable.

The disaster also touched another chord, serving as a wakeup call throughout the United States and even abroad, in England and on the Continent.

Eager to quell the anxieties caused by the enormous loss of lives, municipal officials in America sought to reassure their citizens that every precaution would be taken to avoid a similar disaster occurring within their own city. Crackdowns were evident everywhere. The proprietors of three theaters in Washington, D.C., were issued warrants for failure to comply with building regulations, and the license of one theater was revoked and its owner arrested.[1] The Massachusetts state police began an immediate inspection of every theater in the commonwealth outside of Boston, a scrutiny that involved more than one hundred playhouses.[2] Meanwhile, theater owners in Boston assured theatergoers that their playhouses were safe. Many of the theaters, they noted, had not only asbestos curtains but also so-called water curtains that provided sheets of water from three directions if a fire broke out. Moreover, the owners were quick to point out, stagehands conducted weekly fire drills.[3] One theater manager even threw open his playhouse during the day and invited the public to examine the aisles and exit arrangements. He offered to have the asbestos curtain tested with a blowtorch.[4]

Officials in Milwaukee closed four theaters after inspectors found that their "fire curtains" were made of thin canvas. The city council of St. Louis passed a revision of its building regulations to require a metal skylight or fire vent over a stage. Its fire chief alerted theater managers that all aisles must be kept cleared. All theater proprietors in Omaha were told to increase their exit facilities and install asbestos curtains, and one theater was ordered to remove 150 seats in the rear of its parquet and balconies because they would interfere with an emergency evacuation if a fire broke out.[5] Under orders from the mayor and city council, a special committee in Toledo began an investigation not only of the city's theaters but also of all buildings in the city.[6] The top gallery of a Philadelphia theater was eliminated after a citywide investigation.[7] As a result of the Iroquois calamity, schools and other public buildings in addition to theaters in Racine, Wisconsin, were compelled to have panic locks on exit doors, and the schools were also required to hold periodic fire drills.[8]

The city council in Kenosha, Wisconsin—which had been traumatized by the loss of the Cooper brothers and the Van Ingen children in the Chicago fire—disbanded its volunteer fire companies and hired twelve paid firefighters, the city's first professional fire department. And after visits from Kenosha's mayor and its district attorney, the owner of Rhode's Opera House there announced plans to provide a number of safety measures: a fireproof steel screen across the stage, outward-open-ing doors, exit lights, a sprinkler system, a hose pipe, and extra fire extinguishers.[9]

While the disaster in Chicago spawned unanimous calls for enforce-ment and tougher safety rules in other municipalities throughout the country, it set off in New York—then as now the city most identified with the theater world—a dispute over whether its fire code really needed strengthening at all. There was no consensus about what should be done—if, indeed, any changes needed to be made—to prevent a simi-lar catastrophe. The manager of the Academy Theatre, for one, insisted that a calamity was not likely to happen at any theater in Manhattan, that what had happened in Chicago was a shortcoming inherent in tour-ing companies. "There is always danger in the case of traveling shows that some part of the apparatus will get out of order," he declared.[10] Acting Fire Chief Charles W. Kruger agreed, contending that it was hardly possible for a disaster such as Chicago had experienced to occur in New York. A fire squad inspector periodically checked that a theater was examined by the house fireman every day, Kruger said, and when firearms were used on stage, more than one fireman was stationed and on hand with extinguishers and pails of water.[11]

Such statements raised more than one eyebrow. New York's fire com-missioner, Thomas Sturgis, said he believed that there were really no fire-proof theaters whatsoever in the city: Building regulations were openly defied. Aisles were narrower than permitted, he said, and hose lines are universally rotted. Recently, Sturgis said, a thousand persons had been allowed to stand during a performance of *Parsifal* at the Metropolitan Opera House. "The courts would not allow us to clear the aisles," Sturgis explained. "The managers do about as they please."[12]

The argument over whether New York needed a new set of regulations dragged on for months. The result, signed into law in June 1904, was a revised set of building ordinances that called for wider aisles, open courts in the rear of and on each side of a theater, exit doors that opened out-wardly, and seating arrangements that permitted no seat to have more than six seats between it and an aisle on either side.[13] But there was a catch, as critics were quick to point out. The new rules applied only to the construction of new theaters. Existing theaters were grandfathered and did not have to comply with the revisions.

Americans were not alone in being shocked by the Iroquois disaster. A wave of sympathy swept through England and the Continent. King Edward and Queen Alexandra sent a condolence telegram to Washington.[14] Count Cassini, the Russian ambassador to the United States, left a sick bed to go to the State Department to deliver a personal note from the tsar.[15] Recalling a similar disaster at the Ring Theatre in 1881, the burgomaster of Vienna cabled Mayor Carter Harrison, expressing his sympathy.[16] Kaiser Wilhelm of Germany personally wired President Theodore Roosevelt to express his sorrow.[17]

The reaction of enforcement authorities abroad was similar to the response in the United States. It was immediately clear that adherence to fire regulations was essential if a repetition of the Iroquois fire was to be avoided. Laxity spelled disaster. Rigid theater inspections were ordered in Copenhagen and Stockholm. Authorities in Amsterdam, Rotterdam, and the Hague demanded strict observance of fire codes. A Chicago architect who happened to have just visited Vienna, Paris, and London was impressed by the theaters he saw in Vienna—"the safest in Europe," he said, and undoubtedly so because the fire in the Ring Theatre more than twenty years earlier took anywhere from 580 to 900 lives, according to reports.[18] The architect was less sanguine about the theaters in Paris. They, "except the best ones, are extremely dangerous," he declared. And, just as bad, from what he saw in London, he judged that "fire in many theaters would result in great loss of life. The passages are often so narrow that two people can scarcely pass."[19]

Enforcement was particularly stringent in Berlin, which then was the cultural center of Europe. At performances, the directors of many theaters took it upon themselves to go before their audiences and promise to install the latest fire-protection devices. The city's fire department, meanwhile, began an immediate inspection of all the city's playhouses,[20] and the kaiser even took it upon himself to summarily close the Royal Opera House pending the completion of certain alterations. In all, a dozen music halls and other places of amusements were shut down until safeguards were improved. A visiting American executive was dismayed to find that many auditoriums in German theaters were fifty yards from the street and to reach them entailed a "journey through a labyrinth of courts, corridors and sudden turnings."[21]

Despite the clamor for severe enforcement measures and more stringent safety regulations, there was unanimity in America and abroad about what had led to the terrible loss of life at the Iroquois Theatre. One particular recurrent theme ran through everyone's reaction: It was caused by panic. In fact, scholars who study mass behavior point to the Iroquois disaster as a prime example of what happens when people run amok.[22] As one of them, University of Virginia professor Duane P. Schultz, has pointed out, "Never before had such a disaster occurred so quickly," though, "ironically," the theater itself "did *not* burn."[23] But looking back on the fire a hundred years later, it seems odd that the negligence exhibited by the Iroquois management and the lack of required safeguards were, for the initial moment at least, given lesser importance than the panic that had occurred as a result of the total absence of fire-safety measures. Details about absent hose lines, the locked accordion gates and doors, the lack of exit signs, the impossibly difficult bascule locks—all were reported within days of the fire. Yet, the great loss of life, everyone believed, was due to panic. The flames and fumes would have been ineffectual in causing so many deaths, the reasoning went, if members of the audience had remained calm and left the theater without a fuss. Oscar Hammerstein, a prominent New York theater proprietor and theatrical producer, best summed up that point of view. A woman with a child constituted one of the most dangerous elements inside a theater, he said, and he, for one, would never permit a child to be admitted to a playhouse he controlled.[24]

Panic. That was the reason given by all those connected with the construction and operation of the Iroquois Theatre. It was as though no other factor could have affected the calamity. Those connected with the theater were not responsible. Some of their remarks, in fact, bordered on the callous. It was, despite all the details of what happened that came out over the next few days, a textbook case of denial.

Panic was Benjamin Marshall's answer. The Iroquois architect was in Pittsburgh at the time of the fire, supervising work on a new theater for Nixon and Zimmerman, the co-owners of the Iroquois with Davis and Powers and with Klaw and Erlanger. Marshall first learned of the disaster in a telegraph message from his mother, who reported, incorrectly, that a boiler had exploded. "I cannot understand," he said, "how so many people were caught in the balcony unless they were stunned by the shock of the explosion." He could not understand either, he said, why the audience was not able to leave the theater "except it was because the house was new and the people were not familiar with the fire exits." Marshall made immediate plans to return by train to Chicago. "I have erected many playhouses," he declared, "and in each one I figure I had mastered the details so that the public would be safe."[25]

Will Davis said that there was "no need, so far as I know, of a single life being lost." As far as he was concerned, "if somebody had not screamed 'Fire!' I think that all, as far as those killed in the panic are concerned, could have reached the street in safety." After all, he said, there were more than forty exits in the theater.[26] Davis, incidentally, had been spared a personal tragedy when his own child, who was in the theater at the time of the fire, escaped unharmed.

Once the fire was under control, Davis and his partner Harry Powers made their headquarters in one of the women's dressing rooms at the Iroquois. They immediately canceled evening performances at their two other theaters, the Illinois and the Powers', and issued a statement saying that they had "sacrificed more space to aisles and exits" in the Iroquois "than any theatre in America."

The two men were soon besieged at the theater by people looking for still-missing relatives. One of them, a prominent businessman, approached Davis. He had treated twelve children to seats in two boxes. They were missing. "My God! This is what kills a man," said Davis, who almost fainted. He had to be assisted to a carriage and taken home.[27]

"The panic, as everybody says, was the chief cause of the large number of deaths," said Marc Klaw of Klaw and Erlanger.[28] His office in Manhattan was swamped with the weeping mothers of young actresses who appeared in the *Mr. Bluebeard* company, all anxious for word about their daughters.[29] Klaw was pragmatic. He shrugged off the notion that the Iroquois disaster would have a lasting effect on theater attendance. "Ships go down at sea, and people still cross the ocean," he said. "And I suppose people will keep on going to theatres despite the Chicago fire."

Samuel Nixon learned of the fire from a telephone call while at dinner at home. He collapsed, sobbing.[30] Nixon later issued a statement saying he could not understand the great loss of life. "Every precaution" was taken, he said, "to insure the safety of the patrons."

Nixon's partner, J. Fred Zimmerman, was equally at a loss to explain what had occurred. When first informed of the fire by a reporter, he replied, "Nonsense! Why, the theatre has only been opened. It is fireproof." Once he was convinced that the news was accurate, Zimmerman still could not fathom its meaning. It was, he said, "beyond my comprehension."[31]

13

SAFETY LAST

Sec. 197. Upon the report to the Mayor by the Department of Buildings, or of the Fire Marshal, that any order or requirement of this ordinance . . . has been violated or not complied with, in any such building, the said Mayor shall revoke the license of such theater, or place of public amusement, and cause the same to be closed.

That Saturday, January 2, as all Chicago grieved, the mayor toured the Iroquois Theatre. With him were Alderman William Mavor of the finance committee, Building Commissioner George Williams, and Benjamin H. Marshall. The young architect had told a reporter how upset he was. He had "studied every playhouse disaster in history to avoid errors."[1]

Ironically, the Iroquois was, indeed, fireproof. It had survived the tremendous heat and flames with scarcely any substantial damage. The plush-covered seats in the auditorium had caught fire and been destroyed; so, too, the damask draperies and other decorative furnishings. But otherwise the building—despite the ugly streaks of charred plaster, the broken doors, and the debris—had survived intact.

As he stepped into the lobby of the Iroquois, Harrison accidentally trod on a lock of human hair. It unsettled him for a moment. Then he continued on, leading the group. Stepping over the wreckage that filled the playhouse, he made a point of walking through the entire building. He went out on the fire escapes, mounted the rigged loft above the stage, visited the dressing rooms. Harrison would pause every so often to try the handle of an emergency door, looking toward Marshall for an explanation. He was searching for answers, hoping for some clue that would make sense of what had happened.

Harrison questioned why heavy damask curtains were hung before exit doors. Marshall replied that it was done to improve the appearance of the house.

Why, the mayor asked, did the architect disregard the requirement that balconies above the ground floor have a separate stairway leading directly to the street? Again, Marshall had an explanation: "There was more total space for the people to get out of the gallery than if separate stairs had been provided."

Why weren't there any exit signs posted? They were being made ready, Marshall said, "but temporary signs were not being used, because it was not desired to mar the beauty of the interior with them."

The architect's responses were too much for Alderman Mavor. He was furious. "This theatre was opened on November 23," he burst out. "It has been running fully five weeks. In Heaven's name, how long does it take to make a few signs?"[2]

Two months earlier, in November, before the Iroquois Theatre opened, there had been an opportunity to correct the shortcomings. As he stepped gingerly through the scorched playhouse, an unhappy Harrison might well have pondered what could have been averted if his effort to close down all of Chicago's theaters at that time had been successful. His attempt to do so had been prompted by a citywide investigation that demonstrated a wide assortment of violations in almost every playhouse and music hall in the city. But Harrison was thwarted then by aldermen on the city council. Now, after an almost indescribable catastrophe, he had all the more reason to take some sort of action. And now he also had the unqualified support of the public.

One of the most vociferous of the Chicagoans demanding that he do something was J. E. O. Pridmore, an English-born architect who was becoming known for his church and theater designs. Pridmore's thirty-two-year-old sister, Edith, had been severely burned in the fire and died in a hospital shortly afterwards. Pridmore, for one, urged Harrison to do what he had planned to do in November: close every theater in the city pending inspections and adherence to the fire code. Surprisingly, at first Harrison—despite his intent two months earlier—demurred from taking such a drastic action. He said he saw "no more reason for closing all the theatres than for stopping all railway trains after a disastrous wreck. There is no necessity of getting hysterical about this matter." Instead, the mayor sent a letter to all theater proprietors, calling their attention to safety ordinances and announcing that two firemen would hereafter be assigned to each playhouse at their expense.[3]

However, as the incredible details of the Iroquois Theatre's violations of the fire code became known, Harrison finally realized that a sterner reaction was required. He ordered an immediate investigation of all theaters and places of public assembly, and within hours, nineteen theaters as well as two museums were closed down. The theaters included some of the city's most popular playhouses, among them the Chicago Opera House and the Olympic Theatre, both vaudeville houses that offered matinee and evening performances every day and were ordinarily so crowded that great numbers of standing-room tickets were sold. All nineteen theaters were closed for being in violation of the same single ordinance: They did not have an asbestos curtain. One theater, the Academy of Music, had a curtain of burlap. The others had curtains of linen or canvas.

Harrison was so shaken by this evidence of a single safety infraction in so many playhouses that he finally decided before the New Year's weekend was over to shut down all the rest of Chicago's thirty-six theaters. His order, in fact, covered in addition every place of public assemblage, churches and fraternal halls included. The mayor was "determined," he now said, "to see that every precaution is taken to prevent such occurrences as will alarm the people and start them on a rush for the exits." The fact remained, "and it cannot be denied," he added, "that there would have been no panic if the apparatus in this theatre, which, judged by all ordinary standards, was the best equipped playhouse in the city, had been in proper working condition. There is no getting around that fact."[4]

Chicagoans agreed. How could such a disaster have happened, everyone wondered. How could an "absolutely fireproof" theater become the setting for a "holocaust"?

It was a disaster waiting to happen. So many things were wrong with the theater, so many ordinances ignored, so little attention paid to the basics of crowd control and fire prevention, that fixing responsibility for who was to blame would become a labyrinth of recriminations. It is difficult to point one's finger at any one thing or at any one person. Everything and everyone were at fault.

Incredibly, there had been a few naysayers before the theater opened to the public. *Fireproof* magazine, for instance, had been skeptical of the method of safeguarding the balconies. The fireproofing was defective, the magazine insisted, because metal lath used in what was called exposed construction, where heat could easily affect it, should have been buried in concrete.[5] Moreover, the magazine noted, even the concrete mixture used in the construction—so-called cinder concrete, which "is the cheapest and worst building material on the market"—was employed "in violation" of the rule established after an apartment house built of it collapsed.[6] Such criticism seemed like carping to some, especially because the Iroquois had not, as it turned out, collapsed or been irrevocably damaged. But there was another matter much more important. The magazine's editor, William Clendenin, had inspected the Iroquois before it opened and was so shocked that the building had no sprinkler system that he described it as "one of the worst firetraps in the city."[7]

One of New York City's leading architects—William Beaumont Herts, the man who introduced cantilever construction in building the New Amsterdam Theatre there in 1902[8]—had also raised a concern while the Iroquois was under construction. He wrote Benjamin Marshall, advising him to take special precautions against fire in the theater, a subject on which Herts was especially anxious when designing a playhouse. Marshall should be particularly concerned, he said, that emergency exits open outward and that they be easily opened.[9]

If Marshall ever received Herts's letter, or even paused to think about his warning, there is no record of the fact. But even if he had, even if he had taken into account the danger inherent in not providing easily accessible fire exits, what happened might not necessarily have been materially altered. So many other safety precautions were nonexistent or faulty.

The Iroquois did not, indeed, have a sprinkler system as required by law. In addition, while there were stand pipes fitted for hose connections on the stage, shockingly, there were no hoses and no water because the water supply system had not been completed.[10]

Moreover, except for about a half dozen cylinders of the cheap chemical extinguisher called Kilfyre,[11] the Iroquois did not have any standard fire-fighting equipment anywhere in the building: no hooks to pull down flaming scenery, no axes to break open locked or stuck doors, not even pails of water on stage. In fact, the theater not only did not have an alarm system hooked up to fire department headquarters, again as required by law, but it also lacked a separate electric circuit system controlled by the box office in case the switchboard on the stage blew out.

The deficiencies would come, but too late, as a surprise, but there were other oversights that were easily visible and should have been noted by any inspector walking through the theater. First of all, not only were there no exit signs over any of the emergency doors but there also were no signs or arrows whatsoever indicating which way to turn to find an emergency exit. That was a glaring violation of the law. What exacerbated the inherent danger in having unmarked emergency egresses was the fact that the exits on the north wall—numerous as they may have been—were all hidden behind the decorative damask draperies. Moreover, the doors were operated by an unconventional, complicated bascule lock. In fact, each exit on the north wall consisted of two sets of doors: an inner double-wing wooden door with glass panels, and an outer double-wing iron door. Both sets opened outwards, but both sets were fitted with the bascule lock.[12] The lock consisted of top and bottom bolts attached to one wing of the door and operated by a handle that, when turned, released both bolts. Only one usher at the Iroquois knew how to unlock the emergency doors, and the only reason he knew was that he had once tried to open one "out of curiosity."[13]

Then, too, the theater management was preoccupied with controlling the movements of the audience. Take, for example, the out-of-the-ordinary accordion gates that cut off escape routes at the head of two stairwells. They served a dual purpose: to steer gallery ticket holders up the correct stairs to the upper balcony and, once a performance began, to keep them from sneaking down below to better seats in the dress circle or parquet. The gates were customarily pulled across and kept shut tight with padlocks while the performance was in progress.[14] The gates, incidentally, were not in the theater's plans that were sent over to the city building department for approval.[15]

Other doors were also routinely locked during a performance. All but one of the three triple-wing doors that led from the vestibule, where the ticket windows were, into the Grand Stair Hall were always secured. The idea was to make it difficult for gate crashers to furtively get inside the theater to see the show while clerks in the box office might be busy selling tickets.

There was one dereliction of responsibility that is impossible to explain. Theater fires were not unheard of or rare, usually sparked by some piece of stage business or apparatus. In the midst of a performance, a lamp is inadvertently kicked over or a torch catches a piece of scenery. Or, in the middle of the night, the rags in a store room suddenly combust. A London architect at that time determined there had been a thousand theater fires in the past one hundred years.[16] The most serious ones were reported in newspapers around the world. Conway's Brooklyn Theatre was destroyed in December 1876 when a lantern fell from a catwalk and landed on scenery below. Nearly three hundred persons died in that blaze.[17] The Ring Theatre in Vienna suffered a similar fate when scenery caught fire in December 1881.[18] There were fires in a small trap beneath the stage at the Opera House in Providence, Rhode Island, and in a dressing room at the Casino Theater in New York City in 1900, both of which were, fortunately, quickly extinguished.[19] The Columbia Theatre in Chicago—on which Will Davis once held a ten-year lease—was destroyed by a late-afternoon fire in the autumn of 1899, when Davis was its manager.[20] The theater was closed at the time, but hadn't the incident given Davis any pause in considering the safety of the Iroquois? What might have happened if there had been a performance going on and an audience in attendance at the Columbia? Granted, memories are short, and there had not been a theater fire involving a great life of loss in many years. As one experienced actor explained, "all precautions against such a thing were greatly relaxed."[21] Still, no effort whatsoever had been made to drill or instruct in emergency procedures any members of the Iroquois's crew, the stagehands, or the ushers. The last, by the way, were almost all teenagers. Not a word was said about what they were expected to do in case of fire, where they should position themselves, how they were to direct the audience to the exits.

The most critical omission, however, was the lack of functioning ventilators to carry off flames and fumes if a fire occurred on stage. Almost all theater fires start on stage, and most fire-prevention experts in the United States, England, and the Continent recognized that it was critical to be able to draw off the flames, smoke, and heat, much as they are drawn off in a fireplace hearth. A flue is essential in the process; otherwise the flames, suffocating gases, and heat penetrate the auditorium, endangering the audience. Hence, the positioning of the ventilators in skylights high above in the roof over a stage. The Iroquois had such ventilators positioned above its stage, which, theoretically, could be opened in an emergency. There were two switches that could operate them: one was located near the switchboard on stage, the other in the ticket office in the lobby of the theater. Both, by law, bore the sign "Move switch to left in case of fire, to get smoke out of building."[22] But the skylights that controlled the exhaust ducts were never operational. Their glass covers had been fastened down with wiring when they were being installed, thus holding them rigid, and no construction worker had troubled to remove the bindings. In contrast, ventilator openings in the walls behind the parquet and the two balconies *were* operational, allowing hot and dank air to leave the building. That the critical roof ventilators were sealed but the air-exhaust ventilators in the rear of the auditorium were operational proved catastrophic. There was only one direction the flames and fumes from the stage could take: Because they could not exit through the ventilators in the roof above, they swept straight for the exhaust outlets behind the audience.

The sole fire-safety ordinance that the Iroquois Theatre complied with was the requirement that a fireman be backstage during a performance. The house fireman in this case was William C. Sallers, a retired veteran of the city's fire department. Sallers was well aware that the theater had none of the required apparatus to fight a blaze.[23] At one point, he conducted Fire Chief William Musham through the theater, pointing out that the playhouse was not equipped with the fire-fighting equipment called for by law. But having said his piece, Sallers felt he had done his duty. He felt no obligation to comment further or to make any written report.[24]

How, everyone wondered afterwards, could so many things have gone wrong and not have been detected or prevented? How did the Iroquois ever merit an "O.K." and permission to be open? Who was responsible? It was "painfully clear," the *Chicago Evening Post* declared, "that those responsible for the proper construction and equipment of public buildings allowed a playhouse to open for business when it had not complied either with its own plans or the building laws."[25] The newspaper noted that "some ordinances were suspended in the interest of theatrical managers—something that ought not to have been done—but were those which were in full effect properly enforced?"[26] The prolabor *Chicago Daily News* was certain who was primarily responsible for the disaster: "theatrical managers in Chicago and other cities [who] have been playing with fire for a great many years." It was time, it said, that "this awful lesson must transform the business of amusing the public into something more than a mere thing of surface glitter and blind chance."[27] The antilabor *Chicago Daily Tribune* saw the issue differently. The Iroquois, it said, "had been built by artisans whom, in our moments of national pride, we call the cleverest in the world. It had been inspected by officials whom recent public indignation was supposed to have awakened to some sense of public duty."[28] Aside from trying to affix blame for the fire, there was agreement about one thing: the need for reform. The *Evening Post* said existing ordinances ought to be revised "not to fit the theaters, but so that the theaters will have to fit themselves to the ordinances." That, it added, would be "something new in local legislation, but it is something wonderfully refreshing and encouraging."[29] "Every theater," the *Daily News* demanded, "must be thoroughly overhauled and made safe."[30] "There must be no more reliance on good luck," insisted the *Daily Tribune*. "Chicago theaters must be made safe."[31]

Those connected directly with the construction and management of the Iroquois were astonishingly remiss in the matter of public safety, no matter what they claimed afterwards. Neither Will Davis nor Harry Powers had ever said a word to their stage manager, their house manager, or their head usher about what to do or what to instruct their staffs to do in an emergency. A district fire captain reportedly complained to them and to his superiors about the lack of fire-fighting apparatus but was ignored. "The directness of entrance and the availability of exits," Davis and Powers had boasted in a special souvenir program printed for the opening of the Iroquois, "are a praiseworthy feature of this admirably planned house of amusement."[32] But nowhere in the program or in the playbill ordinarily handed out at performances was there, as required by law, a diagram of the theater displaying the exits.

If Benjamin Marshall had entertained any doubts about the worthiness of the theater he had designed, and whose construction he was supposed to have overseen, he never expressed them. Instead, earlier in 1903, he took up his pen and wrote an article for *Fireproof* magazine in which he acknowledged, "One of the greatest dangers in theaters not fireproof is that if a fire starts on the stage it is like an immense flue, as the distance from the basement to the gridiron and ceiling is generally about 100 feet." Well, his theater had its ventilators and was, moreover, of fireproof construction, so no need to worry. Marshall did admit, though, that the gridiron, from which scenes are shifted, is "hard" to make absolutely fireproof, "because of the sheaves or rollers, which number about 1,500, and the thousands of feet of rope ordinarily used in lowering and raising scenes. Wood strips have to be fastened to the sheaves to permit nailing." What really concerned Marshall, however, was the acoustics of the theater. He was experimenting with the use of glass washers where ironwork came next to the stage in order to "let sound travel direct to the audience."[33]

How does one explain the complete lack of attention to even the most basic fire laws? Simply benign neglect? Hubris on everyone's part? Most likely it was just a matter of business-as-usual. For despite all the excitement about the city's phenomenal growth and economic health, Chicago remained a city of corruption, built as much by greed as it was by steel and cement. "Chicago people are money and pleasure mad," declared the Reverend Hugh F. Given of the Second Presbyterian Church. "In other cities the question is 'Does reform help the community?' In Chicago it is 'Does it pay?'"[34] Not much had changed since 1894, when English editor William Stead found that "questionable resorts"—that is, gambling dens and whorehouses in the so-called Levee south of the Loop in the First Ward—were operated "if not under the patronage of the police, at least with their cognizance." And the men who ran the city government, Stead wrote, were hopelessly corrupt.[35] The religion of the church, he said, had been taken over by the Democratic Party, whose faith was built "upon bribery, intimidation, bulldozing of every kind, knifing, shooting and the whole swimming in whiskey."[36] According to Alderman Nathan T. Brenner, there were only three aldermen in the entire group of sixty-eight on the city council who could not and would not steal a red-hot stove.[37] The Civic Federation, one of the city's few reform groups, listed fifty-seven aldermen as grafters; their take, it said, came to between $15,000 and $25,000 a year,[38] a lavish range.

Progressive Era reformers and the uncovering of scandals by muckraking journalists notwithstanding, Chicago was a wide-open city. Political hacks, open to bribery and influence peddling, were of the ilk of "boodlers" like "Hinky Dink" Kenna and "Bathhouse" John Coughlin—aldermen, many of them saloon keepers, who bought and sold votes or were bought themselves. One of the most disreputable was Johnny Powers, otherwise known as the "Prince of Boodlers," who ruled the Nineteenth Ward. In Kenna and Coughlin's cases, they operated the brothels in the First Ward. Carter Harrison was indebted to them, for the mayor, for all his voiced good intentions, was at heart a conniver and political opportunist. Even he acknowledged, later in writing his autobiography, that the council of aldermen was composed of "saloon keepers, proprietors of gambling houses and undertakers."[39] Harrison, though, forgot to mention in his life story that for his first two terms, his office actually housed the office of the building commissioner, who, as one prominent Chicago builder wrote, "was not expected to exert any particular influence or control over building as such."[40] Just as in the past, payoffs to police, construction inspectors, and other municipal employees were routine at Harrison's City Hall.[41] On a visit to Chicago in 1903, one muckraker, Lincoln Steffens, said, "The wide-openness of protected crime and vice fascinated my bulging eyes. The New York Tenderloin was a model of order and virtue compared with the badly regulated, police-paid criminal lawlessness of the Chicago Loop and its spokes."[42]

Where was Chicago's reform movement in all this? The Municipal Voters League in 1902 chose the son of a well-known Chicagoan as its candidate in the Second Ward. The young man, William Hale Thompson, was going to finance his own run for office and, so the League was told, would do no harm: "The worst that you can say of him is that he's stupid." Thompson, of course, lost, but "Big Bill" would run for mayor as a Republican in 1915, amaze everyone by winning, and then take it upon himself to permit unrestricted gambling in the city with one exception, a sop to reformers: Saloons had to close on Sundays.[43] As Lincoln Steffens put it, the city's "businessmen-reformers were not interested in uncovering or challenging 'sources of privilege.'"[44]

The city's building department, in particular, drew the wrath of *Fireproof* magazine. "Chicago has been afflicted for years with an incompetent and rascal building department," the magazine declared in a blistering editorial in its November 1903 issue, a month before the Iroquois fire. "Chicago builders have made open charges of the connivance of the bureau of buildings with flagrant violations of the law." The magazine went on to quote M. B. Bushnell, a local contractor who had lost the contract to erect the Cleveland Theatre on Wabash Avenue. Bushnell said the architectural plans "in no way conformed to the ordinance." He was in fact responsible, he confessed, for constructing "a firetrap theater which he would not permit his wife and daughter to enter"—the LaSalle on Madison Street. It was built "under a contract by which the owners 'were to stand between him and the building department.'" The LaSalle Theatre, Bushnell charged, was "unsafe in almost every particular, and a menace to the public." He had "violated the building ordinance and evaded building inspectors" while putting up the building. "But I am a builder and contractor, and I must make my living," he explained. There is, *Fireproof* magazine charged, "an infinitude of graft for those who are amenable to the persuasive and seductive charm of the American dollar. There is much graft in firetraps."[45]

It was no wonder that the construction of the Iroquois Theatre did not live up to the law. The magazine's condemnation of municipal corruption was by no means exaggerated. Take the month before the Iroquois Theatre opened. On October 19, 1903, the city council appropriated $5,000 to cover the expense "of uncovering rascality around the city hall."[46] It was already sifting evidence that month against Deputy Building Commissioner Timothy O'Shea, who had allegedly used his authority to have a fire-protection device in which he had a financial interest used in the construction of new buildings.[47] O'Shea denied the charge, but he resigned five days later, saying, "I know too much. I will not say about what I know too much, but it has been plainly intimated to me that I am not wanted in office."[48]

The same committee looking into O'Shea's case was also looking into charges that inspectors in the Boiler Inspection Bureau were collecting illegal fees. Graft had gotten so extensive, the committee reported, that it had only been able to skirt the edges of municipal corruption. It needed the $5,000 to hire detectives to delve further. Four days later, on October 23, that same committee also learned that Fire Chief William Musham was ignoring accusations of corruption made against members of his department.[49]

Musham had already suffered an embarrassment earlier in October when it was disclosed that his son Frank had misrepresented his age when he had applied for a position in the fire department. He swore he was over twenty-one years old when he was not even twenty. Frank Musham escaped indictment for perjury, however, when an assistant state's attorney said he had only six days—not nearly enough time, he insisted—to prepare evidence against the youth before the statute of limitations would run out.[50]

Musham's assistant, Fire Marshal John Campion, had his own troubles. His son, Captain Frank Campion of Engine Company 7, had for the third time been admitted to the county hospital, suffering delirium tremens. Nevertheless, the young man, a plainly evident alcoholic, was being retained in the service, which meant he was still a salaried employee of the department.[51]

Police Chief Francis O'Neill was in the headlines, too. O'Neill was one of the few appointees of Harrison who enjoyed an unsullied reputation. He was perhaps chosen to make up for the man he succeeded, Joseph Kipley, who was one of the worst police chiefs in the city's history. O'Neill, that same month, October, had had to suspend nine detective sergeants for "inefficiency, incompetency, and incapability."[52]

Meanwhile, a subject closer to Chicago's theater community was coming under scrutiny. Before the damning editorial in *Fireproof* magazine had come out, someone must have alerted Carter Harrison to the situation at the Cleveland and LaSalle Theatres. In an apparent attempt to avert an embarrassing brouhaha, on October 14, Harrison, who had recently been elected to his fourth term in office, announced to the city council's investigating committee that he had made a personal inspection of the two theaters and believed a further investigation into them was warranted. He was, he said, sending out his own experts—men in no way connected to the building department—to inspect both playhouses. One thing that bothered him, the mayor said, was that the building department would issue a permit to a theater for a certain seating capacity but never check to see how many seats were actually installed in the playhouse. The Cleveland Theatre was supposedly intended to house not more than one thousand patrons—which, under the city's code, meant it could be constructed of slow-burning material rather than be a totally fireproof—and perforce, costly—structure. But, on the basis of the use of standard twenty-two-inch-wide seats employed in the Cleveland's construction, the theater could easily hold fifteen hundred persons—and that meant it should have been built to fireproof specifications. There were other violations as well: the use of wooden rather than iron latticework in the rigging gallery and fly loft and the substitution of a patent partition for the brick proscenium wall required for the building. Henry Ericsson, a prominent and reputable Chicago builder who nearly a decade later would become the city's building commissioner, ascribed the root of many of the problems in the building department to the "nullification of ordinances by special permits," which allowed construction companies to bypass code requirements.[53] As one city council committeeman remarked, any cost-conscious theater proprietor "could juggle with the city at will."[54]

A few days later, on October 17, Harrison notified the proprietors of the LaSalle Theatre to show cause why their license should not be canceled. The essential charge among the many violations he cited was that the LaSalle's auditorium was higher than street level, requiring steps to leave or enter the theater—a hazard if it was necessary to exit the building in an emergency. In an effort to dramatize his concern, Harrison at the same time gave orders for the rigid inspection of all the city's thirty-five theaters, burlesque houses, vaudeville houses, and musical halls. The inspections "might as well be thorough," the mayor declared. "Any place where lives are being risked will have to make the necessary improvements for safety or close up."[55]

The inspections took two weeks to carry out, and no sooner had Harrison announced them than the city council passed an order staying any action against theater violations until its judiciary committee reported out an amended set of ordinances.[56] So, even though the investigation was ongoing, the aldermen effectively aborted any possibility of theater closings that might result from it.

Despite Harrison's intent, the inspections were handled by inspectors of the building department, apparently because they were totally familiar with ordinance requirements and knew what to look for. On the strength of the resulting report on theater safety submitted on November 2 by Building Commissioner George Williams, the mayor decided that he would have to close nearly every theater in Chicago unless the city council did indeed amend the building ordinances to take into account all the discrepancies. "Practically every theater in Chicago is violating the law," he declared.[57]

It certainly appears likely that the Iroquois disaster would have been averted if Harrison's decision to have all the city's theaters closed until they passed inspection had been implemented, assuming, of course, that the inspections would be thorough and all the ordinances enforced. Surely, the obvious lack of fire-protection equipment and exit signs as well as other violations would have been reported and enforcement insisted upon before the Iroquois Theatre was granted a license and the theater was permitted to open.

The prospect that their playhouses might be closed chilled Chicago's theater owners. The very thought was financially alarming, what with the holiday season in the offing. So they used their influence to scuttle the inspections and closings. Two aldermen were able to quash the mayor's threat and put off the question of theater safety by demanding yet another inquiry into the matter.[58] The aldermen, whose names were not recorded and who hence remained anonymous, were obviously sympathetic to the proprietors of the city's playhouses. The entire matter was referred again to the judiciary committee, which was still wrestling with the series of amendments that, if enacted, would, anyway, modify the severity of existing fire-safety ordinances.[59]

In effect then, the matter of theater inspections and closings was pigeonholed. As a result, an irate editorial in the *Chicago Record-Herald* stated, the report on theater safety "slumbers among the archives, dust-laden and forgotten." It was a simple case of not rocking the boat, the *Record-Herald* went on. "A majority of the places were in violation of the order, but as to close one would mean the shutting down of nearly all, the council dodged the issue."[60]

Nothing further came of the subject. On November 23, almost three weeks after the mayor's unrealized threat, the Iroquois Theatre opened.

14

FINGER POINTING

Sec. 196. The Commissioner of Buildings or Fire Marshal shall have the power to order any building of Class IV and V to be closed, where it is discovered that there is any violation of the provisions of this ordinance, until the same are complied with.

How could the theater with so many deficiencies open? Who had approved its license? What had gone wrong? Chicagoans were mystified. The answers they sought, when answers were forthcoming, failed to explain the disaster. Charges and countercharges flew back and forth to such a degree that it was impossible to pinpoint any single culprit. Everyone put the blame on someone or something else. No one accepted responsibility. What they said was implausible.

Fire Chief William Musham attributed the disastrous results of the fire to the absence of sprinklers. Will Davis and Harry Powers conceded that none had been installed in the Iroquois Theatre. Their justification: "As far as I know," said Davis, "there are no theaters in Chicago with automatic sprinklers." Davis made no excuse for not complying with the fire code. In fact, he admitted, "We have no sprinklers in the Illinois Theatre." And, Davis said, "as far as portable fire extinguishers go," he and Powers thought they had complied with the law by having—on the recommendation of a former fire chief—tubes of Kilfyre on hand. Powers said he did not "care to discuss the matter further."[1]

The theater's fireman, William Sallers, acknowledged that there were no portable fire extinguishers or hand fire pumps available backstage. That being the case, why hadn't Sallers brought their lack to someone's attention? Well, he had shown Chief Musham what the situation was. "It is not up to the fire department to order installation of these sprinklers and other necessary apparatus," said Musham. "I am not trying to shift any blame, for I am always ready to take any responsibility that belongs to me," the chief explained, "but there is no legal requirement on us, as far as I know, to make inspection of these theaters."

To support his contention that neither he nor the fire department was responsible for ensuring that the Iroquois Theatre adhere to the city's fire code, Musham hired an attorney, James T. Brady, who wrote a lengthy brief in Musham's defense. According to Brady, two sections of the city's ordinances provided that a license permitting the operation of a theater was issued by the city clerk's office, "a department entirely separate and distinct from the fire department, one over which the Fire Marshal has not control and with which he can have no legitimate official influence." The only responsibility a fire marshal has, Brady continued, was to sign a certificate detailing the theater's seating capacity and number of exits, a duty the marshal fulfills after he has personally examined the theater. But Musham was not obliged to examine the building until "it had been officially called to his attention" and "he had been officially requested" to do so. After all, "It could hardly be expected that the Fire Marshal in a city of nearly two millions of people could go about making inspections unless he was requested to do so." It was up to the city clerk or "the Executive department" to determine whether the theater had been inspected, Brady wrote, and if no inspection had been made, it was up to them either to instruct the fire marshal to make the examination or to reject the license application. Moreover, Brady continued, "If this theatre was in operation without a license, it was the duty of the Police Department of the City of Chicago to compel a suspension of business until the laws of the city had been complied with."

Brady also said that, under other sections of the city's fire code, it was also not incumbent upon Musham to determine that sprinklers and fire equipment were available. That, he said, was up to the owners or managers of the theater, who were supposed to request the fire marshal to make an inspection. But Musham was never requested to do so "either by the mayor, the Building Department or the theatrical managers." Brady said that "if there is culpability at all, it must rest elsewhere than upon the chief of the Fire Department." The fact was, he concluded, "that such a license was issued and the Fire Marshal's inspection seems to have been dispensed with by somebody in authority."[2] Who that was Brady did not say.

(Despite his insistence that it was not his responsibility, on February 5, 1904, thirty-eight days after the Iroquois fire, Musham would sign an order to all assistant marshals, commanding them to visit "each theatre in your respective inspection districts once each week and inspect all fire appliances and forward a report of such inspections to these headquarters.")[3]

It was abundantly clear that the fire department knew in advance about the lack of sprinklers and proper fire-fighting apparatus. The day after the fire, Musham told a reporter for the *Record-Herald* that he understood that Battalion Chief John Hannan—the same department official who was first to reach the scene of the fire—had earlier made an inspection "to get a personal idea of the theater." Indeed, he had, said Hannan, way back in November. "In order to get an idea of the lay of the theater and exits I went there and looked it over. There were no sprinklers, nor the other apparatus called for by ordinance. I understood that this stuff was to be got." Hannan said he had not reported his inspection to anyone "as I am not required to do so, nor is there any obligation on us to inspect these theaters." And then Hannan added: "There is little doubt that if there had been sprinklers they would have brought the fire to a halt. Those sprinklers always work, and they pour down a great torrent of water." Hannan believed that the "mere appearance of the flood of water" would "in itself" have helped "to quiet the audience and keep it from panic."[4]

Just as incredible as the remarks of Musham and Hannan are those of Deputy Building Commissioner Leon E. Stanhope. The Iroquois, he said, was purposely built so that sprinklers could be left out. Stanhope, an architect by profession, said sprinklers were not called for because of a "provision about the iron doors made it unnecessary." He did not specify what provision he was referring to (and an inspection of Chicago building ordinances fails to find any provision dealing with the matter). "And, anyhow," Stanhope said, "the flames spread so rapidly that no sprinkler system would have availed anything." Stanhope then disclosed that William Cullen, a building inspector who was in the Iroquois a few minutes before the fire broke out, had left the playhouse saying that everything was in good condition. "The theatre and its management were strictly within the law," Stanhope insisted.[5]

Meanwhile, with the likelihood that lawsuits would be filed, the fire department's attorney, Monroe Fulkerson, went to inspect the theater. He came across the two accordion gates, now in battered condition. Fulkerson was surprised to find them. They weren't on the architectural plans approved by the building department. "They proved to be gates of death," he said. Fulkerson asked two policemen to witness the fact of their existence. He wondered why the house manager, George Dusenberry, had not stationed ushers in place of the gates to direct people to their seats.[6] Fulkerson was also alarmed to learn from an attorney whose office windows overlooked the roof of the Iroquois Theatre that the day after the fire two men appeared on the roof of the theater and broke away the bindings that kept the skylights, essential for the venting of smoke and fire, from opening. The two men slid the skylights back, making it appear that they had been opened during the fire. An architect with a view of the Iroquois roof from his office substantiated the attorney's account.[7] R. N. Cummings, a theater carpenter, admitted that the skylights "seem to be open now" but added that "if they are it must have happened during the fire." Fulkerson, however, questioned whether "the officials of the Iroquois Theatre tried to destroy evidence of violations."[8]

That was not the only indication of a cover-up. Victor Falkenau of the Illinois Society of Architects was put off by the lack of knobs, thumb latches, or other "opening appliances" on many of the doors throughout the playhouse when he first inspected the Iroquois the day after the fire. But eight days later, when he returned to the theater, he noticed that "newly supplied" knobs had been fitted to at least one door that previously had had a dead bolt and required a key to open.[9]

There were attempts by many theater employees to put a better face on how they, as members of the Iroquois staff, had reacted to the fire. Their statements were tinged with lies. Although not one survivor attested—either to reporters at the scene or at official inquiries afterward—to having been helped in any way by an usher or other theater attendant, several members of the staff came forward later to tell how they had assisted theatergoers. James Gibbon, an usher stationed on the first floor, took credit for opening two alley exits nearest the boxes on the north side—the very exits that Charles Dexter and Frank Houseman had had to force open. Another usher, Ernest Lovett, claimed to have unlocked the west foyer door—which a survivor, W. M. Claybrook, said he had broken open.[10] A ticket taker named E. Leavitt said he had personally "burst open" the lobby doors and then run outside to find a fire box and pull the alarm.[11] If he had done so, the mob of fleeing theatergoers would not have been impeded from exiting the Iroquois.

Leon Reeves, who worked in the Iroquois's advertising department, told a *Sun* reporter that he had not only assisted members of the audience to escape from the parquet but had also helped to pull down fire escapes in the alley behind the theater and even "rushed to the upper balcony upon the fire escapes" to urge panic-stricken people "to get down," personally rescuing two small girls by "pulling them out."[12] This was clearly impossible because even experienced firemen had not been able to ascend any fire escape.

One theater employee thought he knew who was responsible for the fire: The real culprit was "the person who placed or was operating the arc light," said head electrician Archie Bernard. But then, ignoring the fact that there was no second set of light controls in the box office, he went to declare: "The electric plant of the theater was installed, as I happen to know from personal observation, in accordance with every modern requirement for safety."[13] Bernard himself was criticized for leaving his post at the master switchboard. The general manager of the Standard Meter Company said if Bernard had remained there long enough to turn on the lights in the Grand Stair Hall, there would not have been such a great loss of life.[14]

As might be expected, the company that built the Iroquois Theatre disavowed any blame; in fact, it appeared almost to gloat about how well the theater was constructed—so well that it had survived the fire. W. A. Merriam, western manager of the George H. Fuller Company, insisted that "all the building ordinances were complied with in every detail and more than that there were additional safeguards thrown about it until I do not hesitate to state that there was no theater building in this country or anywhere which was so free from danger." Proof of the theater's invincibility, Merriam added, was the fact that "no part of the structure was burned. A few seats, not more than eight, or ten. All in the parquet seem to have been torn away by the rushing crowd. The backs of the seats in the first and second balconies are scorched, but the roof, the walls, the balconies, and the main floor are there just as we built them, and the exits and entrances are all free and open."[15]

"So free from danger"? This from the man whose workers left the crucial ventilator skylights over the stage roof tied down and inoperable.

Everybody seemed to have an idea of what was at fault or who was to blame. Robert Craik McLean, editor of *Inland Architecture,* believed there were several reasons for the disaster. First of all, he said, there was the lack of a fireproof curtain. McLean himself had inspected the theater the morning after the fire. The proscenium arch was "clean as a bone." He asked a policeman what had happened to the asbestos curtain and was told that "it was burned up. There's the rods of it lying on the stage." In addition, McLean said, there was a plethora of other problems, whereupon he went down a veritable punch list of the assorted violations and unfortunate circumstances: The ventilators were not open; there were no sprinklers nor any exit signs; exits doors were locked; ordinances were violated; faults were apparent in the general plan of the house, in particular the design of the foyer and stairs; outside iron exit doors were opened halfway, blocking a major fire escape; and, lastly, there was "*remiss management.*" (The italics are his.) "This was the darkness, the closed ventilators, the stampede of an audience that was without direction by house employees, and most disastrous in its results when it reached to closed doors that stopped the audience." McLean noted that "there was no one on duty to open" the exit doors, "for the ushers were boys of seventeen years and under, and as there had never been a drill or special instructions issued in regard to emergencies, they made their escape at the first alarm." The "most important feature" and "an explanation of much" that went wrong, concluded McLean, was that the theater was opened "before it was *complete.*" (Again, his italics.) "The absence of a fire alarm in the theater and all 'first aids' in extinguishing fire, the plush-covered seats, stuffed with a sort of hay or sea grass, all contributed to the general disaster that has startled two continents."[16]

R. A. Cavanaugh, secretary-treasurer of the eighteen-thousand-member Illinois Commercial Men's Association, an organization of traveling salesmen, made two inspections of the Iroquois, prompted because two members of the association and their entire families were burned to death in the fire, four other members lost their wives, and a fifth member, his wife and two sons. Cavanaugh's own wife, son, and sister-in-law had attended the matinee performance, seated in a balcony with the other association members. They were badly burned but escaped. Cavanaugh was so exercised by what he saw that he distributed to the membership a twelve-page pamphlet describing his reaction. "I have never seen a place where the exits were more confusing," he wrote. "I know of nothing more fitting to compare it with than the magic maze." One passageway led to a "blind exit, where over 200 poor unfortunates were found dead." Coming out of the balcony, Cavanaugh continued, "you are at a loss to know which way to go." To get downstairs, he said, a person first had to go up four steps, then turn to the left and go down by the grand stairway. "The wall near the top of the grand stairway is the most clever deception I ever saw. It has the appearance of a double door, the upper half of which is made of panes of glass, each pane about 10 by 12. The whole thing really is nothing but a mirror with strips of wood arranged in front to give it the appearance of an exit." Cavanaugh wondered "how bewildering such an exit and such stairs must have been to those poor unfortunates who rushed into it." "They sacrificed safety for beauty," he declared.[17]

J. E. O. Pridmore, the architect whose sister was fatally burned, was critical of the "single entrance" plan of the Iroquois. "After centuries of noble example in safe planning," he wrote in the *Architectural Record,* "the American dollar has decreed that nearly two thousand people shall congregate in a playhouse with but one regular entrance and exit, and that not even located on the main axis of auditorium and stage. For the rear [that is, the east wall of the theater] imposed a cruel barrier, 100 feet wide and almost as high, with not a solitary opening to break the dread prison wall." Pridmore was also critical of the projecting balconies. "Cantilever construction has made an enormous overhang possible without the use of obstructing columns, and here ensues a subtle danger, that of bringing the occupants too close to the dread inflammability of stage equipment." He believed that "the greatest measure of safety lies in a ventilation system specially designed" and *"always open"* [italics his] to vent flames and smoke.[18]

Although it seemed a moot point because it had snagged and never fully isolated the stage from the auditorium, a number of persons raised questions about the asbestos curtain. Before details of how the curtain had been caught by a reflector were known, some persons believed the curtain had gotten fouled in the trolley wire used to swing aerialist Nellie Reed back and forth above the audience.[19] Others questioned whether the curtain in the first place was substantial enough to be effective. A reporter for the *Inter Ocean* received a special permit to examine the interior of the theater the day after the fire. "The stage was completely gutted," he reported. "Only the bare brick walls of the proscenium arch extended up to the roof. On the iron supports the top and bottom of the curtain stretched across the stage opening. Near by were fragments of the curtain, that crumbled to the touch." Alderman Luther P. Friestedt, who was also in the Iroquois that day, picked up a piece "of the supposed asbestos curtain." He said he pulled it to pieces "easily with my finger and thumb. It was a single thickness when it should have been three or four thicknesses at least."[20]

An article in the *Tribune* quoted unidentified insurance men as saying that the asbestos curtain had never worked perfectly and had never been repaired. They also said that a few pails of water on stage might have put out the fire at the start, but that the management of the theater had always opposed placing any pails of water or even patented extinguishers inside the building on the ground that their presence on the stage or in the auditorium tended to alarm patrons.[21]

One thing was clear. Justice demanded that someone or some persons had to be held accountable for the tragedy. But who precisely? Benjamin Marshall for putting esthetics over safety in planning the fire exits and not making them easily accessible? Will Davis and Harry Powers because they had flouted so many laws and common-sense precautions? Musham and the fire department for not being more aggressive in seeing that the municipal ordinances were enforced? The city inspector—whoever he was—who had turned his eye from the violations? Whoever it was at City Hall who had engineered the issuing of the license to operate the theater? Supervisors of the construction company for not seeing that the roof ventilators were operational? The house manager for not instructing his ushers in even a basic fire drill? The operator of the arc light that had touched off the blaze? Or the lighting man who had left the reflector extended when the asbestos curtain snagged? Who? Who was to blame? Who would be held responsible?

15

BLIND JUSTICE

Sec. 193. All gas or electric lights in the halls,
corridors, lobby or any other part of said buildings
used by the audience, except the auditorium, must be
controlled by a separate shut-off, located in the
lobby, and controlled only in that particular place.

The investigations began less than twenty-four hours after the fire.
A veritable legion of individuals passed through the building on
Thursday, December 31. One after another, they stepped carefully
around the detritus inside the still-darkened theater, their paths lit only
by lights on poles provided by the fire department. Pools of water from
fire hoses made walking difficult, too, but the most troubling problem
was the stench. It was overpowering, a nauseating blend of burned flesh,
furnishings, and scenery. Despite the horror of seeing firsthand the devastated ruin of the interior, they came—the mayor; Benjamin Marshall;
other architects; fire, police, and building inspectors; members of the city
council; engineers; building contractors; fire-insurance specialists; rep-
resentatives of the construction company; reporters.

It is safe to say that never before or since has a fire inspired so many
different inquiries, official, legal, and private. The prospect of both criminal action and an untold number of lawsuits led to a struggle between

competing interests that muddied the investigations. There were political considerations, as well. Justice—despite how obvious the truth appeared to be—was not a given.

Promising to prosecute "to the fullest extent of the law" any persons responsible for the fire, on the day after the disaster, Coroner John Traeger impaneled a jury of six businessmen that immediately began hearing testimony in the council chamber at City Hall.[1] There was to be a grand jury inquiry, too. In the rush to fix responsibility for the terrible fire, the police had already taken into custody three members of the Iroquois staff, including stage manager William Carleton. Detectives were hunting down twenty-six other persons—the electrician in charge of the arc light that started the fire, the flyman in charge of the drop curtain that was the first to catch on fire, other electricians, stagehands, carpenters, all of whom were being charged with manslaughter. The police were also seeking members of the men's chorus, whom they wanted as material witnesses, though the reason they in particular were singled out was unclear.[2]

The mayor, meanwhile, set up a special commission composed of building contractors, insurance agents, and members of both the Illinois chapter of the American Institute of Architects and the Chicago Architects Business Association. The *Tribune* formed its own task force of construction experts to look into the disaster. Charles Richard Crane, a wealthy Chicago manufacturer who had lost two young nieces in the fire, asked the president of the American Society of Mechanical Engineers to delve into the causes of the fire and suggest "means for rendering such fearful disasters impossible."[3] Crane's choice, John R. Freeman, a construction engineer by profession, hastened from Providence, Rhode Island, hoping to examine the Iroquois before any of the wreckage had been removed.

The most unusual investigation was undertaken by Louis Guenzel. The architect and his friend, German Consul Walter Wever, had walked away from the scene of the fire on Wednesday afternoon without any idea of what was happening. It wasn't until several hours later—at the very moment that Guenzel purchased an extra edition of a newspaper and learned of the fire—that he received a telephone call from Wever. The consul was certain he would get an order from Berlin directing him to ascertain the cause of the disaster. Wever asked Guenzel to make "a thorough examination of the premises and draw up a statement" of his findings. Guenzel agreed to do so, provided that he could get a pass allowing him access to every part of the theater. Wever arranged for one at City Hall. That Thursday, at ten o'clock in the morning, Guenzel, the pass in hand, obtained his "first glimpse," as he put it, of the interior of the building "where less than 19 hours before one of the most tragic happenings in American Theater history had taken place."[4] Guenzel was to spend several weeks in the Iroquois, measuring, reconstructing plans and sections, taking photographs. He delivered his findings to Wever in January. But his report was written in German and not intended for publication. The only person beside Wever who knew about Guenzel's conclusions was one of the owners of the Iroquois—Guenzel never said whether it was Davis or Powers—who heard about his report and, knowing Guenzel personally, asked to read it. He returned the copy "without comment."[5] It was not until 1945 that Guenzel decided to have the report translated into English and made public.

The investigation of the coroner's jury was closely followed in the city's press. Hordes of reporters jammed the council chamber as the panel was sworn in and began its investigation. That Thursday evening, after the jurors first heard testimony at City Hall, Traeger personally conducted them on a tour of the various morgues in the city, where so many unidentified bodies still lay. They then proceeded on to the theater. It was a grim tour—first, at the morgues, where anguished mothers, fathers, and grandparents were still trying to identify lost children and spouses, then at the ill-starred theater itself. All that was left of the scenery for *Mr. Bluebeard* were small piles of ashes. The steel frames of the floodlights were piled in confusion near the front of the stage. The seats in the first row of the parquet were burned, those in the dress circle completely scarred by fire. The balcony rail in the gallery was bent in several places where spectators had stood on it and then leaped to the parquet below. Grim relics were still scattered between the seats—rubber shoes, muffs, handkerchiefs, gloves, a gold-trimmed comb with an inscription, children's woolen hoods and mittens, a tiny doll. Assistant state's attorney A. A. Heer, who accompanied the coroner's jury, told its members that the theater's "management" was blaming the audience for forcing open exits that caused the great draft of air that swept through the theater, carrying with it flames and smoke. But Heer believed otherwise, he said: "I may be wrong, but from the evidence now at hand I think it will be shown that it was the action of the stage hands or members of the company instead of anything done by the audience in its attempt to escape."[6]

By Friday, two days after the Iroquois fire, warrants for the arrest of Will Davis and Harry Powers were issued. They and Building Commissioner George Williams were among those now being charged with manslaughter. All three were released on bond after being booked.[7]

The coroner's jury held twenty-two days of hearings. To speed its inquiry, three rotating court reporters and four typewriter operators were employed, the latter stationed in a room adjacent to the council chamber. Each reporter took five minutes' worth of testimony, then handed his notes to a typist while another court reporter occupied his place. Altogether, they collected three thousand pages of testimony—more than seven hundred thousand words—from 174 witnesses. The jury heard from survivors, members of the stage crew and theater staff, actors and actresses, policemen and firemen.[8] The only scheduled witness it did not hear was Edith Williams, the member of the women's octet who had fainted on stage during the "In the Pale Moonlight" scene. She took the witness stand and was sworn in, but then swooned again, falling backwards. A stenographer caught her before she hit the floor. Williams revived in an adjoining witness room but was not asked to return to give testimony.[9]

Meanwhile, the state attorney's office held off calling a special grand jury into session, believing that the inquiry by the coroner's jury was being so thorough that responsibility for the fire would be fixed by it.[10] Besides, other inquiries were going on at the same time, providing new details or confirming already suspected failings in the theater's compliance with city ordinances. F. J. T. Stewart, superintendent of the Chicago Underwriters' Association, reported that the building "was incomplete in a number of items." He noted that the stage scenery "was so highly inflammable that the fire reached its greatest degree of intensity very rapidly and within 15 minutes had spent its force, having consumed most of the combustible material on the stage side of the proscenium wall." The building's "unfinished condition," he said, "together with the highly combustible scenery of the 'Mr. Blue Beard' spectacle, combined a remarkable number of very unfortunate circumstances."[11]

The verdict of the coroner's jury was a shock—though perhaps not to anyone attuned to the political machinations at City Hall. Traeger had promised at the outset of the inquiry that the jury "will not attempt to fix the blame of the fire upon anybody, nor will it recommend the punishment of anybody." That, he said, would be left to the state attorney's office.[12] But the verdict of the coroner's jury belied the pledge. Mayor Carter Harrison was held responsible for "a lamentable lack of force" in seeing to it that city ordinances were implemented. The jury recommended that he be held for the grand jury. Those in the know wondered whether the jurors were influenced by the fact that Harrison was a political foe of Traeger's and that the foreman of the jury, the manager of a furniture company, might well have held a grudge against the mayor. Harrison had ordered closed down a number of cheap, crime-ridden hotels that his company had sold furniture to before the manager could collect payment for the items.[13]

The coroner's jury also ruled that seven other individuals be held for grand-jury action. Topping the list was Will Davis, who, the jury said, as president and general manager of the Iroquois was "principally responsible" for all the fire-code violations and for not instructing his employees in what to do in an emergency. Building Commissioner George Williams was held responsible for "gross neglect of his duty in allowing the Iroquois Theater to open its doors to the public when the said theater was incomplete, and did not comply with the requirements of the building ordinances."

The others charged by the coroner's jury, all also accused of gross neglect of duty, were: Building Inspector Edward Laughlin for "glaring incompetency" in reporting the theater "O.K."; Fire Chief William Musham for not enforcing the city ordinances and for "failure to have his subordinate, William Sallers, fireman at the Iroquois Theater, report the lack of fire apparatus and appliances as required by law"; Sallers for not reporting the lack of fire-fighting equipment; William McMullen, who operated the arc light, for "carelessness in performance of duty"; and stage manager James E. Cummings for "gross carelessness" in not equipping the stage with proper fire-fighting equipment.[14]

The mayor surrendered himself to the Cook County sheriff but immediately filed an appeal. His confinement was brief. Within two days, Judge Richard Tuthill—who had earlier served, appointed by Harrison, as the city's corporation counsel[15]—granted the mayor a writ of habeas corpus. The coroner's jury, Tuthill ruled, had committed "a very great wrong" and had placed "an unmitigated stigma" on the mayor. The judge said that the jury's verdict was without any basis in law or in the facts heard by the jurors. Harrison, he said, was no more liable than the president of the United States would be if a calamity befell West Point or Annapolis. The state attorney's office also acknowledged that there was nothing in the testimony that indicated that the mayor was criminally responsible for the Iroquois disaster.[16]

As a result of the coroner's jury's action, the manslaughter charges initially filed by the police against Will Davis, Harry Powers, and George Williams were dismissed. But that still left Davis, Williams, and the others cited by the coroner's jury subject to grand-jury action and prompted a plethora of speculation. Davis and Williams, one unidentified courthouse attorney opined, were the most liable. But no city official, even Laughlin, the building inspector, could be held for anything more than malfeasance, he said. Moreover, it was debatable whether the duties of Cummings and McMullen, the stage manager and the lighting operator, included being personally responsible for safeguarding the theater. As for the house fireman Sallers, the attorney said, "his position is so equivocal I doubt he can be held on any charge."[17]

The grand jury began its inquiry on February 8, and basically, it heard or read virtually the same evidence presented to the coroner's jury; Traeger, in fact, provided it with transcripts of the testimony of the witnesses who had already testified.[18] Unlike the coroner's jury, however, the grand jurors, twenty-three men in all, represented a cross section of the city's male population. There were a number of company executives but also a carpenter, a railway conductor, a stone mason, and a paving contractor. Like the coroner's jury, the grand jurors' first duty was to inspect the Iroquois Theatre.[19] Although the building was sound and had been cleaned up, Harry Powers said no decision had yet been made whether to reopen it as a theater or use it for other purposes.[20]

Within a few days of the opening of the grand jury's hearings, a Chicago businessman named Arthur E. Hull raised a question about its impartiality. He accused two members of the panel of collusion. One, he said, held contracts with the city; the other had laid the stonework in the theater's front.

Hull was an especially embittered person, for an understandable reason. His thirty-two-year-old wife, Marianne, and their three children—

Helen, twelve, and two adopted nephews, Donald, eight, and Dwight, six—had all perished in the Iroquois Theatre. It was the bereaved Hull who had initiated the meeting of relatives of fire victims that was held nine days after the disaster in the Monadnock Building in downtown Chicago. More than one hundred grieving and angry persons attended the gathering, all desirous of finding out what had caused the fire and who was to blame. They decided to form an organization, the Iroquois Memorial Association, and elected Hull as their chairman. Afterwards, it was disclosed that it was he who had prompted the arrest of Davis, Powers, and Williams immediately after the fire. Hull was determined to see "the men that are criminally and financially responsible for our terrible loss and bring them before the bar of justice."[21]

Hull claimed that the presence of two men on the grand jury with connections to the city administration was "a crime and an outrage." "Powerful influences" were trying to prevent the punishment of those responsible for the fire. He said he intended to "keep on collecting evidence until the case is settled one way or another."[22]

The grand jury immediately summoned Hull to prove his charges. He spent an hour in closed session with the jury, admitting, said one juror, that "he had no information to back up anything he had charged." The "powerful influences" were "creatures of his personal opinion only." The grand jurors completely dismissed Hull's accusations and, after he left, they cast a vote of confidence for the two men he had accused.[23]

Embarrassed by public disclosure of his appearance before the grand jury—newspapers had been leaked word of the jurors' reaction to his accusations—Hull resigned from the association. Dispirited, a widower, and childless, he closed his business affairs and left Chicago, ostensibly to spend a year in California, but apparently for good.[24]

It was soon evident that Mayor Harrison was, indeed, not culpable. Deputy City Collector Jeremiah McCarthy told the grand jury that he was present when, after Building Commissioner George Williams submitted his report on safety violations in the city's theaters in November, the mayor summoned Williams to his office in City Hall. There, with City Collector Edward Lahiff and City Clerk Fred C. Bender also in attendance, Harrison instructed that no license was to be issued to any theater without assurance from the building department that the theater was safe. McCarthy said the Iroquois license was withheld until

Williams reported favorably on it. It was, in fact, Williams himself who had endorsed it.[25]

After eleven days of sessions, the grand jury voted indictments of five individuals, and Harrison's name was not among them. Will Davis was again charged with manslaughter. Also charged with manslaughter were Thomas J. Noonan, the Iroquois treasurer and assistant manager, and James E. Cummings, the stage manager. According to the testimony of Harry Powers, both Noonan and Cummings had the authority to order the necessary fire equipment for the theater. In addition, Building Commissioner Williams and Building Inspector Edward Laughlin were charged with malfeasance. All the defendants were released on bonds.[26]

The fixing of responsibility for the Iroquois Theatre fire was an exasperating task, a lesson in courtroom manipulation, a travesty of justice. For one thing, what transpired next was, from the prosecution side, a frustrating and seemingly endless series of delays, one after another after another, as attorneys for the five men entered motions, wrote appeals, asked for postponements so they could have time to prepare their cases, and, after successfully delaying the trials by using those tactics, asked in September 1904 for a change of venue. It was so aggravating that state attorney A. S. Barnes was convinced they were engaged in a conspiracy. At one point, the lawyers for Davis, Noonan, and Cummings submitted affidavits from 150 persons who, they said, were prejudiced against the defendants—proof that they could not get a fair trial in Cook County. Barnes was beside himself. Why had their counsel waited until the very moment before going to trial to ask for a change of venue? How come all those affidavits were dated the night before they were offered in court?[27]

One of the attorneys for the three theater men was a lawyer who had gained a reputation for taking on cases of workers' rights, Clarence Darrow. Darrow always mistrusted the public's desire to find a scapegoat. In the case of the Iroquois fire, he believed that it was not "just to lay the sins of a generation upon the shoulders of a few."[28] Darrow worked behind the scenes to find ways to quash the indictments and, as far as it can be determined, never appeared personally in court. His participation was, in a sense, an ironic twist of fate. He had defended the frustrated office seeker who, at the time of the Columbian Exposition in 1893, had fatally shot Harrison's father, Carter Harrison Sr. The elder Harrison had just been elected to a fifth term as Chicago's mayor.[29]

Prosecutors believed Davis's attorney had "something up his sleeve" when he subsequently withdrew Davis's name from the motion to change the venue of the trial. The state was planning to try Davis first, before the others. It was a wily ploy. If Noonan and Cummings won their appeal to be tried outside of Cook County but Davis was tried in the county, much of the evidence pertaining to their alleged negligence could not then be introduced first in Davis's trial because it would prejudice their trial. State attorney Barnes was dismayed. As it was, the cost of trying the case outside the county was bound to be "enormous." There were 138 witnesses to call, and under state law, Cook County would have to pay all their expenses, including their railroad fares to wherever in Illinois the trial would be held.[30]

Circuit Court Judge George Kersten, who was weighing the change of venue motion, was also upset. He had received a letter threatening him with "dire vengeance" if he moved the trial of Noonan and Cummings out of Cook County. Nevertheless, Kersten granted the motion. It was now certain that their trial would be many months off, because the trial of Davis, who would be tried first, was expected to take two months.[31]

Kersten's decision in favor of the change of venue came in early October 1904, some eight months after the Iroquois fire. Still further legal maneuvers led to more postponements, delaying the start of Davis's trial. Then, on February 9, 1905, Kersten astonished everyone when he, together with a visiting judge from Peoria named Green, granted the latest defense stratagem, a motion to quash the indictment against Davis. Kersten said there was no evidence that Davis—or Noonan or Cummings for that matter—"had ever took upon themselves the duties imposed by the ordinance[s]." Green, in fact, went even further in his opinion. He said he did not consider it even possible that any indictment of the three men could ever justify their conviction. They were not responsible for the fire. The fire, Green declared, was attributable to "a certain electric light close to the stage, and that set fire to the curtains." "There is no evidence," he concluded, "that any of the defendants caused the light to be put there." Green said that he intended to quash the indictments against Noonan and Cummings when they appeared, as scheduled, in his court in Peoria the next day to enter their pleas.[32]

Davis, for one, was ecstatic. The public, he said, "has been unfair and unjust to me. It would be just as fair to hold the president of a railroad company for manslaughter because there was an explosion in one of the railroad trains, and fire ensued and passengers were burned to death." It was no one's fault, Davis contended. "No human agency could have dreamed that on account of some inherent defect in a carbon point, that point would spit out a spark which would ignite the scenery and produce the fire." Everything possible had been done to make the Iroquois Theatre fireproof. "We could do no more," Davis said. "Why should we be charged with murder because an audience stampeded and the ushers lost their reason?"[33]

Davis's joy was short-lived. The prosecutors involved in the case refused to accept defeat. A new grand jury was called later that month and new indictments were issued. As expected, Davis was scheduled to be the first to be tried, but further delays put off the start of his trial until March 1907, more than three years after the Iroquois fire. By then, his lawyers had also applied for and won a change of venue. Davis would be tried in Danville, Illinois, but again apart from Noonan and Cummings. However, no sooner had Davis's trial started than it became bogged down in another bit of courtroom jockeying. This time, the legal jousting had a portentous result, thanks to his newly hired legal counsel, Levy Mayer, whose role in the Iroquois litigation would propel him into being one of the most sought-after attorneys in the theater world nationwide.

Mayer purposely waited until the prosecution had made its opening statement before the trial jury. He then declined to make his opening statement and, before the first witness could take the stand, he objected to the entire proceedings. Mayer questioned the validity of the Chicago ordinances under which Davis was being tried, saying that if they were invalid there was no law to violate.

Mayer was on solid ground. The justification for his argument was a damage suit he had been involved in sixteen months earlier, in November 1905, when he represented the Iroquois Theatre Company. The suit was thrown out because the judge, Kennesaw Mountain Landis—who would later become the commissioner of baseball—ruled that the city's ordinances were incorrectly written and failed to specify who was responsible for what. As an example, Landis said the section on fire escapes failed "to discriminate between owner, tenant, and trustee." He characterized another ordinance, dealing with exits, as "absolutely absurd."[34] Landis's ruling put into doubt the entire building code of regulations.[35]

Observers marveled at Mayer's move. It was evident that his action was purposely timed. If he succeeded in quashing the indictment against Davis after the trial had started—and it had started once the jury was impaneled and the prosecution made its opening statement—then Davis could not be indicted and tried again on the same charges. That would be double jeopardy.

The trial proceedings were suspended while Mayer and prosecuting attorneys argued the point for almost a week before Judge E. R. E. Kimbrough. Mayer presented a printed brief that ran to 231 pages. Behind the substance of his argument was his view that "the defendants did not intentionally produce the fire, nor intentionally cause the death of any one."[36] Pressing his case, Mayer argued that state law limited Chicago's authority to impose certain building regulations because the state's code superseded the city's. Chicago only had the right, for example, to prescribe the thickness and strength of stone and brick buildings. The city was also empowered to prevent the dangerous construction and condition of chimneys, fireplaces, ovens, and boilers, but there its authority ended. Moreover, Mayer said, Chicago had deputed to the Board of Underwriters of Chicago—that is, to insurance companies—the power to approve sprinkler systems, a delegation of power to a civil body that was itself void.[37] The building code, Mayer contended, "in no way declares whose duty it is to put in flues and sprinkler systems." Davis's indictment, he said, "is based on a law which might go in China, but which has no place in this land of constitutional liberty and privilege."[38]

In the end, Mayer prevailed. On March 9, 1907, Kimbrough ruled that, on the basis of the wording of the ordinances, they were invalid. In consequence, the indictment against Davis had nothing upon which to rest. The charge of manslaughter against him was defective. The trial was over. Davis was free. He could not be tried again on the same charges. Moreover, the judge's ruling effectively quashed the manslaughter charges against Noonan and Cummings, as well as the charges of malfeasance against Williams and Laughlin.[39]

State's attorney John J. Healy threw up his hands in despair. He briefly considered prosecuting the case against Davis on what were called common-law counts of manslaughter, but it was pointed out that another judge had a year earlier ruled that such counts were invalid.[40] Healy gave up. Mayer had won. As a result, implausible as it seems, no one was ever tried, no one ever punished, for the loss of 602 lives.

There were, however, still civil actions pending, lawsuits against the city, the theater owners, and the construction company brought by relatives of the victims and the theatergoers who had been injured in the fire. The lawsuits and the trial of Davis had dragged on for so long that in February 1907—more than three years after the Iroquois fire—Professor Frederic C. Woodward of Northwestern University Law School said the delay "in bringing to trial the large number of cases, civil and criminal, arising from a theater fire which caused the loss of nearly 600 lives and shocked the civilized world sows the seed of contempt for law and gives notice to the world of the inefficiency of our judicial system." Woodward believed that Davis could have been brought to trial earlier "but for judicial procrastination." As for the civil suits, half of the lawsuits had been abandoned by plaintiffs who were discouraged by the cost of the dragged-out litigation. There had been pleas of not guilty and pleas of abatement, general demurrers and special demurrers, and the prognosis for the cases remaining, the professor said, was that "none will be tried for some time." The system, Woodward concluded, was too "complicated and antiquated."[41]

Hundreds of lawsuits had been filed. By the time Davis's trial in Danville was aborted, somewhere between fifty and sixty suits were still pending in courts, and so far not a penny in damages had been collected. James J. Reynolds, who had taken over the chairmanship of the Iroquois Memorial Association, said it "seems to be a queer situation" that so many lives "are snuffed out and the responsibility cannot be fixed on anyone." Reynolds, who lost his fourteen-year-old daughter, Dora, in the fire, said the association would "fight for a stronger building ordinance."[42]

Virtually every ruling had gone against the relatives of the Iroquois fire victims. Sixty-one suits against the city of Chicago, totaling an aggregate $8 million, were jeopardized, and finally dropped, in July 1904 when Superior Court Judge Jesse Holm ruled that holding the city liable "would confront every municipality with imminent bankruptcy—the city would in effect be held financially responsible for every mishap not only occurring through the negligent maintenance or operation of all places of amusement, but of every other business and enterprise con-

ducted under a license or permit."[43] Litigation against the Iroquois Theatre Company became moot when a federal court in November 1906
discharged it from bankruptcy; 272 damage suits, representing an aggregate total of more than $2.5 million, were summarily ended.[44]

A great number of damage cases were instituted against Klaw and
Erlanger as producers of *Mr. Bluebeard* and co-owners of the Iroquois
Theatre. Quite a number were tried in Chicago, but the local courts failed
to hold the theatrical company legally responsible and verdicts in its favor
were returned. Forty-four damage suits were subsequently filed against
it in New York City, where its offices were located, but as late as the spring
of 1907, Klaw and Erlanger's attorneys—one of whom was Clarence
Darrow—had succeeded in winning one adjournment after another. A
federal circuit court judge finally dismissed fifteen of the suits in May
of that year when, despite all the time they had for preparation, attorneys for the victims' families announced that they were not ready to
proceed with their cases. At the time, none of the remaining lawsuits were
even on court calendars,[45] and not one civil case was ever submitted to
a jury.[46]

Attorneys for the George H. Fuller Company argued successfully
that the liability of the construction company ceased when the plans for
the building were approved by the city. A circuit court judge threw out
the lawsuits against the company in April 1907.[47] However, the following February, Chicago Superior Court Judge Axel Chytraus ruled in favor of the plaintiffs, saying that the construction firm was not absolved
from liability for violating the building code. His decision affected thirty-
five claims amounting to about $400,000. Instead of appealing the rul-
ing, the Fuller Company decided to settle the suits. In January 1909—
five years after the Iroquois Theatre fire—the company paid the claim-
ants $750 each,[48] and a few weeks later it paid the same amount to settle
four additional suits. Each of the lawsuits had originally sought $10,000
in damages.[49]

In all, then, the Fuller Company—alone of all the defendants who
were sued—was the only one held legally responsible for the disaster. It
cost the company a total of $29,750. Not a penny more was paid to any-
one for the great loss of life that was sustained.

16

CURTAINS

Sec. 190. It shall be the duty of the owner, agent, lessee or occupant of any building of Class V, with accommodations for 1,000 or more persons, to employ one or more competent, experienced firemen. . . . [Such firemen] shall be in uniform and shall see that all fire apparatus required is in its proper place, and in efficient and ready working order.

Many of the members of the cast of *Mr. Bluebeard* found themselves stranded in Chicago, with no money to pay their lodging bills or even enough to buy railroad tickets back to New York City. A hastily put-together Actors' Emergency Relief Association arranged benefit entertainments and concerts to raise funds to help them. One at the Sherman House, at which several minor members of the cast appeared, garnered more than $700, and a similar one was planned at Handel Hall. The most prominent private donor was the widow of meatpacking tycoon Ogden Armour, who contributed $500. However, donors to the fund and to agencies set up to help victims of the fire were advised to be cautious. "Unscrupulous adventurers" were said to have staged phony benefits, and "confidence men and beggars" were pretending to represent fire victims.[1]

Four days after the fire at the Iroquois Theatre, the *Mr. Bluebeard* troupe was able to leave Chicago. Will Davis and Harry Powers had paid each member of the cast the half week's salary that they were due, and nothing more, despite the fact that they were all stranded in the city by the disaster. However, with that pittance and the relief money in hand, the actors and actresses were able to settle their debts and arrange for rail transportation home. Traveling with them, in the baggage car of the train, was a plain white box containing the body of young Nellie Reed. A memorial service for her in Manhattan was already being planned; members of two Klaw and Erlanger musical companies, *The Sleeping Beauty and the Beast* and *Mother Goose* were to sing the hymns.[2]

The scene at the railroad station where the *Mr. Bluebeard* company embarked was bleak. Two of their colleagues were dead, the show had closed, they all had lost clothing and valuables in the fire, the prospect for work was almost nil. To make things even more somber, also boarding the train home was the cast of *The Billionaire,* another of Klaw and Erlanger's traveling acting troupes. It had suffered the loss of three cast members.[3] Two of them, part of the men's chorus, had gone on their day off to the matinee performance of *Mr. Bluebeard* and had died in the fire. The third was Jerome Sykes, the star of the show, who had caught a severe cold at a cast Christmas party and had succumbed to pneumonia the day before the Iroquois disaster. *The Billionaire* had been playing at another theater in the Davis and Powers chain, the Illinois.[4]

An understudy had taken on Sykes's role as the wealthiest man in the world at the matinee on Wednesday, December 30, but after that, with all the theaters in Chicago closed as the result of the fire, the cast of *The Billionaire,* as well as those in every other play in the city, was out of work. In fact, the enforcement of fire laws throughout the country had a severe negative effect on theatrical productions everywhere. With many playhouses shut down until they complied with fire-safety codes, numerous road shows were canceled. Thousands of actors and singers, stagehands, and other theatrical workers were left idle. More than fifty companies in all closed their season's runs, and an estimated fifteen thousand persons were jobless. In Chicago alone during the first two weeks of January 1904, six thousand theater people were out of work.[5]

After thirty days, one by one the theaters in Chicago began to reopen. Inspections had been thorough. In some cases, seats had to be removed, aisles widened. Exit signs were a must. The proprietor of the Garrick Theater, where *The Pit* had been playing, was compelled to close the playhouse's gallery until the pitch of the floor was made less hazardous.[6] Its manager, Jake Shubert, hoped to have the theater ready in time for the scheduled appearance of the Four Cohans in *Running for Office*.[7] The Illinois Theatre was forced to close its upper balcony, too, because of the pitch. The Illinois had a new steel curtain and a complete stock of fire equipment, but uncertainty as to when it would reopen had forced the Anna Held company to cancel its appearance. It was hoped that the theater would be ready when Sir Henry Irving was scheduled to appear. The opening of the Powers' Theatre was delayed for several weeks by the construction of a code-dictated proscenium arch.[8] Finally, building and fire inspectors were making theater managers toe the line.

The McVickers Theatre, which resumed performances on February 1, was the first playhouse to reopen, though its gallery was completely closed off. Red lights and the word "Exit" were prominently blazoned above every door leading to the street, and the theater's asbestos curtain had been replaced by a formidable-looking corrugated-steel curtain that took nearly two minutes to raise and lower. The curtain was backed by a layer of magnesia-covered boards concealed by a sheet of heavy asbestos, all riveted together.[9] Building Commissioner George Williams mandated that such screens had to be able to withstand a fire test of 1,500 degrees Fahrenheit on the stage side for ten minutes without registering more than 500 degrees on the auditorium side. The new steel curtain at the Powers' Theatre, which weighed two tons, passed the test without difficulty. It could be lowered in an emergency by switches in five different parts of the building.[10]

Despite an appeal from the Iroquois Memorial Association that the Iroquois site be used for a special emergency hospital that the association was raising funds for, the theater was sold in the spring of 1904 to an amusement company with a chain of playhouses in New York, Newark, and Pittsburgh. The association fought to keep the Iroquois from reopening, outraged that the theater where so many had died would again echo with laughter and applause. It seemed a sacrilege. Architect J. E. O. Pridmore represented the association when Chicago authorities conducted an inspection of the theater on September 17, 1904. Pridmore objected to "an old flimsy three-quarter inch railing" on one of Couch Place fire escapes and the narrowness of an aisle in the auditorium. But the authorities considered his objections minor, and they issued a license to operate the theater as an amusement place.[11]

The new owners changed the theater's name to Hyde and Behman's Music Hall, and any outward connection to its former title was obliterated. A bust of a laughing woman replaced the head of the Indian that had graced the theater's classical portico. The words *Vaudeville Theater* in ten-foot-high letters now graced the Dearborn Street side of the theater's west wall, and when the theater reopened on Monday, September 19, 1904—263 days after the fire—the word *Vaudeville* blazed brilliantly in lights outside its Randolph Street entrance.

The once-lavish interior of the playhouse was no longer evident. The renovation was mundane, with no attempt made to refurbish it in the style of the original. The gallery was eliminated, and some boxes were in place of seats in the rear of the orchestra. Excluding the boxes, the theater now sat 1,135 persons, 74 fewer than the orchestra and dress circle originally held.[12]

The reopening was so controversial that fifteen police officers and twenty plainclothes detectives were on hand to handle the crowd of protesters on Randolph Street, which was made up of many persons who had lost relatives or friends in the fire. One, a working man, shook his fist and cursed the playhouse, its proprietors, and city officials. "My wife and my sister-in-law were burned to death in that place," he said with a sob in his voice, as he was led aside by detectives.

Inside, the theater management went to elaborate pains to restrict ticket holders from roaming like sightseers through the playhouse. Arrivals were ushered immediately to their seats and told they could only stroll into the foyer. By choice, only men sat in the dress circle. One woman who discovered that her ticket was for the balcony refused to sit there. There was a moment of stunned silence when a drop curtain caught briefly on the same side of the proscenium arch that the asbestos curtain had snagged on the day of the fire. Actors watched helplessly as a stagehand stumbled about for a minute, trying to untangle the curtain with a pole. When he finally freed the canvas, a deep sigh of relief was heard on both sides of the footlights. A reporter who covered the reopening said the vaudeville show included only one clever performer, a pantomimist who silently danced his way through the five acts of the opera *Carmen*.[13]

It is not clear whether it was public resentment over reopening the theater or simply the lack of exciting vaudeville acts that led Hyde and Behman to close down the house and sell it to Harry Powers and A. L. Erlanger before a year was up. They renamed it the Colonial and abandoned its previous vaudeville pretensions. The Colonial opened in October 1905 with Victor Moore and Fay Templeton in *Forty-Five Minutes from Broadway*. Over the next nineteen years, until 1924, plays and musicals were staged at the Colonial. Then the theater was torn down to make way for the building that now houses the present Oriental Theater.[14] The Oriental occupies a substantial part of the plot on which the Iroquois Theatre once stood.[15] Its stage door exits on the narrow alleyway called Couch Place, though no street sign bears the name.

Many individuals and every investigative body, whether official, semi-official, or private, had something to recommend to correct or add to the city's fire code. All agreed that basic to the success of any ordinances was strict enforcement of the rules and regulations. If nothing else, the Iroquois fire had demonstrated what can happen when violations are permitted to go unchallenged.

The coroner's jury that had accused Mayor Carter Harrison of shirking responsibility urged that all city officials and employees be required to pass a rigid examination testing their familiarity with the ordinances they were empowered and supposed to enforce.[16]

The inquiry initiated by the *Tribune* considered "one of the most vital points" to be the rendering of "all scenery and stage paraphernalia" nonflammable.[17]

The report the mayor received from the Illinois chapter of the American Institute of Architects and the Chicago Architects Business Association urged the elimination of "blind passages" and called for "an independent run of fire escape stairs from each and every fire exit above the first floor."[18]

City Engineer John Erikson said he believed that a sprinkler system "would add greatly to the safety of life and property," but he conceded that it might have been less effective in the Iroquois fire because of the rapidity with which the gaseous fumes and flames swept through the auditorium.[19]

The editors of the magazine *Inland Architecture* recommended that "the main lines of exits should be continuous with the aisles leading from the stage, with entrances that can not be locked leading (without steps) into foyers or corridors that will hold the entire seating capacity of the part of the theater with which they connect." When such was done, the magazine said, "when the architect has made a natural plan instead of an ingenious one, then the almost certain laxity of inspection by public officials and careless management will not place the lives of thousands of people in jeopardy."[20]

Bishop Samuel Fallows, who had served as chaplain of an infantry regiment during the Civil War, wanted ushers to be "drilled like soldiers to keep their places and allay confusion."[21]

A columnist in *Fireproof* magazine wondered whether any thought would be given to "churches, the hospitals, the hotels and great apartment houses where thousands of people abide and sleep or congregate, and where dangers ever lurk."[22]

Louis Guenzel, who wrote the report for the German consul, made a point of saying that fire escapes were "a nuisance and should not be permitted on any building, unless they are arranged in such a manner, that they do not pass openings, and the use of them cannot be endangered by fire on any floor."[23]

John Freeman, the mechanical engineer asked by Charles Richard Crane to recommend ways to avoid a repetition of the Iroquois disaster, made the most sweeping study of the fire and the theater. He was highly critical of the use of the bicarbonate-of-soda mixture Kilfyre, which he said "gives a false sense of security."[24] He put samples of the gauze drops and asbestos curtain through rigorous tests. He questioned whether the paint used on scenery could be made fully nonflammable. "The foremost problem of safeguarding life in theaters," he said, "is to give prompt and certain vent" to the smoke and suffocating gas "elsewhere than through the proscenium arch." Venting would "probably have saved" all those who had died of suffocation in the Iroquois. "This remedy," concluded Freeman, "is so simple, so sure and so cheap that it is a crime not to apply it."[25]

J. E. O. Pridmore agreed wholeheartedly, calling a proper ventilation system "the greatest measure of safety." In an essay entitled "The Perfect Theatre," published in the *Architectural Record*, Pridmore declared that the ideal was a system that would enable flames and smoke to be "drawn through the stage opening and out through ventilators—*always open* [italics his]—in the stage roof." The trouble was that, "in contrast, all our present measures are left absolutely in the hands of an undisciplined and ever changing stage crew, and we expect safety!"[26]

The campaign waged by the Iroquois Memorial Association to bolster Chicago's fire code and the legal pressure to revise the code once the current one was declared spurious led to a new set of regulations that went into effect in 1905. Within a week after the fire, Mayor Harrison himself had sought ways to toughen the city's code, for one thing, writing to and receiving from the mayor of New York City its building code and fire department rules.[27] But the regulations finally adopted by the city council were less strict than many proponents of the revision hoped for. The memorial association had tried, and failed, to forestall the watering down of new wording supposedly designed to strengthen the existing building laws. Theater managers had prevailed on aldermen from making some of the suggested changes.[28]

Among others, both John Freeman and J. E. O. Pridmore were upset by several of the provisions of the new set of ordinances. Freeman could not get over the fact that "within a few months of the appalling disaster," the city council rescinded the requirement for sprinklers over the stage and rigging loft of a theater "because the managers believed they 'wouldn't do any good,' and 'might start a panic should one happen to open prematurely.'" Even though the old Chicago building code required automatic sprinklers, Freeman pointed out, not one had ever been put in. "Then, in an effort to perfect the enforcement of the law," he added in amazement, "they cut out its requirement for sprinklers over the stage" altogether.[29]

With similar incredulity, Pridmore pointed out that Chicago "is the only city in the world which recently has lowered the number of its exits."[30] The entire revised code, he said, "is in important points distinctly inferior to its predecessor." Like Freeman, Pridmore objected to dropping the requirement for sprinklers above the stage. He questioned a new requirement that a theater front on only two public places. The previous ordinance prescribed fronting on three public areas. One less frontage required under the new code meant reducing the availability of egress in an emergency. "In this way," Pridmore declared, "the revision legalizes an increased element of danger." "If the saying is that man's greed has violated the first law of humanity," he declared, "it has also played havoc with the artistic ensemble of our theatres."[31]

Their objections notwithstanding, the new code did include a number of improved safety features. Each balcony had to have "distinct and separate places of exit and entrance." Aisles had to be at least thirty inches wide, and hallways or corridors no less than four feet wide. There could not be more than fourteen seats in any one row between aisles, and the rows had to be at least thirty-two inches apart, back to back. No exit door could be "obscured by draperies" or "locked, or fastened in any manner during the entire time any such room is open to the public." Moreover, "every passageway, or court, or corridor, or stairway, or exit, or emergency exit stairway" now had to be provided "with signs, indicating the way out of the building." Scenery would have to be treated "with a paint or chemical solution" to "make it non-inflammable," and such treated scenery "or stage paraphernalia, or both," would be tested and approved by the fire marshal. And all flues and vents were to "be opened by a closed circuit battery" and controlled by two, newly situated switches, "one at the electrician's station on the stage, which station shall be fireproof, and the other at the city fireman's station on the opposite side of the stage." As in the past, each such switch was to "have a sign with plain directions as to the operation of same printed thereon."[32]

Could a fire like the one that occurred at the Iroquois Theatre happen again? Were the new rules strong enough to prevent a repetition of the tragedy? Was the burden of responsibility for fire safety in a theater clear now? Those questions seemed secondary to the issue of to what extent the fire-safety rules would be observed. Revised or not, enforcement of the city's ordinances was still going to be the key to compliance with safety regulations in Chicago. The Iroquois Memorial Association—concerned primarily with preventing any future disaster—felt that it, for one, could never relax its vigil. "Theaters now appear to be patronized more largely than ever before," its president, James Reynolds, noted in 1907, "and the managers are becoming careless again."[33]

17

ASHES AND EMBERS

Sec. 195. The Commissioner of Buildings or Fire Marshal, or their respective assistants, shall have the right to enter any building of Classes IV and V, and any and all parts thereof, at any reasonable time, especially when occupied by the public, . . . and it shall be unlawful for any person to refuse admission to such officers or to throw obstacles in the way of such officers. . . .

On June 12, 1904—nearly six months after the fire—the last victim was buried. She was a woman whose body was burned beyond recognition. Her body had rested first at Rolston's undertaking parlor and later at the county morgue. Although several frantic searchers who were looking for relatives had several times claimed the body, it turned out that they were in error. No one had ever come forward to identify correctly the woman and to bury her, so the Iroquois Memorial Association took it upon itself to see that she was given a decent funeral and interment.

Five hundred persons, many of them survivors or relatives of victims of the fire, attended the ceremony as the mystery woman's remains were lowered into a grave in Montrose Cemetery. A simple inscription on the coffin read: "THE UNKNOWN, DECEMBER 30, 1903."[1] The association later erected a memorial tablet over the grave, a large diamond-shaped monument that read: "SACRED TO THE MEMORY OF 600 PEOPLE WHO PERISHED IN THE IROQUOIS THEATRE FIRE DEC. 30, 1903." It can be seen in Section 14 of the graveyard, about one hundred yards from the cemetery's office.

A stained-glass window was installed at the Forrestville School, at 45th Street and St. Lawrence Avenue, in memory of twelve pupils and one teacher from the grammar school who died in the fire. But no one knows what happened to the window after the building was closed and torn down.[2] A memorial plaque once graced the lobby wall of the building erected on the site of the Iroquois Theatre. It was removed and was gathering dust in a storage cabinet of the building in 1972, but since then, its whereabouts are unknown.[3]

In 1910, with funds raised by the association, the Iroquois Memorial Hospital, a four-story building designed to handle emergency cases, was erected at 87 Market Street (now Wacker Drive). The hospital later became a treatment center for indigent tuberculosis patients, and during World War II, it was the headquarters of the city's civilian defense agency. The edifice was torn down in 1951.

There had been a large plaque in the main reception room of the hospital listing the names of the men, women, and children who died in the fire. By then, the total number of known victims had reached 602. What happened to the plaque is unknown. However, above it was a bas-relief done in the flattened style known as *stiacciato* by the noted Chicago sculptor Lorado Taft.[4] It depicts a woman representing Sympathy dominating a scene showing a child on a litter carried by two bearers and surrounded by sorrowing figures. Although there is no inscription on the piece, a building engineer recognized the grime-covered bas-relief when he came across it in a storage room in the basement of City Hall in the late 1960s.[5] It now rests on the wall to the left of a revolving door that is the most northwesterly entrance to City Hall off LaSalle Street.

Two songs were written about the fire and published in 1904. Thomas Quigley, who was walking down Randolph Street with Bishop Peter Muldoon soon after the fire started, wrote the words and music to one of them, "The Iroquois Fire."[6] Mathew Goodwin wrote the words, Edward

Stanley the music, to the other, "The Burning Iroquois."[7] Neither song, however, appears to have made a lasting impression on Chicagoans.

For more than half a century, the city council set aside December 30 as Mercy Day in honor of all the agencies that had helped the living and the dying at the fire. Memorial services for the victims of the fire were held in the Grand Army of the Republic Hall at the old Chicago Public Library, and Fire Box No. 26, which had signaled the initial alarm, was ceremoniously pulled at 3:32 P.M., usually by the same fireman who had originally pulled the alarm, Michael J. Corrigan. Over the years, Corrigan rose from rookie fireman to become Chicago's fire commissioner. The commemoration always drew a number of survivors, but as they grew infirm or died off and the memory of the disaster faded, the last of such observances was held in the early 1960s, and the association itself quietly disbanded.

Other than the monument in Montrose Cemetery and the Taft bas-relief on the wall at City Hall, nothing else exists as a reminder of the tragedy that took so many lives. And except for fire buffs and local historians, few people even in Chicago are aware of the Iroquois Theatre fire.

Eddie Foy never forgot. The memory of the fire tormented him. "Never elsewhere did a great fire disaster occur so quickly," he wrote in the chapter he devoted to the disaster in his autobiography, *Clowning Through Life*. He always minimized the part he played in trying to calm the audience. "What I did was little enough, Heaven knows," he wrote.[8] Foy testified before the coroner's jury that investigated the fire, then he and his family left Chicago to return to New York City. Back east, for a few weeks he did an adaptation of his scene as Sister Anne with the Pet Elephant as a vaudeville act. The two young men who had played the fore and hind legs of the animal joined him, but Foy had to acquire a new elephant costume. The fire had cremated the old one.[9]

Foy continued to enjoy enormous success in both musical comedies and on vaudeville stages. By 1912, he and his wife Madeline had seven children, and together Eddie Foy and His Seven Little Foys toured the country. After fifty-seven years of performing, he was appearing in 1928 in a farewell tour entitled *The Fallen Star* when he died in a Kansas City hotel room of heart disease. He was seventy-one years old. A noted theatrical impresario said Foy was probably "the favorite of more entire American families than any other stage artist."[10]

All three principals in the drama surrounding the playhouse—Will Davis, Harry Powers, and Benjamin Marshall—enjoyed successful careers afterwards, too. Davis was the only one who expressed anything resembling a mea culpa, though he couched it in a way that, on reading his words, sounds as if he never accepted his responsibility for what had happened. He told the first grand jury in March 1904: "I don't want to blame any one else, and my own conscience doesn't accuse me, but when it comes down to the question of responsibility, I was the manager of that house, and if anybody connected with it is to blame for what happened, why I suppose I am the man."[11] The only other time Davis ever even alluded to the Iroquois disaster in public after that was when he retired in 1914 and was honored at a testimonial dinner given by the Chicago theatrical community. His face ashen, he told his colleagues that few people in the world could know "the sorrow" he had experienced. He hoped, he said, that "none present would ever face such trouble."[12] Davis died five years later at the age of seventy-five.[13]

Harry Powers subsequently allied himself with A. L. Erlanger in purchasing and operating the Blackstone and Erlanger Theatres in Chicago. He retired in 1931 but continued to attend first-night openings until he left the city to reside in New Jersey eight years later. Powers lived until 1941, when he died at the age of eighty-one.[14]

Benjamin Marshall's reputation was unsullied by the Iroquois fire. He came to be considered one of the nation's outstanding architects, and he was hailed in Chicago as one of its most significant innovators. His impact on the design of theaters, hotels, and sumptuous high-rise apartment buildings in the city was felt for decades. Among others, he designed the famed Blackstone Hotel and was both the architect and developer of the Edgewater Beach and Drake Hotels. Several of his spacious, high-ceilinged apartment buildings on Lake Shore Drive still exist. Marshall also became known for his extravagant lifestyle and his friendships with luminaries in the theater world. He died in 1944 at the age of seventy. It is not surprising that news of his death, like the deaths of Davis and Powers, made the obituary page of *The New York Times*. They were all prominent and nationally known in their fields. But what is remarkable is that there is no mention in *The Times* article that Marshall had designed the ill-fated Iroquois Theatre.[15] It is as though the tragedy had never happened.

Perhaps it was Marshall's death—and the absence of the architect's connection with the Iroquois Theatre—that led Louis Guenzel to translate into English and make public in 1945 his report on the fire that he had made for the German consul, Wever, more than forty years earlier. Guenzel said, in his introduction, that he had "repeatedly" attended the annual memorial observances of the fire in the Chicago Public Library. "From observations made at these meetings, from conversations and discussions with eye-witnesses of the fire but, primarily, in consequence of the adverse court decisions rendered at the trials of the damage suits," Guenzel said he had decided that "knowledge of the actual conditions prevalent in the Theater at the time of the fire has been maliciously withheld from the public by clever and successful manipulation."[16] His conclusion:

"The Theater was erected by one of the largest contracting firms in America in accordance with plans produced by a young and, as the layout shows, rather inexperienced architect, whose sacred duty should have been to prevent by all means the opening of a public building in an unfinished condition."[17]

Notes

Bibliography

Index

Notes

The epigraphs at the opening of each chapter are from *Ordinance Relating to the Department of Buildings* (Chicago: Moorman and Geller, 1903), Municipal Reference Collection, Chicago Public Library. The ordinances include all those enacted on March 28, 1898, as well as subsequent amendments in force and in effect on September 1, 1903.

The following abbreviations are used in the notes:

BRADY—William A. Brady, *Showman.* New York: E. P. Dutton, 1937

CHS—Chicago Historical Society

DIS—Marshall Everett, *The Great Chicago Theater Disaster.* Chicago: Publishers Union of America, 1904

FOY—Eddie Foy and Calvin F. Harlow, *Clowning Through Life.* New York: E. P. Dutton, 1928

FREEMAN—John R. Freeman, *On the Safeguarding of Life in Theaters.* New York: American Society of Mechanical Engineers, 1906

GUENZEL—Louis Guenzel, *Retrospects: "The Iroquois Theater Fire."* Elmhurst, Ill.: Theatre Historical Society of America, 1993.

MRC—Municipal Reference Collection, Chicago Public Library

NYPL—New York Public Library for the Performing Arts

SOU—Souvenir Program, Iroquois Theatre: Dedicatory Performance, November 23, 1903, Special Collections and Preservation Division, Chicago Public Library

SCPD—Special Collections and Preservation Division, Chicago Public Library

THS—Theatre Historical Society of America

Prologue

1. *Chicago Times,* February 13, 1875.
2. Excerpts from the newspaper article also appear in DIS, 317–24.

1. Warning Signs

1. FOY, 276.
2. DIS, 153.

3. DIS, 156.

4. DIS, 160.

5. FOY, 276.

6. Playbill, Iroquois Theatre, SCPD.

2. "Absolutely Fireproof"

1. *Chicago Daily News,* December 31, 1903.

2. Irving Cutler, *Chicago: Metropolis of the Mid-Continent* (Chicago: Geographic Society of Chicago and Kendall/Hunt Publishing, 1982), 30.

3. Cutler, 29.

4. Cutler, 46.

5. Cutler, 45.

6. Larry A. Viskochil, *Chicago at the Turn of the Century in Photographs* (New York: Dover, 1984), ix.

7. Viskochil, ix.

8. Frank A. Randall, *History of the Development of Building Construction in Chicago* (Urbana: University of Illinois Press, 1949), 11.

9. Randall, 17.

10. Perry R. Duis, *Challenging Chicago: Coping With Everyday Life, 1837–1920* (Urbana: University of Illinois Press, 1998), 26.

11. Duis, 34.

12. *Unrivaled Chicago and How to See It* (Chicago: Rand McNally, 1896), 29.

13. Jonathan J. Keyes, "The Forgotten Fire," *Chicago History* 26 (fall 1997): 56.

14. *Unrivaled,* 30.

15. William H. Musham, "Fire Extinguishment in Chicago: The Fire Department," *Journal of the Western Society of Engineers* 7 (January–December 1902): 599. Musham presented the talk to the society on November 19, 1902.

16. Musham, 603.

17. Musham, 618.

18. *Chicago Daily News,* December 31, 1903.

19. *Inter Ocean,* December 31, 1903.

20. SOU, 90–91.

21. Details of Powers's early life are from obituaries that ran in the *Chicago Tribune* and *The New York Times* on February 22, 1941. The former says he was eighty-two when he died, the latter gives his age as eighty-one.

22. Details of Davis's life are from SOU, 89–91.

23. *Inter Ocean,* December 31, 1903.

24. SOU, 20.

25. Miles L. Berger, *They Built Chicago: Entrepreneurs Who Shaped a Great City's Architecture* (Chicago: Bonus Books, 1992), 161–62.

26. Henry A. Withey and Elsie Rathburn Withey, *Biographical Dictionary of American Architects (Deceased)* (Los Angeles: New Age Publishing, 1956), 392.

27. *Chicago Chronicle,* December 31, 1903.

28. *Inter Ocean,* December 31, 1903.

29. GUENZEL, 5.

30. *Chicago Evening Post,* November 21, 1903.

31. *Chicago Chronicle,* December 31, 1903.

32. Newspaper clipping, apparently from the *Toledo Blade,* dated March 7, 1907, Robinson Locke Collection, NYPL.

33. FREEMAN, 12. Freeman delivered his report in an address at the annual meeting of the American Society of Mechanical Engineers in New York on December 4, 1905.

34. The *New York Tribune* of December 31, 1903 gives the figure as $500,000. The *New York Sun* of the same date quotes the theatrical firm of Klaw and Erlanger as saying it cost nearly $1 million.

35. *Chicago Chronicle,* December 31, 1903.

36. SOU, 20–33.

37. Emmett Dedmon, *Fabulous Chicago* (New York: Atheneum, 1981), 219.

38. SOU, 24.

39. Roebling Construction Company, *The Baltimore Fire . . . The Iroquois Theatre Fire* (New York: Roebling Construction, n.d.), 51.

40. Roebling, 51.

41. *Chicago Evening Post,* November 24, 1903.

42. Roebling, 51.

43. The three steps that were added were cited by Frederick Bulley, a building contractor on Mayor Carter Harrison's committee that probed the disaster, as reported many years later in the *Chicago Daily News* of December 29, 1948.

44. GUENZEL, 8–10.

45. SOU, 27.

46. SOU, 29.

47. Roebling, 51.

48. *Chicago Chronicle,* December 31, 1903.

3. Play and Players

1. David Pickering, ed., *Encyclopedia of Pantomime* (Hants, England: Gale Research International, 1993), 25–26.

2. Pickering, 26.

3. Uncited newspaper article, Clipping Files, *Mr. Bluebeard,* NYPL.

4. *Chicago Record-Herald,* December 31, 1903.

5. Uncited newspaper article, Clipping Files, *Mr. Bluebeard,* NYPL.

6. *New York Herald,* qtd. in the *New York Dramatic Mirror,* January 31, 1903.

7. SOU, 11.

8. *New York Herald* review, qtd. in *New York Dramatic Mirror,* January 31, 1903.

9. *New York Times,* January 22, 1903.

10. *New York Clipper,* January 31, 1903.

11. *New York Times,* January 22, 1903.

12. *New York Times,* January 22, 1903.

13. *New York Sun,* qtd. in the *New York Dramatic Mirror,* January 31, 1903.

14. *New York Sun,* qtd. in the *New York Dramatic Mirror,* January 31, 1903.
15. Uncited newspaper clipping, Clipping Files, *Mr. Bluebeard,* NYPL.
16. FREEMAN, 14.
17. Roebling, 52.
18. FREEMAN, 55.
19. FREEMAN, 14.
20. FREEMAN, 274.
21. *Chicago Tribune,* December 29, 1983.
22. Roebling, 51–52.
23. *Chicago Tribune,* October 22, 1903.
24. FOY, 274.
25. Ruth Thompson McGibeny, "The Iroquois Theatre Fire," Iroquois Theatre Fire of 1903 (McGibeny), CHS. McGibeny's remark also appears in her account under the same title in *Chicago History* 3.3 (winter 1974–1975): 178.
26. FOY, 274.

4. Opening Night

1. Iroquois Theatre playbill, SCPD.
2. *Chicago Tribune,* December 30, 1950.
3. *Chicago Tribune,* November 23, 1903.
4. *Chicago Tribune,* November 16, 1903.
5. *Chicago Daily News,* November 23, 1903.
6. DIS, 297.
7. *Chicago Tribune,* November 24, 1903.
8. *Chicago Evening Post,* November 24, 1903.
9. *Chicago Daily News,* November 24, 1903.
10. *Chicago Tribune,* November 24, 1903.
11. *Inter Ocean,* November 22, 1903.
12. *Chicago Daily News,* November 24, 1903.
13. *Chicago Evening Post,* November 24, 1903.
14. *Chicago Tribune,* November 24, 1903.
15. *Chicago Tribune,* November 24, 1903.
16. DIS, 299.

5. 3:15 P.M., Wednesday, December 30, 1903

1. *New York Clipper,* January 2, 1904.
2. *New York Clipper,* January 9, 1904.
3. *New York Clipper,* January 9, 1904.
4. FOY, 275.
5. DIS, 302–3.
6. DIS, 256.
7. DIS, 303.
8. *Inter Ocean,* December 31, 1903. Herbert Cawthorne, the actor, says there were more than five hundred persons backstage.

9. Testimony of William H. Patterson, Illinois Society of Architects Papers, CHS.

10. The description of the arc light is based on two accounts, that of Chicago's chief electrical inspector, H. H. Hornsby, DIS, 112–13, and Fire Chief William Musham in his *Annual Report* (1903), 10, MRC.

11. *Inter Ocean,* December 31, 1903.

12. DIS, 106.

13. *New York Times,* December 31, 1903. In his account, McMullen (DIS, 105–6) does not mention Farrell by name.

14. *New York Times,* December 31, 1903.

15. DIS, 111. Sallers's name is sometimes misspelled Sellers in accounts of the fire.

16. DIS, 105–6.

17. DIS, 298–99.

18. DIS, 200–201.

19. DIS, 115.

20. DIS, 307.

21. The account of the sequence of events on the stage are an amalgam of FOY, 275–80; DIS, 220–22, and *The New York Times,* December 31, 1903.

22. DIS, 307–8.

23. DIS, 309.

24. DIS, 103.

25. *Chicago Tribune,* December 31, 1931.

26. DIS, 308–9.

27. DIS, 310–11.

28. DIS, 309.

29. DIS, 311.

30. DIS, 308.

31. DIS, 294–95.

32. *New York Times,* December 31, 1903.

33. *Inter Ocean,* December 31, 1903.

34. DIS, 99–101.

35. *New York Dramatic Mirror,* January 16, 1904.

36. DIS, 307.

37. DIS, 255.

38. DIS, 97–99.

39. *New York Evening Post,* January 5, 1904, and DIS, 110–11.

40. DIS, 290–91.

41. The account of the problem with the asbestos curtain is an amalgam of DIS, 109–10, and the *Chicago Tribune,* February 12, 1904.

42. *Inter Ocean,* December 31, 1903, and DIS, 102–3.

43. *Inter Ocean,* December 31, 1903.

44. *New York Tribune,* December 31, 1903.

45. *New York Sun,* December 31, 1903.

46. *Chicago Tribune,* December 27, 1953.

47. DIS, 207–8.

48. DIS, 268–69 and 271–72. Murray identified the screaming girl as Nellie Reed, but it could not have been her. She was trapped in the fly gallery.

49. The account of Viola McDonald's experience is an amalgam of the *New York Sun,* December 31, 1903, and *The New York Times,* January 2, 1904.

50. *New York Tribune,* December 31, 1903.

51. *Chicago Tribune,* December 27, 1953.

52. FOY, 280–84.

6. In the Parquet and Boxes

1. Dimery worked for the T. W. Wilmarth Company, which advertised on page 62 of the souvenir program, SCPD.

2. Iroquois Theatre Fire of 1903 Collection (manuscript, Dimery), CHS.

3. One girl was the daughter, unnamed, of Henry Parker, superintendent of the Plamondon company; the other was the daughter, also unnamed, of W. R. Davis, head foreman. The Davis girl died as a result of the fire. Her name, however, does not appear on the list of victims that was published by the coroner's office in the latter part of January, 1904, so she must have died later than that.

4. The story of Emily and Charlotte Plamondon is an amalgam of accounts in DIS, 129–32, and the *New York Sun* and the *New York Tribune* of December 31, 1903. Some of the details do not jibe, apparently because Charlotte, for one, had trouble remembering her exact movements.

5. S. C. Thompson, *All-Time Rosters of Major League Baseball Clubs* (New York: A. S. Barnes, 1974), 7. Houseman was in only one game, which he lost, in 1887. He batted .250. It was his first and last appearance in the major leagues.

6. DIS, 260–64.

7. DIS, 257–59.

8. Iroquois Theatre Fire of 1903 Collection (manuscript, Dreher), CHS.

9. *Chicago Tribune,* December 28, 1952.

10. *New York Tribune,* December 31, 1904.

11. Iroquois Theatre Fire of 1903 Collection (manuscript, Brown), CHS.

12. DIS, 194–95.

13. *New York Times,* January 20, 1904.

14. The account of Winnie Gallagher's experience is an amalgam of DIS, 128–29, and the *New York Post,* December 31, 1903.

15. *Chicago Tribune,* December 31, 1931.

16. DIS, 134.

17. DIS, 292–94.

18. The account of Mrs. William Mueller's experience is an amalgam of DIS, 133, 195–96, and the *New York Tribune,* December 31, 1903. The youngest daughter's age is given as three years in the latter DIS citation.

19. DIS, 305.

20. DIS, 257.

21. DIS, 252–53.

22. DIS, 304–5.

23. DIS, 133, 196.

7. In the Dress Circle and Gallery

1. James M. Strong's story is an amalgam of DIS, 127–28, and *The New York Times,* January 1, 1904.

2. DIS, 197.

3. Samuel Fallows, *Lest We Forget: Chicago's Awful Theater Horror* (Chicago: Memorial Publishing, 1904), xv. Except for this introduction by Bishop Fallows— who is usually credited in bibliographic references as the author of the book—this book is exactly the same in every word and every page number as *The Great Chicago Theater Disaster* by Marshall Everett, which was also published in 1904 but by the Publishers Union of America. It is not clear which was published first, or the reason for the different titles, or whether Everett should also be credited as the author of the one for which Fallows wrote the introduction. Everett is described on the title page of *The Great Chicago Theater Disaster* as "The Well Known Editor and Descriptive Writer." Interestingly, the same copyright owner for both books is given as D. B. McCurdy.

4. Iroquois Theatre Fire of 1903 Collection (manuscript, Whitney), CHS.

5. DIS, 199.

6. *New York Times,* January 1, 1904.

7. *Chicago Tribune,* December 30, 1950.

8. *New York Times,* December 31, 1903.

9. *New York Sun,* December 31, 1903.

10. *Chicago Tribune,* February 13, 1904.

11. DIS, 264–67.

12. *Chicago Tribune,* December 31, 1973.

13. The account of Ruth Michel's experience is an amalgam of DIS, 269–70, and the *Chicago Tribune,* December 31, 1903.

14. DIS, 101.

15. *Chicago Tribune,* December 31, 1903.

16. Formal Dedication of the New Professional School Building, Buildings— Chicago Campus—Tremont House, Northwest University Archives.

17. DIS, 101–2. The other engineer was M. J. Tierney.

18. *Chicago Tribune,* February 12, 1904.

19. DIS, 291–92.

20. The account of the students and painters is an amalgam of the *New York Sun* and the *New York Tribune* of December 31, 1903, and DIS, 289–90.

8. The Rescuers

1. *Chicago Tribune,* December 21, 1958.

2. *Chicago Daily News,* December 31, 1903.

3. FOY, 287.

4. *Chicago Daily News,* December 30, 1967. Remer was near Madison and State Streets when he spied the smoke.

5. DIS, 290.

6. *Chicago Tribune,* December 31, 1903.

7. "The Iroquois Fire" (sheet music), CHS. Quigley's experience is recounted by his niece Eleanor Quigley Youngblood, who wrote on free space on the sheet music.

8. The account of Brady's experience is an amalgam of his autobiography (BRADY, 252–54), the *New York Tribune,* December 31, 1903, and the *Milwaukee Journal,* March 28, 1925.

9. DIS, 94–96.

10. The account of Michael J. Corrigan's experience is an amalgam of the *Chicago Herald-American,* July 7, 1950 and the *Chicago Tribune,* December 30, 1951.

11. *Chicago Record-Herald,* December 31, 1903.

12. Musham gives the total number of fires in 1903 as 6,054, Chicago (Ill.) Fire Marshal, *Annual Report,* 1903, 13, MRC.

13. *New York Times,* December 31, 1903.

14. GUENZEL, 3.

15. *Chicago Record-Herald,* December 31, 1903.

16. The account of Walter J. Raymer's experience is an amalgam of the *Chicago Tribune* and the *Inter Ocean,* December 31, 1903.

17. *New York Sun,* December 31, 1903.

18. *New York Post,* December 31, 1903.

19. *New York Times,* December 31, 1903.

20. *Chicago Tribune,* December 21, 1958.

21. *New York Tribune,* December 31, 1903.

22. BRADY, 255.

23. *New York Times,* December 31, 1903.

24. DIS, 96–97.

25. The account of Fire Chief William Musham's experience is an amalgam of the *Chicago Record-Herald* and *The New York Times,* December 31, 1903.

26. Chicago (Ill.) Department of Police, *Annual Report,* 27, MRC.

27. *New York Sun,* December 31, 1903.

28. The account of the experience of Fire Chief O'Neill and his assistant, Herman F. Schuettler, is an amalgam of the *Chicago Tribune, The New York Times,* and the *New York Tribune,* December 31, 1903.

29. *New York Times,* December 31, 1903.

30. *Chicago Record-Herald,* December 31, 1903.

31. *Chicago Daily News,* December 30, 1967. Max Remer's experience was related by his brother, Theodore G. Remer.

32. *Chicago Tribune,* December 21, 1958.

33. *Chicago Tribune,* December 31, 1903.

34. *New York Tribune,* December 31, 1903.

35. *New York Times,* January 1, 1904.

36. *New York Times,* December 31, 1903.
37. *New York Sun,* December 31, 1903.
38. *New York Times,* December 31, 1903.
39. *New York Post,* December 31, 1903.
40. FREEMAN, 15–16.
41. Fire Marshal, *Annual Report,* 12, MRC.
42. FREEMAN, 11, 15–16.

9. The News Spreads Rapidly

1. *Milwaukee Journal,* March 28, 1925.
2. *Chicago Record-Herald,* January 1, 1904.
3. *Chicago Tribune,* December 28, 1952.
4. *Chicago Tribune,* December 28, 1952.
5. The account of William McLaughlin's experience is an amalgam of *The New York Times,* January 1 and 2, 1904.
6. McGibeny, "The Iroquois Theatre Fire," CHS, 178.
7. The account of the scene inside Thompson's Restaurant is an amalgam of DIS, 202–3, 206, the *New York Post, The New York Times,* the *New York Tribune,* all of December 31, 1903, and the *Chicago Tribune,* December 28, 1952.
8. *Inter Ocean,* December 31, 1903.
9. *New York Post,* December 31, 1903.
10. *New York Sun,* December 31, 1903.
11. *Chicago Tribune,* December 28, 1952.
12. FOY, 287–89.

10. Morgue Scenes

1. *New York Sun,* December 31, 1903.
2. Except as indicated, the account of the scenes at the morgues are an amalgam of the *New York Post,* December 31, 1903, and *The New York Times,* December 31, 1903, and January 1, 1904.
3. *New York Post,* December 31, 1903.
4. Chicago (Ill.) Department of Police, *Annual Report,* 28, MRC.
5. *New York Times,* January 2, 1904.
6. DIS, 199–200.
7. DIS, 196–97.
8. *New York Times,* January 2, 1904.
9. *New York Tribune,* December 31, 1903.
10. *New York Times,* January 1, 1904.
11. DIS, 135–36.
12. DIS, 136.
13. DIS, 213.
14. The Van Ingens's story and background are an amalgam of DIS, 212, and *The New York Times,* January 1, 1904. There are minor discrepancies in the ages given for some of the children.

15. DIS, 199.

16. *New York Times,* January 2, 1904.

11. In Mourning

1. Carl Sandburg, *Abraham Lincoln: The War Years* (New York: Harcourt Brace, 1939) 408–12.

2. *Chicago Record-Herald,* December 31, 1903.

3. Inquest No. 28462, Mary Edna Torney, et al., Cook County Coroner's Inquest Records, Illinois Regional Archives Depository (at Northeastern Illinois University).

4. DIS, 356.

5. Coroner. Iroquois Theater Fire, Chicago. List of Victims. MRC.

6. DIS, 137.

7. DIS, 139.

8. *New York Times,* January 1, 1904.

9. *New York Times,* January 1, 1904.

10. *Inter Ocean,* January 1, 1904.

11. *New York Sun,* January 1, 1904.

12. Chicago (Ill.) Department of Police, *Annual Report,* 28–29, MRC.

13. BRADY, 259.

14. *Chicago Tribune,* December 28, 1952.

15. The account of the livery drivers' response is an amalgam of the *Chicago Tribune,* December 31, 1903, and *The New York Times,* January 1, 1904.

16. Except as noted, all funeral services are from DIS, 144–51.

17. *New York Times,* January 2, 1904.

18. DIS, 137–42.

19. DIS, 143–51.

12. A State of Shock

1. *Chicago Record-Herald,* January 1, 1904.

2. DIS, 233.

3. *New York Times,* January 2, 1904.

4. FOY, 293.

5. DIS, 233–34.

6. *Chicago Herald American,* January 7, 1904.

7. FOY, 293.

8. Edwin F. Sanders, undated, single-page typed manuscript, Theaters: Iroquois Theatre, CHS.

9. Undated *Kenosha Evening News* clipping, Clippings—Iroquois Theatre Fire, THS.

10. *New York Times,* January 1, 1904.

11. *New York Times,* January 2, 1904.

12. *New York Tribune,* December 31, 1903.

13. *Chicago Record-Herald,* June 7, 1904.

14. *New York Times,* January 1, 1904.

15. *New York Times,* January 1, 1904.

16. DIS, 241.

17. *New York Times,* January 2, 1904.

18. The death toll in the Ring Theatre fire in Vienna is given as 580 in *The New York Times,* December 31, 1903, but as 900 in the *New York Tribune* of the same date.

19. DIS, 238. The Chicago architect quoted is W. Carbys Zimmerman.

20. *New York Times,* January 1, 1904.

21. DIS, 240–41.

22. Jerome M. Chertkoff and Russell H. Kushigian, *Don't Panic: The Psychology of Emergency Egress and Ingress* (Westport, Conn.: Praeger, 1999). The theories regarding panic are discussed on pages 7–16 and the Iroquois Theatre fire in particular on pages 19–31.

23. Duane P. Schultz, *Panic Behavior* (New York: Random House, 1964), 9.

24. FOY, 292.

25. *New York Tribune,* December 31, 1903.

26. *New York Tribune,* December 31, 1903.

27. *New York Tribune,* December 31, 1903.

28. *New York Times,* January 1, 1904.

29. *New York Times,* December 31, 1903.

30. DIS, 211.

31. *New York Sun,* December 31, 1903.

13. Safety Last

1. DIS, 120.

2. *New York Times,* January 2, 1904.

3. *New York Times,* January 1, 1904.

4. *New York Times,* January 2, 1904.

5. *Chicago Tribune,* December 31, 1903.

6. *Fireproof* 4.2 (February 1904), 17.

7. Undated *Kenosha Evening News* clipping, Clippings—Iroquois Theatre Fire, THS.

8. Henry A. Withey and Elsie Rathburn Withey, *Biographical Dictionary of American Architects (Deceased)* (Los Angeles: New Age Publishing, 1956), 280.

9. *New York Times,* January 1, 1904.

10. GUENZEL, 18.

11. FREEMAN, 84–85.

12. GUENZEL, 17.

13. GUENZEL, 20.

14. DIS, 300–302.

15. DIS, 303–4.

16. FREEMAN, 10.

17. The death toll at the Brooklyn fire is given in *The New York Times,* December 31, 1903, as 294, but the *New York Tribune* of the same date gives it as 295.

18. *New York Times,* December 31, 1903.

19. FREEMAN, 35.

20. SOU, 91. Also, see the *New York Sun,* December 31, 1903.

21. FOY, 274.

22. Edgar Lee Masters, *Levy Mayer and the New Industrial Era: A Biography* (New Haven: 1927; printed under direction of Yale University Press), 74.

23. *Chicago Record-Herald,* January 1, 1904.

24. *Chicago Tribune,* January 17, 1904.

25. *Chicago Evening Post,* January 8, 1904.

26. *Chicago Evening Post,* January 2, 1904.

27. *Chicago Daily News,* December 31, 1903.

28. *Chicago Tribune,* December 31, 1903.

29. *Chicago Evening Post,* January 6, 1904.

30. *Chicago Daily News,* December 31, 1903.

31. *Chicago Tribune,* December 31, 1903.

32. SOU, 27.

33. Benjamin H. Marshall, "Fireproof Construction of Theaters," *Fireproof* 1.2 (August 1902), 26.

34. Emmett Dedmon, *Fabulous Chicago* (New York: Atheneum, 1981), 257.

35. Richard Lindberg, *To Serve and Collect: Chicago Politics and Police Corruption from the Lager Beer Riot to the Summerdale Scandal* (New York: Praeger, 1991), 120.

36. Dedmon, 257.

37. Dedmon, 258.

38. Dedmon, 259.

39. Dedmon, 258.

40. Henry Ericsson, *Sixty Years a Builder: The Autobiography of Henry Ericsson, Written in Collaboration with Lewis E. Meyers* (Chicago: A. Kroch and Son, 1942), 298.

41. Donald L. Miller, *City of Century: The Epic of Chicago and the Making of America* (New York: Simon and Schuster, 1996), 540.

42. Miller, 516.

43. Dedmon, 285–86.

44. Miller, 540.

45. *Fireproof* 3.5 (November 1903), 5–6.

46. *Chicago Tribune,* October 20, 1903.

47. *Chicago Tribune,* October 10, 1903.

48. *Chicago Tribune,* October 15, 1903.

49. *Chicago Tribune,* October 23, 1903.

50. *Chicago Tribune,* October 4, 1903.

51. *Chicago Tribune,* October 10, 1903.

52. *Chicago Tribune,* October 7, 1903.

53. Ericsson, 305.

54. *Chicago Tribune,* October 15, 1903.

55. *Chicago Tribune,* October 17, 1903.

56. Carter H. Harrison, *Stormy Years: The Autobiography of Carter H. Harrison, Five Times Mayor of Chicago* (New York: Bobbs-Merrill, 1935), 236.

57. *Chicago Tribune,* November 2, 1903.

58. *Chicago Daily News,* December 29, 1948.

59. Harrison, 237.

60. *Chicago Record-Herald,* January 4, 1904.

14. Finger Pointing

1. *Chicago Record-Herald,* January 1, 1904.

2. Musham Family Papers [manuscript], 1869–1965, CHS.

3. Musham Family Papers.

4. *Chicago Record-Herald,* January 1, 1904.

5. *New York Times,* January 1, 1904.

6. DIS, 303–4.

7. *Chicago Record-Herald,* January 4, 1904.

8. *Chicago Record-Herald,* January 1, 1904.

9. Testimony of Victor Falkenau, Illinois Society of Architects, CHS.

10. *Chicago Tribune,* February 13, 1904.

11. The account of E. Leavitt's role is an amalgam of *The New York Times* and the *New York Tribune,* December 31, 1903.

12. *New York Sun,* December 31, 1903.

13. *Chicago Chronicle,* December 31, 1903.

14. DIS, 106–7.

15. *Chicago Tribune,* December 31, 1903.

16. Robert Craik M'Lean, "The Iroquois Theater Disaster in Chicago," *Inland Architect and News Record* 42.6 (February 1904), 41–42.

17. To Members of the Illinois Commercial Men's Association, 3–8, Theaters. Iroquois Theatre, CHS.

18. J. E. O. Pridmore, "The Perfect Theatre," *Architectural Record* 17.2 (February 1905), 101–12.

19. *New York Times,* January 1, 1904.

20. *Inter Ocean,* January 1, 1904.

21. *Chicago Tribune,* December 31, 1903.

15. Blind Justice

1. *New York Times,* January 2, 1904.

2. *Chicago Sun,* January 2, 1904.

3. FREEMAN, author's note.

4. GUENZEL, 3.

5. GUENZEL, 4.

6. *New York Times,* January 2, 1904.

7. *Chicago Sun,* January 2, 1904.

8. *Chicago Sun,* January 2, 1904; grand jury verdict transcript, John E. Traeger Papers [manuscript], 1900–1940, CHS.

9. DIS, 308.

10. *New York Evening Post,* June 7, 1904. The newspaper was obviously misdated and should have been dated January 7, 1904.

11. Superintendent of Inspections, Report of Fire, 2–4, CHS.

12. *New York Dramatic Mirror,* January 16, 1904.

13. *Chicago Tribune,* January 28, 1904.

14. DIS, pages B–C.

15. Henry Ericsson, *Sixty Years a Builder: The Autobiography of Henry Ericsson, Written in Collaboration with Lewis E. Meyers* (Chicago: A. Kroch and Son, 1942), 297.

16. *Chicago Tribune,* January 28, 1904.

17. *Chicago Tribune,* January 29, 1904.

18. *Chicago Tribune,* February 10, 1904.

19. *Chicago Tribune,* February 9, 1904.

20. *Chicago Tribune,* January 28, 1904.

21. DIS, 312–13.

22. *Chicago Tribune,* February 13, 1904.

23. *Chicago Tribune,* February 14, 1904.

24. *Chicago Tribune,* February 23, 1904.

25. *Chicago Tribune,* February 17, 1904.

26. *Chicago Tribune,* February 21, 1904.

27. *Chicago Tribune,* September 29, 1904.

28. Kevin Tierney, *Darrow: A Biography* (New York: Thomas Y. Crowell, 1979), 195.

29. Tierney, 40–42.

30. *Chicago Tribune,* September 30, 1904.

31. *Chicago Tribune,* October 5, 1904.

32. *Chicago Tribune,* February 10, 1905.

33. *Chicago Tribune,* February 10, 1905.

34. *Chicago Tribune,* November 3, 1905.

35. *New York Times,* March 7, 1907.

36. Edgar Lee Masters, *Levy Mayer and the New Industrial Era: A Biography* (New Haven: 1927; printed under direction of Yale University Press), 82.

37. Masters, 77–78.

38. *Toledo Blade,* March 7, 1907, Robinson Locke Collection, NYPL.

39. *Chicago Tribune,* March 11, 1907.

40. *Chicago Tribune,* March 11, 1907.

41. *Chicago Tribune,* February 8, 1907. Woodward's remarks appeared in that month's issue of the *Illinois Law Review.*

42. *Chicago Record-Herald,* March 11, 1907.

43. *Chicago Record-Herald,* July 7, 1904.

44. The account of the theater company lawsuit is an amalgam of the *Chicago Tribune* and *The New York Times,* November 13, 1906.

45. *Chicago Record-Herald,* May 29, 1907.

46. Masters, 86.

47. *Chicago Record-Herald,* April 14, 1907.

48. *Chicago Tribune,* January 18, 1909.

49. *Chicago Tribune,* February 7, 1909.

16. Curtains

1. *Chicago Tribune,* January 29, 1904.

2. *New York Dramatic Mirror,* January 16, 1904.

3. H. D. Northrop, *The World's Greatest Calamities* (N.p.: n.p., 1904), 443–44.

4. *Chicago Tribune,* December 30, 1903.

5. FOY, 291–92.

6. *Chicago Tribune,* February 2, 1904.

7. *Chicago Tribune,* January 31, 1904.

8. *Chicago Tribune,* February 1, 1904.

9. *Chicago Tribune,* February 2, 1904.

10. *Chicago Tribune,* January 29, 1904.

11. *Chicago Tribune,* September 18, 1904.

12. Colonial Theatre (Iroquois) diagram, *American Architect,* December 31, 1913, Clippings—Theaters of Chicago, THS.

13. *Chicago Tribune,* September 20, 1904.

14. Uncited clipping, Clippings—Iroquois Theatre Fire, THS.

15. Richard E. Schmidt, typescript dated January 14, 1942, Chicago. Theaters. Iroquois Theatre, CHS.

16. Traeger Papers, CHS.

17. Roebling Construction Company, *The Baltimore Fire . . . The Iroquois Theatre Fire* (New York: Roebling Construction, n.d.), 62.

18. Illinois Society of Architects, CHS.

19. DIS, 247–48. Erikson's name is misspelled in the book.

20. Robert Craik M'Lean, "The Iroquois Theater Disaster in Chicago," *Inland Architect and News Record* 42.6 (February 1904), 41.

21. 3. Samuel Fallows, *Lest We Forget: Chicago's Awful Theater Horror* (Chicago: Memorial Publishing, 1904), xiv.

22. F. W. Fitzpatrick, "Whittlings," *Fireproof* 4.4 (February 1904), 51.

23. GUENZEL, 28.

24. FREEMAN, 84.

25. FREEMAN, 16.

26. J. E. O. Pridmore, "The Perfect Theatre," *Architectural Record* 17.2 (February 1905), 112.

27. George B. McClellan to Carter H. Harrison, January 6, 1904, Harrison Papers, Newberry Library.

28. *Chicago Tribune,* January 26, 1904.

29. FREEMAN, 10.

30. *Chicago Tribune,* September 18, 1904.

31. Pridmore, "Perfect Theatre," 116.

32. *Revised Municipal Code of Chicago of 1905* (Chicago: Lawyers' Co-operative Publishing Co., 1905), 95–100.

33. *Chicago Tribune,* March 11, 1907.

17. Ashes and Embers

1. *Chicago Tribune,* June 13, 1904.

2. Alan D. Whitney Papers [manuscript], ca. 1885–1976, CHS.

3. The account of the fate of the memorial plaque is an amalgam of the *Chicago Daily News,* January 13, 1972, and the *Chicago Tribune,* November 4, 1981.

4. James L. Riedy, *Chicago Sculpture* (Urbana: University of Illinois Press, 1981), 184–86.

5. *Chicago Sun-Times,* August 11, 1967.

6. "The Iroquois Fire" (sheet music), CHS.

7. "The Burning Iroquois" (sheet music), THS.

8. FOY, 289.

9. FOY, 293.

10. *New York Times,* February 17, 1928.

11. Uncited newspaper clipping, March 1, 1904, Robinson Locke Collection, NYPL.

12. *Chicago Record,* October 6, 1914.

13. *New York Times,* May 17, 1919.

14. *New York Times,* February 22, 1941.

15. *New York Times,* June 20, 1944.

16. GUENZEL, 4.

17. GUENZEL, 22.

Bibliography

Manuscript Sources

CHICAGO PUBLIC LIBRARY

Municipal Reference Collection

Chicago (Ill.) Department of Police. *Annual Report.* 1903.

Chicago (Ill.). Fire Marshal. *Annual Report.* 1903.

Clipping Files—Fires—Chicago—Iroquois Theatre Fire.

Cook County (Ill.). Coroner. Iroquois Theater Fire, Chicago. List of Victims.

Municipal Code of Chicago, from April 2, 1890, to July 10, 1894. Chicago: E. B. Myers and Co., 1894.

Ordinance Relating to the Department of Buildings. Chicago: Moorman and Geller, 1903.

Revised Municipal Code of Chicago of 1905. Chicago: Lawyers' Co-operative Publishing Co., 1905.

Special Collections and Preservation Division

Iroquois Theatre programs.

CHICAGO HISTORICAL SOCIETY

Chicago Teachers' Federation.

Clippings—Iroquois Theatre (photocopies and typed transcriptions).

Clippings—Theaters. Iroquois Theatre.

Cook County (Ill.). Coroner. Iroquois Theatre Fire, Chicago. List of Victims.

William James Davis papers [manuscript], 1879–1914.

Sarah Knisely Dreher interview transcript [manuscript], March 1985.

Illinois Society of Architects Papers.

"The Iroquois Fire" (sheet music).

Iroquois Theatre Fire of 1903 collection [manuscript], 1904–1978.

> Bessie M. Letts Brown
>
> Joseph Dimery
>
> Rose G. Payson
>
> Harry J. Powers

Musham family papers [manuscript], 1869–1965.
Superintendent of Inspections, Report of Fire.
John E. Traeger papers [manuscript], 1900–1940.
Alan D. Whitney papers [manuscript], ca. 1885–1976.

ILLINOIS REGIONAL ARCHIVES DEPOSITORY
(AT NORTHEASTERN ILLINOIS UNIVERSITY)

Cook County Coroner's Inquest Records.

NEWBERRY LIBRARY

Carter H. Harrison Papers, 1901–1909.

NEW YORK PUBLIC LIBRARY FOR THE PERFORMING ARTS

Clippings Files, *Mr. Bluebeard.*
Robinson Locke Collection.
Program, Knickerbocker Theatre.

NORTHWESTERN UNIVERSITY ARCHIVES

Buildings—Chicago Campus—Tremont House.

THEATRE HISTORICAL SOCIETY OF AMERICA, ELMHURST, ILLINOIS

"The Burning Iroquois" (sheet music).
Clippings—Iroquois Theatre Fire.
Clippings—Theaters of Chicago.
Collection of Michael R. Miller.

Books

American Art Annual. Vol. 21. New York: American Federation of Arts, 1924.
American National Biography. Vol. 6. New York: Oxford University Press, 1999.
Berger, Miles L. *They Built Chicago: Entrepreneurs Who Shaped a Great City's Architecture.* Chicago: Bonus Books, 1992.
Bordman, Gerald. *American Musical Theatre.* New York: Oxford University Press, 1978.
Brady, William A. *Showman.* New York: E. P. Dutton, 1937.
Chertkoff, Jerome M., and Russell H. Kushigian. *Don't Panic: The Psychology of Emergency Egress and Ingress.* Westport, Conn.: Praeger, 1999.
Chicago Blue Book . . . for the Year Ending 1904. Chicago: Chicago Directory Co., 1903.
Cronon, William. *Nature's Metropolis: Chicago and the Great West.* New York: W. W. Norton, 1991.
Cutler, Irving. *Chicago: Metropolis of the Mid-Continent.* Chicago: Geographic Society of Chicago and Kendall/Hunt Publishing, 1982.
Daily News Almanac and Year-Book 1905. Chicago: Chicago Daily News Company, 1904.

Bibliography

Dedmon, Emmett. *Fabulous Chicago*. New York: Atheneum, 1981.

Duis, Perry R. *Challenging Chicago: Coping with Everyday Life, 1837–1920*. Urbana: University of Illinois Press, 1998.

Ericsson, Henry. *Sixty Years a Builder: The Autobiography of Henry Ericsson, Written in Collaboration with Lewis E. Meyers*. Chicago: A. Kroch and Son, 1942.

Everett, Marshall. *The Great Chicago Theater Disaster*. Chicago: Publishers Union of America, 1904. (See also Bishop Samuel Fallows, *Lest We Forget,* below.)

Falk, Peter Hastings, ed. *Who Was Who in American Art*. Madison, Conn.: Sound View Press, 1985.

Fallows, Alice Katherine. *Everybody's Bishop: Being the Life and Times of the Right Reverend Samuel Fallows, D.D.* New York: J. H. Sears, 1927.

Fallows, Bishop Samuel. *Lest We Forget: Chicago's Awful Theater Horror*. Chicago: Memorial Publishing, 1904. (Although many catalogues list Fallows as the author of this book, he wrote only the introduction. The remainder is word for word and page for page the same as Marshall Everett, *The Great Chicago Theater Disaster,* above. And although printed by different publishers, both books bear the name of D. B. McCurdy as copyright holder.)

Farr, Finis. *Chicago: A Personal History of America's Most American City*. New Rochelle, N.Y.: Arlington House, 1973.

Foy, Eddie, and Calvin F. Harlow. *Clowning Through Life*. New York: E. P. Dutton, 1928.

Freeman, John R. *On the Safeguarding of Life in Theaters*. New York: American Society of Mechanical Engineers, 1906.

Green, Abel, and Joe Laurie Jr. *Show Biz from Vaude to Video*. New York: Henry Holt, 1951.

Guenzel, Louis. *Retrospects: "The Iroquois Theater Fire."* Elmhurst, Ill.: Theatre Historical Society of America, 1993.

Harrison, Carter H. *Stormy Years: The Autobiography of Carter H. Harrison, Five Times Mayor of Chicago*. New York: Bobbs-Merrill, 1935.

Henry, Mae Felts. *Herringshaw's City Blue Book of Current Biography*. Chicago: American Publishers' Association, 1913.

Lakeside Annual Directory of the City of Chicago, 1903. Chicago: Chicago Directory Co., 1903.

Laurie, Joe, Jr. *Vaudeville: From the Honky-Tonks to the Palace*. New York: Henry Holt, 1953.

Leonard, John W., ed. *Book of Chicagoans*. Chicago: A. N. Marquis, 1905.

Lindberg, Richard. *To Serve and Collect: Chicago Politics and Police Corruption from the Lager Beer Riot to the Summerdale Scandal*. New York: Praeger, 1991.

Lowe, David. *Chicago Interiors: Views of a Splendid World*. Chicago: Contemporary Books, 1979.

Mantle, Burns, and Garrison P. Sherwood. *The Best Plays of 1899–1909*. New York: Dodd, Mead, 1947.

Masters, Edgar Lee. *Levy Mayer and the New Industrial Era: A Biography*. New Haven: 1927. (Printed under direction of Yale University Press.)

Mayer, Harold M., and Richard C. Wade. *Growth of a Metropolis*. Chicago: University of Chicago Press, 1969.

Miller, Donald L. *City of Century: The Epic of Chicago and the Making of America*. New York: Simon and Schuster, 1996.

Northrop, H. D. *The World's Greatest Calamities*. N.p.: n.p., 1904.

Pickering, Davis. *Encyclopedia of Pantomime*. Hants, England: Gale Research International, 1993.

Randall, Frank A. *History of the Development of Building Construction in Chicago*. Urbana: University of Illinois Press, 1949.

Riedy, James L. *Chicago Sculpture*. Urbana: University of Illinois Press, 1981.

Roebling Construction Company. *The Baltimore Fire . . . The Iroquois Theatre Fire*. New York: Roebling Construction, n.d.

Sandburg, Carl. *Abraham Lincoln: The War Years*. New York: Harcourt Brace, 1939.

Schultz, Duane P. *Panic Behavior*. New York: Random House, 1964.

Slide, Anthony. *Encyclopedia of Vaudeville*. Westport, Conn.: Greenwood Press, 1994.

Smith, Carl. *Urban Disorder and the Shape of Belief*. Chicago: University of Chicago Press, 1995.

Stryker, Lloyd P. *Address: The Gerry Society*. New York: Gerry Society, 1912.

Thompson, S. C. *All-Time Rosters of Major League Baseball Clubs*. New York: A. S. Barnes, 1974.

Tierney, Kevin. *Darrow: A Biography*. New York: Thomas Y. Crowell, 1979.

Trow's General Directory of the Boroughs of Manhattan and Bronx, City of New York, Vol. CXVL for the Year Ending July 1, 1903. New York: Trow Directory, Printing, and Bookbinding, 1902.

Unrivaled Chicago and How to See It. Chicago: Rand McNally, 1896.

Viskochil, Larry A. *Chicago at the Turn of the Century in Photographs*. New York: Dover, 1984.

Weinberg, Arthur and Lila. *Clarence Darrow: A Sentimental Rebel*. New York: G. P. Putnam's Sons, 1980.

Withey, Henry A., and Elsie Rathburn Withey. *Biographical Dictionary of American Architects (Deceased)*. Los Angeles: New Age Publishing, 1956.

Newspapers

The following newspapers are those that were employed extensively, chiefly to recreate the events surrounding December 30, 1903, and their aftermath but also as otherwise cited in the notes:

Chicago Chronicle.
Chicago Daily News.
Chicago Evening Post.
Chicago Herald-American.
(Chicago) Inter Ocean.
Chicago Record-Herald.
Chicago Sun.

Bibliography

Chicago Tribune.
New York Clipper.
New York Dramatic Mirror.
New York Evening Post.
New York Sun.
New York Times.
New York Tribune.

Articles

"Armour Fire." *Fireproof* 1.1 (July 1902): 26–28.

DuciBella, Joseph R. "Iroquois Theatre—Chicago, Illinois," *Marquee, Journal of the Theatre Historical Society of America* 25.4 (1993): 29–34.

"Editorial: Building Scandals in Chicago." *Fireproof* 3.5 (November 1903): 5–6.

"Fireproof Theater Curtain." *Fireproof* 4.4 (February 1904): 31–33.

Fitzpatrick, F. W. "Whittlings." *Fireproof* 4.4 (February 1904): 47–51.

Foy, Eddie. "A Tragedy Remembered." *NFPA Journal* July–August 1995: 75–79.

"Iroquois Theater Disaster." *Fireproof* 4.4 (February 1904): 15–22.

Keyes, Jonathan J. "The Forgotten Fire." *Chicago History* 26 (fall 1997): 52–65.

King, Donald C. "Theatre Disasters . . ." *Marquee, Journal of the Theatre Historical Society of America* 8.3 (1976): 3–6.

Luce, C. K. "Fire Escapes and Fire Protection." *Fireproof* 2.2 (July 1903): 31–33.

Marshall, Benjamin H. "Fireproof Construction of Theaters." *Fireproof* 1.2 (August 1902): 26.

McGibeny, Ruth Thompson. "The Iroquois Theatre Fire." *Chicago History* 3.3 (winter 1974–75): 177–81.

M'Lean, Robert Craik. "The Iroquois Theater Disaster at Chicago." *Inland Architect and News Record* 42.6 (February 1904): 42.

Musham, William H. "Fire Extinguishment in Chicago: The Fire Department." *Journal of the Western Society of Engineers* 7 (January–December 1902): 596–622.

Parkes, Albert L. "The Chicago Stage Before the Fire." *The New York Dramatic Mirror* December 19, 1903: 40.

Pridmore, J. E. O. "The Perfect Theatre." *Architectural Record* 17.2 (February 1905): 101–17.

Westerberg, Julia. "Looking Backward: The Iroquois Theatre Fire of 1903." *Chicago History* 7.4 (winter 1978–79): 238–44.

Index

A veteran journalist, Nat Brandt has worked for CBS News and for a number of newspapers, including *The New York Times,* where he was an editor on the national news desk. He was subsequently managing editor of *American Heritage* magazine and editor-in-chief of *Publishers Weekly.* A freelance writer since 1980, he is the author of nine books dealing with episodes in American history. One of them, *The Man Who Tried to Burn New York*—about a Confederate plot to burn the city in the fall of 1864—won the Douglas Southall Freeman History Award. Brandt was the creator of the PBS television series *Crucible of the Millennium,* for which he also served as head of research.

Other Books by Nat Brandt

The Man Who Tried to Burn New York
The Town That Started the Civil War
The Congressman Who Got Away with Murder
Con Brio: Four Russians Called the Budapest String Quartet
Massacre in Shansi
Harlem at War: The Black Experience in WWII
Mr. Tubbs' Civil War
When Oberlin Was King of the Gridiron: The Heisman Years

With John Sexton

How Free Are We? What the Constitution Says We Can and Cannot Do

With Yanna Brandt

Land Kills
Murder in Bulloch Parish